Leading, Managing, Ministering

MODEM – Managerial and Organizational Disciplines for the Enhancement of Ministry – was founded in 1993 to serve both the Church and the business communities at large by promoting dialogue and sharing insights on best practices.

John Nelson, formerly Head of Management Studies at Liverpool Polytechnic (now John Moores University) is editor of the MODEM newsletter, *MODEM Matters!* and edited MODEM's first book, *Management and Ministry*, also published by the Canterbury Press.

What the reviewers said about *Management and Ministry*:

'this book contains a feast of good things'.

Ministry Today

'an extremely important book . . . should be read by all who take ministry within the Church seriously.'

The Door

'A high quality book from an exciting new venture.'

Crucible

'There is much to explore in the book . . .'

Methodist Recorder

Leading, Managing, Ministering

challenging questions for
church and society

A MODEM Handbook

Edited by John Nelson

CANTERBURY
PRESS
Norwich

© Modem 1999

First published in 1999 by The Canterbury Press
Norwich (a publishing imprint of Hymns Ancient &
Modern Limited, a registered charity),
St Mary's Works, St Mary's Plain,
Norwich, Norfolk, NR3 3BH

British Library Cataloguing in Publication Data

A catalogue record for this book is available
from the British Library

ISBN 1-85311-238-0

Typeset by Rowland Phototypesetting,
Bury St Edmunds, Suffolk
Printed in Great Britain by
Biddles Ltd, Guildford and King's Lynn

Contents

Foreword

It is a real pleasure to write this foreword for I have long been deeply interested in the issue of leadership in the churches. I am grateful for this opportunity to reflect and think aloud about the field so ably and seriously covered in this book.

As I read its contributors and their predecessors in *Management and Ministry*, I feel that I am listening to a conversation. My ear is now quite practised in listening to conversations about leadership and management, their natures and differences, within an extremely wide range of organizational and cultural contexts. I can now sense the level or quality of any such discussion.

There has been a great debate on both sides of the Atlantic about the meanings of the two key concepts of leadership and management. Although it flickers on, at least I am much clearer in my own mind as to how they overlap and how they differ, even if only in nuance or overtone.

We know that working organizations are going to look for leadership rather than for management if they find themselves in serious situations, namely those where a great deal of change is required, where there is uncertainty and fear and where ideals such as service, truth or excellence are being pursued.

We know that although all working groups and organizations are unique, they all share certain things in common. One breakthrough has been to identify among their common factors the three interacting and overlapping needs of the task (why do you have an organization – because there is a task that one person cannot do on his or her own), the group or team maintenance or uniting needs, and the individual needs we all have as persons and which we bring to work with us.

The application of this body of knowledge to the churches is actually very problematic. Are the churches working organizations or are they communities (extensions of the family or clusters of families), or both? How do concepts like leadership and management relate to ministry – the work of those holding public office in the churches? That is what the initial conversation has to be about.

At least there is some agreement here. All organizations exist in time and space and also in a money economy. Although not businesses, churches – like universities, schools and the armed forces – have to be businesslike. That calls for an element of what we now call managerial skill: administrative ability and paperwork; use of organizational systems to ensure effectiveness and efficiency; information technology; and, the most important, husbandry of scarce resources, especially money. Notice, however, that *administration* – be it *business administration* or *ecclesiastical administration* – is always secondary to the main purpose. If it usurps the first place you end up with a bureaucracy.

In this sense all ministers need to be managers for, shall we say, 20 or 30% of their time. It is part of the package deal. Sometimes lay members with expertise in the management fields – finance, marketing, information technology, organizational restructuring – are seen as potential contributors and asked to write reports or carry out consultancy work by the churches.

Too often, however, their contributions are seen to relate only to that 'unimportant' 20 or 30% of ministerial work. For example, when I did my own study of the Diocese of York in 1970, a number of cartoons appeared in the national press. One of the two originals I acquired hangs on my study wall. It shows a conveyor belt in the central aisle of a church, with about-to-be-married couples moving on it rapidly towards the altar rails. The caption – the vicar's remark to his curate – reads, 'Things are certainly speeding up now!' In other words, the press saw my work as that of a time-and-motion man, or efficiency expert being called in to streamline a piece of Victorian ecclesiastical machinery.

That is not how I saw the exercise. I began by asking the Archbishop of York to write down for me in one sentence his vision for the diocese. The object then was to try to realign the diocesan roles and responsibilities so that they served the vision. Much of my report was accepted and it acted as a reference point for a decade or more in the diocese. Incidentally, my report on the Diocese of Chichester, a year or two later, was technically a better one – one learns by experience – but its effect was completely negated by a change of diocesan bishop! Positive change needs leadership.

If, however, 20 to 30% of a minister's time goes on management, what about the rest? What is the core role? A variety of answers can be given to those questions and examined in this part of the conversation, and they will obviously reflect the particular church's tradition. In the Church of England, for example, the answer might be, in various permutations, preacher and teacher, priest, pastor and carer for individuals. The notion that a minister should also be the leader of the congregation has come more to the fore of late. Thus we may now properly ask what is the nature of such leadership, how does it relate to secular concepts of leadership and how, granted its importance, can it be identified in the selection process and nurtured and developed? That, then, is another area of the conversation, one which is now, I am pleased to report, receiving some attention within the new field of leadership studies.

Vision has now become central to some of the main schools of thought about leadership. Leadership and vision go together. Whilst I am not entirely in that camp – not all visionaries are leaders and not all leaders are visionaries – it is certainly true for some of those universally recognized as great leaders.

For me, Jesus is the supreme example. The concept of the Kingdom of God functioned, I think, as his leadership vision. He lived the vision and he made others to be partners with him in its service. And the extraordinary thing is that the vision of Jesus is still there, as it were, hanging in the air before us.

I cannot help wondering what effect this vision – the legacy of Jesus – has upon the churches today, upon their concepts of purpose and their understanding of leadership. And so I paused with particular interest where I came across some mention of the Kingdom of God in this book. It is not easy – at least for me it isn't – to grasp how a mystery such as the Kingdom, like a few lines of a master's sketch and no more, can provide purpose for these churches that still look to Jesus for inspiration as their author and leader. That is where I, speaking personally, need a lot more conversation to help me to see it more clearly.

John Adair
September 1998

Introduction

An editor has the special privilege of working with contributors to prepare a book for publication. This is how our second book has come about. The Canterbury Press Norwich judged that a successor to what has become a best-seller in religious book terms – a reprint within six months of publication – had a good chance of being as successful – providing, of course, that it continued the lively debate produced by its predecessor.

What, then, made *Management and Ministry: Appreciating Contemporary Issues* (our first book, published in October 1996) so successful? There were a number of reasons. First, it faced up to the issue of actually linking management with ministry. Indeed, we made this the title of our book. Management is still a dirty word for many clergy. For them it has connotations of manipulation and profiteering inextricably linked to private sector big business. We might easily have been persuaded to soft-pedal on this point. But we didn't. Secondly, it was timely. It caught the mood of the time when a growing number of lay people keen to participate in the ministry of the church needed encouragement in discovering how to organize themselves locally and synodically. Reorganization was the order of the day with the much publicized Turnbull review of the Church of England and other less well-publicized structural reviews of some of the Free Churches. There was a growing recognition of the need for appropriate expertise at all levels in the churches.

Thirdly, what was inside the book's front cover was judged to meet a need – and continues to do so. I was persuaded, against the wishes of my wife, to reveal in the back of the book my home telephone number and to invite people to ring me up about the book and about MODEM – an acronym for 'Managerial and Organizational Disciplines for the Enhancement of Ministry'. This proved to he a Godsend for the book, for MODEM and for me. I reckon I have received on average one phone call a week since October 1996 when the book was published. I could never have imagined the sheer pleasure I continue to get from picking up the phone and hearing people whom I have never met and from all over the country enthuse about having discovered *Management and Ministry*. Thankfully, most of them expressed an interest in MODEM and what it stood for, which led, in most cases, to them joining. So we gained many new members through our book. Fourthly, we were very fortunate to have a household name from the business world providing the Foreword. Sir John Harvey-Jones MBE, a former Chairman of ICI and star of the BBC TV series *Troubleshooter* wrote a marvellous tribute to our book (and to MODEM). I have no doubt this helped materially in getting the book more widely known. Calls are still welcome; the number is 01704-873973.

Fifthly, MODEM went to great lengths to promote it. With the support of our publisher, we held a series of midday launch programmes in the two months immediately following its publication These were held in London (in the London office of the Institute of Management), Milton Keynes (in the ecumenical church of Christ the Cornerstone), Liverpool and Manchester (in their Anglican cathedrals), Cambridge (in the boardroom of the David Ball Group PLC), Oxford (in Westminster College), Nottingham (in its Town Hall), Birmingham (in the central URC church complex), York (in a parish church hall), Bradford (in the diocesan offices) and Ambleside (in the Diocese of Carlisle's Conference Centre).

I suspect we would have been content to rest on our laurels for a little while if we hadn't been approached by Canterbury Press

Norwich and invited to produce a successor to our book – and as soon as possible to maintain momentum and to keep us in the public eye.

We were flattered and keen to respond positively to this unexpected invitation. But the value of the invitation lay not only in boosting our morale but also in causing us to reconsider MODEM's aims, objectives, and especially, its vision. We even reflected on the appropriateness of our title – MODEM.

The very success of the book, followed by the publisher's invitation to produce a successor to it, led us to realize that there was an incongruence between our title (MODEM) and the book's title with our vision. To have a successor to our first book published might add to this incongruence and increase our dilemma of having a title which was beginning to be widely recognized and yet which conveyed an incomplete, one-sided message.

As Norman Todd, a founder MODEM trustee, puts it,

> The acronym stands for **M**anagerial and **O**rganizational **D**isciplines for the **E**nhancement of **M**inistry. But, as with a modem, communication is in both directions. It also stands for Ministerial and Ontological Disciplines for the Enhancement of Management (that is, exploring what it is to be a manager).
>
> MODEM depends upon and seeks to generate *dialogue* between people engaged in management (mainly secular) and people engaged in ministry (mainly religious or charitable). There is, of course, considerable overlap. There can be good or bad management, good or bad ministry or both. Each can learn from the other.

This aim of generating two-way dialogue is reflected in MODEM's vision. MODEM aims to set the agenda for management/ministry issues so that by the year 2000 the values and disciplines of those engaged in the management of secular and church organizations will be mutually recognized and respected.

We decided, therefore, to respond to the publisher's invitation by producing a second book which continued the thrust of the first book, so that it could genuinely be promoted as a successor to it and also broaden the dialogue to cover the issue of managing in society as well as in the church. This led us to identify the relationship between managing and leading as the key challenging question common to both secular and sacred organizations/institutions.

Hence, our statement of aim as a guide for all our potential contributors:

> A follow-up to our very successful book *Management and Ministry: Appreciating Contemporary Issues*, with the aim of pursuing the questions raised in it. In a series of major chapters a carefully chosen group of contributors will engage in an in-depth exploration of the range of concepts between managing and leading.
>
> The editorial team believes the issues of managing and leading are fundamental at a time when belief in institutions is being questioned and many individuals feel little sense of commitment to large-scale secular organizations and the churches. It also believes these issues have a particular relevance to an understanding of the nature of authority, both exercised and accepted.
>
> The book is aimed at making a significant contribution to contemporary thinking at a time when churches and companies, with statutory and voluntary organizations, need to cooperate in sharing expertise and demonstrating how various groupings in a society can move forward through deliberate collaborative effort.

There is a desperate need to identify appropriate management and leadership for our institutions – secular and sacred – when our confidence and trust in them is so low and cynicism towards them is so rampant.

A recent survey by the Henley Centre (noticed in the *Client Jogger* newsletter of our contributor from the business world,

Leonard Collinson), found that Britons say they trust brand names and retailers more than any state, cultural and religious organizations. Whereas the percentage of people saying they trusted Marks & Spencer, Heinz and Sainsbury were 83, 81 and 74 respectively, the percentages saying they trusted the police and judiciary, church and parliament to be honest and fair were 62, 43, 26 and 10 respectively.

Who can doubt the need to recognize the relevance of managerial skills where scarce resources are involved (and that includes the churches)? Maybe, though, the need is at last beginning to shift away from having to argue the case for management towards helping to ensure that an *appropriate* use of managerial skills and know-how is recognized as different from managerialism (as the NHS is now discovering). One of the Church of England's most senior diocesan bishops – Rt Revd Eric Kemp, Bishop of Chichester – devoted a recent presidential address to his Diocesan Synod (9 May 1998) to what he called 'Management in Perspective'. He recognized that:

> there are two elements in the concept of management. One is efficiency – that one should do what has to he done in a businesslike, professional manner ... The other ... is that of purpose, having a goal to aim at, which generally involves doing so in an efficient and economical way. It is in connection with that concept that I think much of the current criticism of what is happening in the Church today arises. There is a feeling that we are now concerned more with organization than with our spiritual calling. The Church exists to worship God, to proclaim his truth and to serve his people, that is everyone. Any organization in the Church should be strictly subordinated to these ends.

We decided to continue the same winning format for this book as we had employed in our first book – an editor plus a team of contributors. But we took great care to alert our members to our positive response to Canterbury Press' invitation and invited them to offer to be contributors. If MODEM is becoming an authoritative body to speak on management/ministry issues, we must ensure that our members with the appropriate expertise and writing ability don't remain hidden and unused. It was this strategy which uncovered Chris Burkett and Anthony Hawley, whose competence in the field of the organizational culture of congregations and whose insights into leading in urban priority areas (UPAs) respectively came to light.

Interestingly, word got round that we were getting together a team of contributors for a second book and we received unsolicited offers from Bruce Reed, Director of the Grubb Institute (on organizational transformation), from an American professor, Jayme Rolls (on transformational leadership) and Julian Cummins, a nonstipendiary minister and managing director of a management consultancy (on mission, ministry and marketing).

We invited a number of those members of MODEM who had been contributors to our first book to contribute again: Norman Todd and Gillian Stamp ('The hidden depths of organizations'), Malcolm Grundy ('The challenge of change'), Alan Harpham ('Why would a businessman study theology?'), Christopher Bemrose ('Learning from charities'), Elizabeth Welch ('Who sees the vision?'), Peter Brierley with Heather Wraight ('Christian leadership in a postmodern society'), Bernard Kilroy ('A new spirit in leadership').

To do justice to our aim, we needed, in addition, contributions from a successful businessman and from a senior member in government at either central or local level. We were pleased to have recommended to us Leonard Collinson from the business world, and David Henshaw from local government, both of whom accepted our invitation to contribute.

To provide continuity with our thinking, we invited John Adair, an eminent authority on leadership with a world-wide reputation, to provide our Foreword. We were delighted when he agreed.

It was when my editorial advisors and I reviewed the insights provided by our contributors that we realized that the key issue facing organizations was not just that of managing and leading, but their interrelationship with ministering. Our book is actually about managing, ministering and leading. It is about ministering in management, managing in ministry and of both in leading an organization. One without the other is useless, and both are included in the responsibility of leading (and following). Hence our title, *Leading, Managing, Ministering: challenging questions for church and society*. (Note, by the way, we have retained the word 'managing' in our title. This is not just to preserve the link between the two books but also to continue to face head-on the need to argue for its relevance to the churches.)

We offer, therefore, a rich variety of perspectives on the challenging questions of managing and leading in the church and in society. However, the chapters in our book provide neither a consistent nor comprehensive answer to important questions about the organization of church and society, but their variety does point towards an emergent consensus. They all demonstrate the value of dialogue between the disciplines. Herein lies the importance of the book: the invitation it offers the reader to engage in the same sort of dialogue. After all, every one of us is involved in a variety of organizations and we need to understand how organizations work and interact. It is the stuff of life – and the raw material of the Kingdom of God.

Finally, I thank Malcolm Grundy and Norman Todd for their editorial advice; Christine Smith, Publisher of Canterbury Press Norwich, for her invaluable help and guidance in getting this book published; and my team of contributors for the high quality of their contributions.

John Nelson
Editor

I

Why would a businessman study theology?

ALAN HARPHAM

I have been a Christian longer than I have been a businessman. However, in many Christian circles that I move in, one would be forgiven for thinking that anything to do with business was corrupt, evil, came from the devil and was wholly un-Christian! This I have found difficult to take – did I choose to enter an evil profession, despite being a Christian? The Church seems to have little difficulty engaging with the 'caring' professions but it relates far less well to the worlds of business, industry and commerce. It seems to have great difficulty accepting that there is the potential for good and evil in *all* professions and forms of work. It is not the nature of the profession or business, it is the nature of the individual and his or her beliefs and behaviour that leads to good or evil conduct and transactions. In fact, I believe that my Christian faith has added value to my contribution and working practice. It has sustained me through difficult times and helped me to think and pray through dilemmas. It is an integral part of the ME that presents himself for work each day, not something I leave behind for my 'days off'.

I have both theoretical and practical experience of the world of business. I spent sixteen years with a major British construction company, John Laings, formed by a practising Christian who, in a paternalistic way, imposed many of his values throughout the

organization; four years teaching a Masters degree in Project Management at Cranfield University aimed at contractors and process
contractors operating internationally on multi-million pound contracts; and eleven years growing and eventually directing a leading
UK management consultancy focused on project management. In
that time I came across many issues that required difficult
decisions and that often caused me to look into my own beliefs
and values. However, I found nothing in the MBA degree I
studied, nor at work, that looked to religious beliefs and understanding for an answer. Indeed, the MBA looked to disciplines
other than management and organization such as psychology, sociology and economics to help train and inform future managers,
but certainly not to theology or Christology.

Why not? Perhaps, because the formation of management education in the early part of the nineteenth century was established
at Harvard University by two professors drawn from the faculties
of law and medicine. These two professors brought with them
the notion of learning by case study – the idea of examining a
past case study and developing principles that could be applied
to future cases. In practice their idea did not work precisely as
they intended. It was not found possible to derive general principles that could be applied to all future cases. Each case was
different, in a different context and general principles could not
be applied. However, the notion of studying by case study, as an
experiential form of learning through practising being a manager
in a case study, was found to be very effective. Similarly, the
disciplines used in the formation of managers were drawn from a
limited range as described above.

The context of leadership and management has moved on a
long way in the last century and we have arrived at a time where
the interest in ethics is a new area of study for business schools.
The idea of the individual's interpersonal skills and behaviour
being influenced by his or her early formative years is being utilized by some of the leading business schools, such as Cranfield,
and a few management writers – for example, Charles Handy –

are increasingly pointing to the need for people to find meaning and purpose in their work communities.

In parallel, the Church is wrestling with re-organization, changing roles within its membership; the role of its non-stipendiary ministers and even more so with its ministers in secular employment (MSEs) for example – worker priests. The theology of the role is constantly being evaluated by MSEs through vehicles such as Chrism (Christians in Secular Ministry) and recent consultations such as those held at St George's House, Windsor.

I will therefore look at a number of management issues to explore their theological significance and whether and how theology (our understanding of God) might bring its insights to bear on the issues.

Profitability and wealth creation

Profitability is the byword of business and the capitalist system. The wealth it generates can be used to serve society or to exploit it in a corrupt way, where wealth provides unfair power and influence. I remember that era when we regularly heard about 'the unacceptable face of capitalism' as various aspects of its excesses were revealed in public. This reached such proportions that many of us in the '70s were beginning to believe that capitalism was of itself an evil invention. In reality, most of us did not understand the capitalist system, how it worked and what it meant. This is not surprising since most of us who had been educated in the UK, at no matter what level or expense, had never had it explained to us. It was not until I studied for my Masters degree in Business Administration, at nearly thirty years of age, that I had it explained to me! Indeed, I can remember asking my Professor of Civil Engineering on my first degree what the budget was for a suspension bridge he asked us to design, and being told that it was irrelevant. Years later, I can remember visiting a student's company and being entertained to lunch by the chairman. He was also president of one of the main engineering institutions at the time. During lunch he said what a shame it was that engineers these days had to have an awareness of cost!

What I now know is that 'profit' is the way the capitalist system measures the added value of an enterprise – its wealth creation and growth. Wealth creation, as Malcolm Grundy argues in his book *An Unholy Conspiracy* (Canterbury Press, Norwich 1992), is not itself evil but open to both good and bad motives. As Jesus says in Mark 8:36, 'What good is it for a man to gain the whole world, yet forfeit his soul?' 'Growth' is key for all of us as individuals and this I believe to be equally true of enterprises. Companies and organizations are either growing or else they are shrinking – standing still is not generally an option. If organizations are to have opportunities for their staff to develop and grow as individuals, then typically the organizations must be growing themselves. If they want to 'look after' their staff and give them more rewards they will again generally need growth to achieve this.

The difficulty with 'profit' is that it is a blunt instrument of measuring growth and performance. First and foremost, the unit of measure is money and as we all know money is not the sole measure of real values and personal growth. Secondly, when is enough 'profit' enough? What Charles Handy calls the 'theology of enough'. What he has found, through debating this question in enterprises with their management teams, is that there are other values at play in human beings and their enterprises. These need to be discovered and made more explicit if the enterprise is to survive; the profit motive alone is seldom enough for most of us. We need to understand the true meaning and purpose of our work to be fulfilled.

God does not use the measure of financial profitability as his test for the success of our mission on earth. Despite some extreme Christian views that claim God financially rewards those who believe in Him, most of us can see from experience that this is blatantly untrue.

I believe that we are more likely to discover these other measures of growth and success if we were to add theology to those other subjects that illuminate this topic, such as psychology. Whilst psychology can help us to understand ourselves and our needs, theology – our understanding of God – can help us to explore his purpose for us as individuals and communities, including the work community.

Personal development and growth

I believe that our most fundamental purpose in life is to grow and develop as whole human beings and to help others to do the same. By growth and development, I mean the life-long learning about ourselves – our bodies, minds and spirits. Our striving to become ever more effective and whole as individuals and as active members of the various 'communities' in which we exist – home, work and other interests.

Of my own values, the one I cherish most is helping others to develop and grow for themselves. Anyone who has ever watched a child developing will have observed and hopefully felt this wonderful mystery of learning and development. Those things that we have learnt, often the hard way, become a part of our common sense – those things that we now know and have often forgotten how we learnt. But if we have yet to learn them, or discover them, they are not a part of our 'common sense', or at least not yet.

In management, the in-word is competence, that combination of knowledge and the experience of applying the knowledge. Organizations are spending more and more time analysing the competencies they need, measuring the competencies they have acquired and looking at the gaps to determine the organization's and individual's training and development requirements.

This is undoubtedly a shared responsibility, particularly as fewer and fewer of us will spend a career with one employer, but rather a career or careers spread over a number of employers or even self-employment. So each individual should evolve his or her own development plan or life plan, having identified the competencies needed to develop for this career step and the ones beyond. They need to discuss this with their employer in order to determine a mutually agreeable plan that the employer can help with, or at least some of it.

Enlightened employers are also recognizing the value of offering 'personal development' as part of its portfolio of 'rewards'. Ex-employees can become ambassadors for the firm long after they have moved on, and in some cases can become excellent customers and/or suppliers. The employer therefore needs to design a development plan for the company that also addresses as much of the individuals' plans as possible and provides the benefits of economies of scale, for example, in training.

Supporting the idea of personal development and growth, some employers are beginning to use mentors, coaches and counsellors to support individuals along their own development paths, in the different ways that these three roles imply. The mentor is usually internal, someone who is ahead on the development path and can provide advice and guidance on the way ahead. The coach, often external, is there to help the individual improve his or her competence by discussing how the individual can enhance performance at work. The counsellor could be internal or external and is someone with whom the individual can reflect on difficulties and behaviour at work. To do any of these effectively requires precise and accurate feedback on our present performance, so that we can see how to improve ourselves. The most pay-back comes from focusing on the things we do badly, where there is the most room for improvement.

This is often difficult for Christians who in their pastoral work – the Christian equivalent of mentoring, coaching and counselling – are often nurtured to be over gentle with each other. The idea of giving direct and negative feedback is often strongly resisted by them. Why, I do not know, as there are many examples in the Bible of Jesus giving very direct feedback to individuals and groups, from remarks to Peter through to overturning the tables of the money lenders in the Temple (John 2:15).

I believe the Bible also has much to say about growth and development, and in particular its importance in our mission on earth. As the Messiah's handbook puts it in Richard Bach's book *Illusions* (Heinemann, 1977), 'here is a test to find out if your mission on earth is complete. If you are still alive it is not.'

Organizational structures

At the outset of my career I worked for a large organization employing over 25,000 people. It was run by a large hierarchical organization with many layers, from the then Chairman, Sir Maurice Laing, to the site tea boy. Each of us knew our place in the hierarchy, who our boss was and Adam Smith's concept of the 'span of control' and traditional pyramid structure was the norm.

The current wisdom is the de-layering of organizations and the creation of flat, non-hierarchical structures. The idea of flatter organizations is to reduce the number of layers in the organization and reduce the numbers of middle managers, particularly where they are not seen to add value. This has given rise to many social problems, as many fit and healthy men and women (but mainly men) have been given early retirement, or worse still put out of work, when many would see themselves at the prime of their careers. Organizations have often lost their company memory (and history) in the process and now find themselves with age gaps – often most short of those who could do the mentoring, coaching and counselling referred to earlier. The flatter organization also requires the staff remaining to become more self-sufficient – the 'buzz word' is empowered.

A lot of recent management effort and education has been focused on empowering lower grades of staff to manage themselves with less direction and management from middle management. Many such staff question whether they have been given the necessary authority and preparation for this empowerment. Many observers see empowerment as being one-sided in favour of the organization, rather than the individual and his/her development. It is widely accepted that the age of self-sufficiency (the Thatcher legacy), has given rise to unacceptable behaviour in some management structures. In other words, those who cannot survive the new ethos are removed from it, often with little or no cushioning.

In the world of projects, the flatter structure has become the 'network' organization, consisting of numerous project teams that come together to undertake specific tasks and then part to re-form on a new project or projects. Each of the projects has links to certain of the other projects that it influences or is influenced by. This is a very dynamic form of organization, constantly changing. It is often difficult for people in these organizations to feel a member of a 'community', one of our basic needs as identified by Charles Handy.

The institutional Church has long consisted of a flat organization with wide spans of control. In the diocese where I live there is one diocesan bishop, a small senior staff team of seven or eight, including two suffragan bishops and three archdeacons; twenty-three deaneries, each with a rural dean and lay chairman and over 300 paid clergy and many more unpaid part-time clergy. Compared with the secular world the span of control between levels in the structure of the Church is much greater. Furthermore the idea of hierarchy is complex. Each member of the clergy undertakes allegiance to their bishop when he or she is presented with a parish, but in effect is being given a 'franchise' to run that parish in their own style. Although there are 'hierarchical' links to the rural dean, most parish clergy do not and would not consider themselves as reporting to the rural dean. In addition and in many cases, they also receive the freehold of the parish church and vicarage in 'trust' for as long as they remain as the vicar of that parish. Unless they do something very bad they cannot have it taken away from them. In practice, the granting of the freehold is reducing as the need for flexible staffing and new amalgamations of parishes under one priest becomes a necessary and growing trend.

There should be much that secular and Church organizations could learn from each other and this of course is one of the prime reasons for the existence of organizations such as MODEM. The majority of Christian Churches in England belong to Churches Together in England. A prime requirement of membership is to be a Trinitarian Church (that is, a Church that believes in the Trinity – God, the Father, Son and Holy Spirit). The nature of the Trinity is one that I find inherently very complex. These three 'individuals' co-existing as One, sometimes sounding in a hierarchical relationship with the Father at the top and in-charge and at other times being entirely equal and representative of each other, indeed each being present in the other. We are told we can come to know the others through the Son. Is there something in learning about the nature of the Trinity that can provide insights to the way hierarchies work in our own church and secular organizations? The Church of England has had three separate hierarchies at work within it – synodical, episcopal and the Church Commissioners, although the recent Turnbull report, *Working as One Body – the Report of the Archbishops' Commission on the Organization of the Church of England* (Church House Publishing, 1995), has worked hard to pull them closer together in a more easily understood structure. Is this a reflection of the complexity of the Trinity or again does it have something to say to secular organizations? For example, what should be the relationship between the owners, who provide the capital, the workforce, who provide their intelligence and labour and the customers, who provide the income in return for goods and services?

One of the major difficulties facing flatter, non-hierarchical organizations is how to bind them together. The older hierarchical model worked by layers of management relating to the layer below them and interpreting senior management's directions into objectives and activities for the next level; the organization being held together through these layers of relationships. In the more dispersed and newer structures, empowered to make their own decisions, there is less to bind the structure together. One of the 'glues' being used is a clear set of 'agreed' values that all members of the organization buy into.

Values and ethics

As Professor Gillian Stamp has written, 'the secular world is stealing the Church's clothes'. One area she referred to is that most companies and indeed organizations now have a mission statement, company prayers and sets of values. More and more organizations are making these more explicit, both for the benefit of their staff – to provide the organizational 'glue' in the flatter, less hierarchical structures – and for the benefit of their customers – to know what kind of organization they are dealing with, and in the case of larger, international and global companies – to provide information to their wider 'publics' of their values and attitudes to the environment, politics and so on.

Many organizations develop their initial values from their founding owners, who doubtless will start with the values and ethics they were taught at home, in church (or equivalent) and at school. As fewer and fewer secular managers will have had the experience of church teaching and as schools are encouraged to reduce the amount of the curriculum they spend on these matters, a vacuum will be created for the development of values and ethics.

Is this why we see that an Institute of Business Ethics has been created in the last decade? This is a vibrant organization with patrons drawn from the senior members of most of the organized religions in the UK. They are providing advice and guidance in highly practical forms to those who are searching for ethics. Many of us carry deep seated Judeao-Christian values from the fact that we were brought up in the UK, which has a culture based on Judeao-Christian values that goes back over 1300 years, since they were brought here by St Augustine and St Columba.

It is good to see that the major business schools in England are now beginning to include ethics in their curricula. They will require the help of our churches and other religious groups to achieve this, but not exclusively.

One of the values that has been much heralded in recent management writings is the 'search for excellence'. Those organizations who pay attention to detail and doing the little things with excellence have been held up as having a trait that marks out the successful organization. The Church too often seems to make a virtue out of being extremely amateur and turning its back on a quest for excellence. Is this really God's plan for us and his Church?

Trust and conflict resolution

Trust has been a keyword in business and management from the very beginning. It is a very fragile and elusive commodity. Once broken it is difficult to re-establish. It is the ultimate form of 'actions speaking louder than words'. Trust requires us to believe what another person says is true or what they say they are going to do is true and to 'act in faith' that they will do what they said. If they do not do what they promise, or worse, if we do not do what we promised, then the trust is in danger of being undermined. In the final analysis, without 'trust' and faith in that trust, communities, society and its operating systems will all breakdown. The consequences of this are terrible; we have all witnessed this in this century between different nations and communities in the world. Even as I write, there has just been an agreement made on Northern Ireland and the plea is for people to look forwards and not backwards, that is, to re-build trust in each other by basing it on future actions and not those of the past.

In business trust is crucial between companies and their customers and clients, and between companies and their suppliers. Companies need to be able to trust that they are paying a fair price for goods and services and that the goods and services are fit for purpose and of an agreed quality and that agreements will be honoured.

In my first career in the construction industry, there were many signs of mistrust. As the rule of economics on the law of supply and demand altered, so some companies got drawn into taking advantage of others: sometimes the buyers squeezing the sellers too hard, and at other times the sellers taking advantage of the buyers. Often such behaviour produced adverse consequences for the so called 'winner' – that is, the contractor under bidding to win the work in competition, but intending to recover the under bidding through claims later. In another example, the buyer squeezes too hard and pushes his contractor into liquidation and finds himself with the project back in his own hands, which proves much more difficult and expensive to complete, often with consequential delays and problems.

The construction industry has regularly reviewed its performance since the early 1960s with reports by the National Economic Development Office (now disbanded), and the government. Nearly every single report, from the Wilson report in the 1960s to the Latham report this decade, has highlighted the need for contractors and clients to work together with common and agreed goals – trusting each other, which requires honesty and integrity. It is only now, after decades of mistrust, that this matter is beginning to be seriously addressed by both parties and we have the advent of 'partnering', the current buzzword of clients and contractors in the industry. I have spent over thirty years in construction – why has it taken so long to get this far? The cynics would say it is the state of the market – a buyer's market – and the fact that the buyers have come together to push the issue and the contractors are following along. Will they revert again, if times change and it becomes a seller's market? Is this just human nature?

Historically, there was also much mistrust in the construction industry between management and the employees. At an early stage of my career I spent one year as a PA to the yard director for the first North Sea oil rig and worked on a variety of 'special projects'. As a young engineer I had tremendous freedom of access to meetings on both sides of the management/union divide. I used to listen to these groups – management and unions – discussing their strategies for future joint meetings and negotiations. What always struck me was the degree of deviousness they could credit to their hypotheses of what the other group was planning. Generally these were way beyond the intellectual capacity of the other group and were born out of years of mistrust. I am very glad to say that this situation has been greatly improved in the industry since then, with the establishment of national agreements and new structures. These have provided the 'formal bridge' for mediation and reconciliation and closure of the culture gap. Alternatively, this may be because the market has changed to a buyer's market with the consequent pressures on labour to conform to the wishes of employers. Once more, as for company-to-company relationships, people ask whether this will revert if the market changes. Is this just human nature?

The quest to understand trust, how it works and what makes it last, are therefore focused on human nature. Whilst psychology and sociology can give us many insights into this area, so too I believe can theology. Christian values and creativity aim to build up rather than destroy, to heal and reconcile rather than cause destruction.

Christians believe that God is the epitome of trust. He created the world and all there is in and on it – including mankind and human nature. He gave us free will and the power to steward the earth. What better example of trust than that he made over the world he created for mankind?

What greater examples of trust than that a Father gives over His only Son? Christ's mission was to reconcile the relationship of human beings with God. This ultimate vision of harmony and working together as co-creators should be the vision for our human society and human transactions – then our prayers would be answered and His Kingdom come on earth, His will be done.

Conflict and its resolution requires us to explore our differences, to put ourselves in the other person's position and to try to understand their position, always remembering that it's easier to change ourselves than the other person. When we approach conflict in this way it can become a wholly positive force. We, and those we are in conflict with, can use it to aid our personal development; we often find that tackled in this way we can move forward together on a new and more effective path. In many places in the Bible Jesus shows us how to use conflict effectively, so why is it that so many of us are frightened to try?

Meaning and purpose in life

In my lifetime those of us in work have become better off financially and have undoubtedly moved up Maslow's 'hierarchy of needs'.* Indeed, we have become so well off that many of us appear to be approaching the top-level of his hierarchy – 'self-actualization', whatever that meant when he wrote it or indeed, what it means now. I think it has something to do with our spiritual well being, and that that is what he meant by it. I was recently recommended a book on NLP – neuro-linguistic programming. This too has a hierarchy on how to address our development needs, culminating in our 'spirituality'. Is the spiritual dimension beginning to come to the fore in the world of work? We in MODEM certainly believe so and have recently launched a research project, entitled 'The Hope of the Managers', to test our hypothesis.

Charles Handy has regularly concluded his recent books or talks by saying the fundamental human need of our times is for people to find meaning and purpose in their lives, and to be in community – not alone. If this is true, and I certainly believe it to be the case in my own experience of work, then a fundamental role of the leader or manager is to try to provide meaning and purpose to

---

* Maslow, an American sociologist, ordered human needs into a pyramid with seven levels. The base level was food, shelter, water and clothing; the top level was 'self-actualization' which might be renamed 'the search for the inner soul'. Neuro-linguistic Programming (NLP) lists six levels – environment, behaviour, capability, belief, identity and spirituality.

the communities that they work with, or to help the individuals they work with search out their own meaning and purpose.

All religions address the meaning and purpose of life and community life. Our job is to discern God's meaning and purpose for the world of work and our place in it. I believe theology can help us achieve this aim. People who have meaning and purpose in their work are generally much happier in their work, more effective and more productive – this must be a good enough reason on its own for a businessman to study theology!

There is a link here with values and ethics. Many organizations now espouse the value that their employees should have balance in their lives – particularly between work and home and play. Workaholics are not generally good for themselves nor those they work with. Managers and leaders in the secular world are more open to encouraging their staff to lead balanced lives, with time for God, families, leisure and health. This may be no more than motivated self-interest as a workforce with balance in their lives are likely to be healthier – both physically and mentally – and be more productive in their working time.

Relationships

This is becoming an increasing area of interest in business, as relationships have changed between customers and suppliers in the widest possible sense. There is much more often the notion of 'partnership' between the two these days. This is true whether we look at the buyer/seller, the employer/employee, the main contractor/sub-contractor, or any other kind of business relationship.

The marketing profession is now making a whole business out of 'relationship marketing', with marketing and behavioural specialists working together to understand how the relationships in marketing work and how to nurture and develop these relationships. As we move to a business world where the largest growth area is the 'service' sector, so this will become even more important.

The Jubilee Trust from Cambridge, a Christian-based charity, has had a lot of recent success undertaking 'relationship audits' for many diverse organizations. As I understand it, they look at the state of an organization's relationships with the other organizations and individuals it deals with. From this better understanding of its relationships the organization can develop plans to improve them.

Theology is founded on the most fundamental relationship of all – our relationship with God and each other. Since we are all made in the image of God, it has much to teach us about the development of our relationships – with God, with each other and with other communities. There is one very particular relationship we can learn about and that is the Father relationship that Jesus so often spoke about – a loving, caring, nurturing father, so unlike some people's experience of human fatherhood.

In the early part of the Industrial Revolution there were also many examples of a 'paternalistic' management style. Many of the early industrial entrepreneurs brought their own values into the work place and often imposed them on their employees. Even in the 1960s, when I joined John Laing, there was no smoking on company premises and no authorized expenditure on alcoholic drinks – and that in the construction industry! The Industrial Fathers – Rowntree, Cadbury, Wills (tobacco!), Sainsbury, Laing and many others – ran their companies with great care and love for their fellow men, often with great determination and drive. They bred a sense of loyalty, almost a family loyalty, where they were seen as benign dictators at work who gave a fair day's pay for a fair day's work, and expected to employ their employees for their whole working lives. In return for this job security the employee often had a very loyal view of his employer and worked often over and above the call of duty. More recently many of these great companies have gone through hard times and have had to shed staff. The notion of loyalty has been severely tested. Some of the early prophets would recognize the notion of their Father forsaking them – read Jeremiah!

Managing cultural differences

In the past, many Western countries have made the mistake of offering aid and practical technological help to developing countries, as 'experts' teaching local people that 'our way is the best way'. Attitudes conveyed dominance, superiority and paternalism and insufficient effort was made to affirm and draw on the indigenous culture and local 'way of doing things'.

What is culture? I like to think of it as the set of common understandings and answers, patterns of behaviour and mind sets that a society develops to answer the common questions faced by each and every society. Therefore, often over long periods, each society has developed its answers and they form deep-seated values in that society. Many of these 'answers' derive from the underlying religious beliefs of that society and as we know these vary around the world. If one truly explores the 'conflict' of different values and beliefs, that is to say explores the differences in an open way, constantly putting oneself in the other person's shoes and trying to understand things from their perspective, then we will all become more tolerant, less prejudiced and more open to learn from other cultures. At that point we can discover the richness of other cultures, their art, drama, poetry, religion, family life, political life and business. There are many examples of the negative effects of ethnocentrism in the Bible, particularly in the Old Testament. In the New Testament, Jesus used the Good Samaritan as his example of the 'outsider' demonstrating more of God's values than their own people did – those who considered themselves His people. We constantly see how God encourages us to love one another – the difficult part is to live it!

Cross-cultural communications need care, otherwise misunderstandings and resentments develop. Many overseas projects have 'imported' a large labour force, the vast majority on a bachelor basis, who have been very different from the local people of that region and which has had an enormous social impact on that local community. In the late 1970s, I spent two years with a construction company which had taken over a thousand Englishmen out to Poland to work on a petro-chemical project. There was a similar perception to the image the American forces had in England during the war – 'over-paid, over-sexed and over here'. I once spent an hour explaining to the client, after a complaint by him, about the morals of our lads away from home, only to discover that he was talking about their morale. The importance of language when you work in someone else's country! However, the main point is that to be effective away from home there are a number of considerations that have to be taken account of.

As a general rule, workers dislocated from their own society and roots require more support and pastoral care. Many of them will feel homesick, not a word we readily use in adult, macho male environments, but none the less very real. I recall a French foreman in Hartlepool (where we had an Anglo-French joint venture), complaining, after we had all had a few drinks, of being lonely and not having anywhere to go. Of course, the assembled British foremen all demanded to know why he had not said so, they would have invited him around! Indeed, as a result of his statement they did, and I hope other Frenchmen got invited too. Homesickness is very real and is about being disorientated by being in another culture, often with different values and beliefs, as well as being away from one's loved ones, family and friends. It is often best overcome by focusing on the host culture and trying to understand it from their point of view – in other words being other-centred or cosmopolitan. Ethnocentrism, the inherent belief that ours is a superior society, will not help us at all. Many of us forget that in that other culture their 'strange' behaviour is their 'norm' and it is us, with our 'different customs', that appear as 'odd'.

If we are to work effectively in another culture, there is a real need to know something about the culture we are going to live and work in. This is made up of a number of characteristics including the economic system, the governmental system, the family system, the work system, and so on. One of the most critical characteristics is the belief and value system usually determined from the prevailing religion in the country. This means we need to look at and try to understand these other religions and their followers. At a personal level, I have found this exploration, when in the company of true cosmopolitans, a truly worthwhile and enlightening experience. I recall a role-play exercise used on a ministerial training course. In the role-play a young university student arrives home at the end of the first term to tell her parents, mother first, of course – that she has become so interested in her roommate's religion – Hinduism – that she is going to become a Hindu herself. Needless to say the parents are horrified – 'How can you do this to us?' – much hand-wringing, and so on, before the girl eventually explains that her room mate has decided to become a Christian and is telling her parents this weekend. She just wanted her parents to 'feel' for the other parents. Many of the students had never seen 'evangelism, ministry and mission' in this way before and it was a great eye-opener!

When we consider our own religious beliefs it is often helpful to try to strip away from our own church (in my case the Anglican Church) those things that derive from our English culture rather than Christianity, in order to get back to the fundamentals of our religious beliefs. As Bishop Trevor Huddleston once put it, what he loves about the Church is its continuity and what he hates is its tradition. So often the tradition becomes too precious.

From another perspective, one of my former managing directors read a book on 'Jesus the man'. He said to me how amazing it was that Jesus was espousing the same values that he was trying to inculcate into his company. Need I say more!

Jesus encouraged his followers to avoid cultural dominance and the building of social stratification which devalued certain groups and their contribution to society. This created second-class citizens. The gospel affirms and celebrates the diversity of the human race, encouraging the valuing of the unique contribution of *every* person and cultural group and the need to draw on and learn from their different gifts and insights. This is equally important whether we are forming partnerships in multi-national cooperative ventures, or in a purely social context.

Management consultancy and its use

As organizations have slimmed down and as the business world has become increasingly competitive, so companies have turned to management consultants. These can take the time that line managers have increasingly less of, to help the organization think strategically. They can fill the gaps in the short term that exist in the organization that has pared off its specialists and spare capacity.

When I was a young man company directors would arrive at work mid-morning, have a large business lunch and depart mid-afternoon. Most of the directors I know these days are first in each day, last out each day, often work evenings and weekends and certainly do not have time for big lunches. Of course we often look back and think how 'idle' our predecessors were, but in fact they spent much of this 'spare time' thinking strategically about their business and the way to help it grow and expand. Without this time, management consultants have an increasingly important role to play in helping to plan and implement new business strategies.

I recently attended a consultation at St George's House, Windsor, on the role of MSEs. In other words, ordained priests who have full-time secular positions. During the consultation a few of us strategic consultants discussed the amount of money paid by the institutional church to its priests for the various roles undertaken.

Interestingly, many of the MSEs thought that the outcome indicated where many of them felt, on the fringe or even outside of the institutional church, misunderstood, unloved and unwanted. Some of us consultants saw them in a much more positive light as the potential keepers of the interface with the great un-churched. Recent polls of the secular world have indicated that 70% of the UK believe in a God, and 70% of those believe Jesus was His

Son, yet less than 5% attend a regular church! There is certainly room for a church that is part of our work and other communities.

We also saw the possibility of the church providing consultancy services to the secular world, even if we thought that this may be some way off. Therefore I was fascinated to read afterwards in a recent copy of *The Times* that a retiring dean of one of our cathedrals is to join a company to advise it on its 'culture' – presumably its values and ethics. One of the Church of England's bishops is already an advisor to the Institution of Civil Engineers on its ethics committee. I suspect that in the former case he will be paid by the company, rather than the Church, and probably at a much better set of rates! It is clear, however, that the church could offer such services and for a fee.

God at work

Herein probably lies the most difficult part of theology – discerning God's action in the world and particularly in the world of work and business. As I said at the beginning there are those who do not believe that God would have anything to do with the world of work. There are those who share with the many theologians who have tried the intellectual and philosophical difficulties of discerning God's actions in the world and I do not wish to start another chapter on God's providence and how we can recognize it.

Nevertheless, if God is at work in our world, by whatever means, then I am certain He does not ignore us in our work. Indeed, I would argue that part of God's providence is that He created us and the notion of work in order for us to produce things for ourselves and our fellow beings.

If this is the case, how can we ignore theology – the study of God and the development of our understanding of God, when it comes to learning more about management and leadership in the secular world?

2

Management isn't mysterious, it's just difficult

LEONARD COLLINSON

Are management and leadership the same thing?

First of all, I would like to emphasize that management and leadership are *not* the same thing. Leading is not managing, and managing is not leading. Managers are not necessarily leaders. Leaders are not automatically managers, nor are they required to be. John Adair says, 'Management is prose; leadership is poetry'.

However, we need leaders and managers. Leaders are few in number, and organizations have to have many more managers. Managers offer continuity. Leaders have crucial, and often temporary, tasks in predicting, interpreting and responding to circumstances. They paint the pictures of the future and set and preserve standards.

A great deal of everyone's time is spent managing or being managed. A manager is the key figure in an organizational scheme of things. Management is concerned with delivering measurable results. One thing is certain: a person is not a manager if the job cannot be measured in some way. Managers marshal resources to produce agreed outputs. This brings a proper bureaucracy: records and structures, systems for information, disciplines, sanctions and accountabilities. Patrick Engellau reckoned that, 'Bureaucracy functions according to the bacteria principle. If you place bacteria in a test-tube filled with nourishment, the bacteria will expand until the nourishment is finished. The same with bureaucracy: as long as it gets funding, it expands.' That is the behaviour of overheads. Managers must have not only objectives but the obligation to meet them.

Leadership is about the way forward; having the vision. It ensures that followers understand it and are persuaded to accept it. Sometimes this means sacrifices. It is not easily tested or assessed.

What are the qualities needed for managing? They may be elusive and tenuous things, but should be under ceaseless examination. When all is said and done, a primary managerial quality is almost certainly inborn. We seek the priceless component called 'character'. The manager's job can be analysed in systematic ways. With training and experience, much of it can be learnt. But 'character' illuminates the whole process. It adds a unique lustre to competence because it opens up the scarce vistas of courage, imagination and adventure.

But leadership is not charisma. Hitler, Mussolini and Stalin were three great charismatics of this century. Leadership is hard, mobile and visible work. We think of Attlee, Montgomery, Roosevelt and Mother Teresa. Leadership is not a right. It is the congruence between words and deeds, behaviour and professed values. The word integrity comes to mind. A leader takes things seriously, not herself or himself. Leaders do not point towards some place and tell people to go there. They go to that place and make a case. But leadership seems to be discussed only when it is absent. Those who think about it a lot are not leaders. Natural leaders are those who do not think about leadership, but have never considered any other job. Leaders know what needs to be done, can articulate it and get it accepted by others. True leadership is for the benefit of the followers, not the enrichment of the leader.

Leadership is not always connected with job titles, particularly at the top; for example, chairman, archbishop, Prime Minister, general, and so on. This is especially so in large organizations.

People in less prestigious positions in hierarchies frequently exercise leadership.

However, there is a danger in staying with this question of whether management and leadership are one and the same thing. We can get bogged down in the issue, becoming prisoners of the words and incurring the wrath of those to whom 'management' is a turn-off. We can be side-tracked from ways of doing things better, using resources efficiently and effectively. This can include unpleasant duties. The *New York Evening News*, 20 June 1933, had a piece entitled 'A Business Man's Philosophy' by William Feather.

An old man once observed that in every successful organization there is a thoroughly mean man who exercises a good deal of authority. The founder and president of the company might be the soul of geniality, a pillar of the church and a leader in all civic enterprises, but in deciding hard and ugly questions the mean man is given his way.

'Mean problems must be met', continued the old man. 'Suppliers become indifferent. Salesmen grow lazy. Faithful but useless employees must be discharged. Expenses rise. Profits dwindle.' The mean man says what he thinks and insists faults be corrected. Perhaps someone must be demoted. Or dividends must be suspended. Or salaries must be cut. The mean man may or may not have initiated this unpleasant business, but to him is voted the nasty job of effecting these new policies.

Success is partly the consequences of willingness to undertake unpleasant duties. Postponement of the pain of an operation sends sick people to an early grave, and by the same process, sick businesses drift into receivership. The mean man, who may be president, vice-president or a director, refuses to put off until tomorrow what should be done today. His meanness keeps the business healthy and is a great asset to the firm.

This is worth thinking about, but managers must expect the best of others. They can accept and respect others as they are, with all their strengths and weaknesses, and then challenge them to become more. In fact, if we do not go beyond what we have already accomplished, we will never grow. Managers should expect other employees to deliver their best and provide opportunities for excelling.

Whatever it is or is not – it's difficult

When Prince Charles saw fit to criticize managers in a newspaper article, he became the latest of a long line of critics who have an undistinguished managerial record. However, to be blamed for economic plights does concede that good management is a valuable asset and that is a step forward. But managers are too soft on their critics. They bend over backwards to avoid offence to anyone. They allow concentration on peripheral activities. The socially responsible manager demands economic performance and abhors waste of all resources. Nothing less will do, and they should say so.

All decisions are held in the tension between expediency and morality. Otherwise, there would be no need for them. Those of us who have the privilege of responsibility have an obligation to face the associated conflicts and problems . . . and opportunities. Often, it is alleged that managerial skills are deliberately mysterious and there is a demand for them to be 'demystified'. But there is nothing mysterious about management. The techniques used are simply those that try to detect patterns in events and to discern sensible choices of action so that judgements can be made, often in situations of intractable complexity.

Management is not mysterious, it is just difficult. Nor is it a process that can be wished away. Integration has to be carried out in some fashion, whether it be by a centralized elite or by being distributed throughout a non-hierarchical collective. Problems of organization are not dissolved by being dispersed. Whether the manager is dealing with a hospital, a ship or a business, the resources have to be marshalled to perform aims and objectives in the face of dilemmas. Management is not an authority-form for suppressing spontaneous and natural efficiency.

Excellence in management is brute perseverance: time, repetition and simplicity. There ought to be constant pressure on creating an organization with fast responses: then there is less reliance on forecasting and other planning techniques. But Peter Drucker says, 'systematic management practices are very much a feature of today's best entrepreneurs. Entrepreneurs of an earlier generation neither had nor wanted to acquire the weight of accumulated knowledge on managing people, communications, team formation, marketing, cash flow and even innovation itself.' That is why the persistent cries that British industry is underinvested have often not rung true. Managerial skill is the key, not just plant and equipment. It is how plant and equipment are managed which draws the line between corporate success and failure. A lot of managers have their own 'pet' theory about how things ought to be managed. The most common feature of these advocacies is the confidence of each manager that his or her problems are more intransigent than those of everyone else.

What is the nature of management? Much has been said and written about this issue. Analyses, models, theories, cracker-barrel philosophies and empirical evidence are available to everyone. Managers are crucial, highly visible (they wear posh suits) and have enjoyed a spectacular and relatively recent rise numbers and importance. They have specialist journals, dedicated pages in 'quality' newspapers, degree courses, unique training schools and professional bodies. Managers are blamed, praised, researched and paid. Boyatzis, in his book, *The Competent Manager* asserts that outstanding performers have certain characteristics. They

- push others to find better or less expensive ways of doing things;

- seize opportunities and do significantly better than is usually demanded on a job;
- apply concepts and are able to see similarities and differences between situations;
- develop visions or an understanding of what has to be done, without necessarily using existing rules or wisdom;
- calculate carefully the best ways for influencing others' actions or thinking;
- catch imaginations, either in one-to-one conversations or large groups;
- are able to present viewpoints that are diametrically opposed to their own;
- demonstrate a feeling of certainty and being in control.

Mikhail Gorbachev reflected, 'Difficulties arose largely due to the tenacity of managerial stereotypes'. What management does, what it is supposed to be doing, and if it does a good job, has been widely misunderstood. While the theorists (Brech, Renold, Barnard Drucker, Fayol and the like) agree that managers plan, organize, control and motivate, there are two popular conceptions: managers are the people at the top of an organization, and they direct the work of others. But these only say who belongs to management – maybe! Remember the old joke: the secret for top managers is to obtain the 'glider quality', the skill to rise higher and higher by going round in circles, supported by a constant stream of hot air.

Management is still quite a primitive notion. As is common in rapidly evolving disciplines, the gap between the leading practitioners and the majority is enormously wide and closing slowly. Not enough of today's managers realize that management is defined by responsibility and not by power. Even fewer fight the debilitating disease of bureaucracy; the belief that big budgets and huge staffs are accomplishments rather than incompetence.

We must analyse what managers do. If, for example, a company decides to build a new plant, lays off workers or change prices, this is to speak of managerial decisions, actions and behaviour. A company can only act as its managers do; by itself, a company has no effective existence.

Most managers prefer the label of 'technocrat' – totally apolitical, with private lives and views separate from managerial actions. This is an inadequate stance. The rise of new stakeholders – public interest groups in particular – can be traced in part to the ideological abdication of managers. The vacuum has been filled by others who neither understand the nuances of business activity nor are impressed with the material benefits of modern business. Marxists have been successful in contrasting their ideals with those of capitalism. The concept of competition goes against the educational bias to equality of anyone who has grown up since 1945. As a result, many managers retreat into technocracy rather than endure the ambivalence of 'hard-nosed management'. They have refused to engage in arguments about the conflicts between equality, co-operation and an individual's rights. Managers must develop an ideology which is clearly in closer harmony than Marxists with the rest of society, education, the church and the political ideas of western democracy. Until this happens, and managers engage in the argument, real legitimacy will not be won and the management of stakeholder forces – consent from governments, managers, workers, unions, customers and consumers' groups – will be an essentially rearguard action.

There are two major parts to management: making and implementing decisions. As Percy Barnevik, former head of Asea Brown Boveri, suggests, 'In any business decision, ninety per cent of success is execution, ten per cent is strategy. And of that ten per cent, only two per cent is really analysis and eight per cent is the guts to take uncomfortable decisions.'

The question is, 'How do you mobilize people?' First, by making decisions. Decisions are meant to achieve something, and objectives are the boundaries within which the decisions are made. Once these limits are recognized, progress can be made and it can be seen that management has no absolute power, and that the power it does have can and should be challenged – the reasons for a decision can be requested, the nature of the problem to be solved can be defined, options with their possible consequences can be set out and everyone can understand that hopes, fears and internal policies prejudice decisions.

Secondly, by implementation. Managers have to organize, communicate, control and motivate, and often fail because panaceas are sought based on incorrect assumptions about motivation. Incentives for managers should be linked to actual results against a dated and costed plan. My experience suggests finding four or five ratios essential to improved performance in the forthcoming financial year. Aim high.

Management is not and can never be an exact science. It can be analysed and classified and this is beneficial, but achievement rather than knowledge remains, of necessity, both proof and aim. To deal with this reality is at the core of the manager's task. The term 'manager's task' is chosen carefully. Those who see management as a status will get into more and more difficulties. They believe themselves to be different in kind from their subordinates rather than different in degree. They pursue a more offensive restrictive practice than the worst craft union. A manager takes decisions about the beneficial use of scarce resources. If a manager cannot furnish guidance in the technicalities of doing a particular job because of generalist pretensions and distaste for detail, then it will be natural for workers to seek leadership elsewhere. The Swedes have noted that British managers are often self-conscious about their titles as managers, regardless of what it is they are managing.

Robert Heller has concluded that managing is a far more homely business than its would-be scientists admit; that it's more closely allied to cooking than any other activity. Like cooking, it rests on a degree of organization and enough resources. But just as no two chefs run their kitchens alike, so no two managers are identical, even if they all went to the same business (cookery) school. You can teach the common rudiments of a subject, but you cannot make a great cook or a great manager. In managing and cooking, you ignore fundamentals at grave risk – but sometimes succeed. In both, science can be helpful but is no substitute for the art itself. Inspired amateurs can outdo professionals. Perfection is rare, and failure is more common than is realized by customers. Practitioners of managing and cooking do not need recipes which show timing down to the last second, procedures to the last flick of a wrist and all ingredients to the precise fraction of an ounce. They need reliable maxims, instructive anecdotes and no dogmatism.

Managers tend to defend the marketing status quo with might and main, even though the one unchanging characteristic of markets is that they change. Suggest that a little market research would not come amiss and all too often you receive appeals to long, arduous years of experience in the trade and grumpy concessions that dubious assumptions are 'obvious' – in short, a refusal to contemplate the turbulence of thinking and acting anew.

Management is a practice rather than a science or a profession, though it contains elements of both. As a practice, not a lot is known about it because it varies by function, level and the situation of the organization. This is why it is doubtful if the 'good manager' can manage anything and why it leads to an over-emphasis on similarities at the expense of differences; and why most descriptions of managers' jobs are so general as to be universally valid. Is management an art? A US baseball coach gives good advice: 'The art of management lies in keeping the people who hate you away from the people who have not yet made up their minds.' The move to lay down professional qualifications for managers has overtones of a holy ritual. The suggestion goes that in charting their ways up a ladder of qualifications, British managers would learn how to negotiate the zoo-ground in organizational life. Well-constructed rungs might even produce guileful corporate snakes. Other professions set out stringent tests for entry into their protections and privileges (law and accountancy come to mind). That they are not noticeable for their spirit of enterprise seems to have held no sway.

Managers are concerned with three processes: seeking change for beneficial growth; the application of managerial techniques and systems and the selection, training and motivation of better calibre people than themselves. Change will be a main factor for management in the next twenty years. Teaching a manager what he ought to read and how he ought to behave and think emphasises particular results. Today's managerial skills for success may pave the way for tomorrow's failure. These may not apply when she or he is given the opportunity to use her or his knowledge. Timeless wisdoms is how to learn, how to diagnose situations and how to profit from experience.

Directors and senior managers in businesses thrash themselves about management development. Everyone is an expert. However, the belief that managers can develop subordinates to be more skilful in interpersonal competence and accurate diagnosis of managerial situations has been replaced by the belief that no one can develop anyone except himself or herself. Therefore, the purpose of developmental programmes has shifted to assisting managers to become aware of themselves and the consequences of their actions. Equally, the responsibility of managers is not to develop people. It is to establish the climate and the opportunities for self-development. But we must have learning managers, not learned ones. Then their successors will think of resolving issues, not simply possessing the answers.

Some of the reasons for this change are as follows: (1) that the former implies that a person's present behaviour is wrong. Who knows what is the correct leadership? (2) That research reveals that there is not a preferred form of leadership for all situations. Effective leadership may require a number of different patterns. The argument between democratic and autocratic style is sterile. It should be replaced by the concept of reality-centred leadership. (3) That change will be the main challenge for managers in the next decade.

Management is a business concept

Management is the specific organ of an enterprise. This is so obvious that it has been taken for granted. It is the function of securing measurable outputs. Managers tend to emphasize similarities between organizations, whereas they ought to be paying attention to the differences. It is in the mastery of detail that good managers excel and these differ from organization to organization.

Management is charged with supplying goods and services whilst discharging its duties in accordance with society's political and ethical beliefs. But these social responsibilities are the conditions which limit, modify, encourage or retard the activities of the enterprise. These constraints change from time to time and it is vital to know when they are changing or about to change. This is not to condemn previous practices. In their time, they were accepted as appropriate and relevant.

The central principle that determines the nature of the management is measurable performance. Management has failed if it does not satisfy the demands of customers or stakeholders at a price they are prepared to pay and if it does not enhance the resources entrusted to it.

There are several hard-won lessons from the practice of management:

- distrust analysis;
- keep in touch with operations and markets;
- face up to issues;
- recognize change and the need to change; to do nothing and expect nothing to change is a recipe for disaster;
- it is a mistake to assume that change only comes about through the actions of top people.

Managing a non-business organization

All too often, however, institutions like the church refuse to contemplate plans for measurable results. They condone sloppy approaches to setting priorities and demanding outcomes, calling on alleged difficulties and differences instead of searching for equally stringent controls and targets. The more liberal the protests, the less they change. The alleged experts in human activity can give the impression of not being a bit interested in the church. They do not even see it. It is the place that enables them to do what they like with their careers. The idea that the institution is not created to enable them to lead a good life has not occurred to them. Politicking absorbs a great deal of time, but they use dummy ammunition; nobody gets fired. Performance really means getting a bigger budget out of the system, one does not measure it by the service given. Fortunately, churches are short of money. This will become their salvation – it makes them think.

In the churches, sector ministry – especially Industrial Mission (IM) – might have been expected to be among the first to appreciate the need for an organ similar to business management, if the aims were to be met. Industrial Mission has not, so far, explored seriously the nature and objectives of management. In 1988, an appraisal of Industrial Mission in the Church of England (and other churches) painted a controversial picture of IM. It was said to lack a sense of direction, ownership, accountability, support and management. Even where there had been management committees – the recommended model for local IM – there was little evidence of clarity by industrial missioners of the contribution of management.

As chairman of one such committee, I see the former ethos of well-meaning effort being seen as sufficient. But if you do what you have always done, you get what you always got. Personal choice dominates actions. There is no pride in extending the influence of parishes. Empowering lay people is comfortable jargon, not an imperative. Indeed, I suspect the ability to recruit and motivate lay people towards agreed outputs is a neglected and resisted skill.

Nonetheless, it is lay people who will promote a balanced theology for Industrial Mission. They know work is the means by which we live. The economic process for designing, producing, marketing and distributing goods and services is vital to our existence and central to our daily lives. Work (or lack of it) is by far the biggest, single defining factor in life for individuals and families. It governs where people live, the style and cost of living, the time-patterns of families. It consumes personal energy, and holds out prospects of positive growth – personal, family and corporate. It moulds opinions, influences values and plays a part in a perception of self-worth. The church has to be where the work is done, embedded in the structures that organize the economic community. This is a pivotal place, responding to God and co-operating in his work of transformation. We have to be alongside the people who are in the process. The mission in this context is to find out what God is doing and do it with him.

Much of life gets its meaning from work. The workplace matters and it does have a theology. Yet there is no celebration of those people who create jobs. We do little to persuade those at work of their obligations to deal with social exclusion.

Ethics in the workplace went on to boards' agendas years ago. Yet the church seemed blissfully unaware of it; certainly it hadn't filtered through to IM. IM is not averse to taking on projects, but never with the commitment to seeing them through at agreed deadlines/outputs. And yet they willingly serve on committees of all kinds as advisers.

A keen lay person is absorbed into a labyrinth of committees that claim to oversee a diminishing presence in all parts of the community. He or she becomes worn out by words, paper and inactivity. Senior clergy, suffragan bishops, archdeacons, area deans seem to do their own thing. The assumptions are pastoral, reliance on the promises clergy make on their ordination (the ordinal), on love (not truth in love) and on the absence of a relevant theology. That is, they are doing things for the right reasons, results can be left to God and in God's good time.

The church is fighting hard to remain clericalized. The clergy are busy, not lazy, but busy working in inward-looking bureaucracies and probably reacting to declining numbers of 'clients' by decentralizing.

The realignment from top-down to bottom-up will not stop. It is an inevitable and proper reaction to the shortage of monies and people and a more sophisticated 'consumer'. The specialists will have to market themselves and parishes will be free to buy in services. Sector ministries and 'clusters' of parishes will be demand-led, not producer-pushed.

3

The new public management

DAVID HENSHAW

Not so very long ago, I had the opportunity to sit down for lunch with a local authority chief executive I first worked with as a young executive assistant in the middle 1970s. He has long since retired but does keep a healthy interest in all matters of local government. He has been fascinated by the developments over the last few years and particularly with the end of what seemed a near-permanent Conservative government and the arrival of a new fresh-faced Labour government with what seems a passion for turning over many of the fields of public policy. As ever, our conversation drifted back to local government; this time he was probably more pithy and direct than I had heard before in terms of how he remembered his own role as a local authority chief executive and how he tried to understand mine as another local authority chief executive some twenty years later. The one constant when we talked seemed to be change, with the good news being that a lot of change was over with, but the bad news being that there was more to come. (I should mention that he is and was a lawyer who progressed to the role of town clerk and then chief executive, whereas I am a general manager with a background of management training and experience who perhaps sees the role of a chief executive in today's times very much more in pro-active terms than was certainly the case in the 1970s.)

It is worth reflecting, though, before getting into the substance of this discussion, about how one might best understand local government from some distance. Stepping back and looking at the structure of the local government you could be forgiven, in the words of my former mentor Professor John Stewart of the University of Birmingham, for thinking that local authority departments generally seem to be monuments to past problems. It is not very complicated. If you look at some of the great reforms of the late 1800s and some of the emerging problems in our then rapidly industrializing society, organizations or departments were set up inside local authorities devoted to a pretty focused group of problems. Look, for example, at public health, and the way in which the public health problems of the late 1800s demanded a response from local government; thus the public health departments of yesteryear – and today, in many cases – were formed.

Of course, monuments to past problems have strengths as well as weaknesses, in the sense that there is a huge base of experience built up with the talent and capacity of dealing with many of the fundamental problems which still pertain in much of our urban and indeed, for that matter, rural context today. However, departments are also, at the core, one of the fundamental weaknesses of our system in the sense that they constrain thinking, limit perspective and can be a major force for conservatism with a small 'c'. But the trap that many fall into, in confronting this issue of departments as monuments to past problems, is believing that the answer lies in structural change, whether it be by re-organizing local government or re-organizing within local government, in particular local authorities.

There is another perspective, though, that is worth reflecting on, and that is what we are seeing now in a more substantial sense across the public sector – the development of the 'new public management'. It is worth reflecting on the new public management, which I believe is central to the leadership of local government and local authorities in the UK and indeed elsewhere, as it now forms a base-line for a very different approach to managing public services, leading local governments and leading local government areas. In this rather brief opportunity the term 'new public management' will be considered and enlivened by reference to how it should, in my judgement, be actioned in the new local government setting that we have today. There are some examples drawn from my own local authority, where I have sought to illustrate how the new public management is having a major impact on others, with a wider or general perspective in the UK and outside.

The development of the term 'new public management' has accelerated dramatically over recent years. It is in some senses a contradiction. At one level there is nothing new in these changing approaches to public management: they import ideas from other sectors – private, voluntary, political – and reform and recast them in models and approaches appropriate to a public sector norm. That said, the new public management is having a dramatic effect on bureaucracies throughout the world.

The pace of change varies considerably, with some of the mature Western democracies in some sectors accelerating rapidly with the introduction of the new public management, whilst in others there continues to be a high level of resistance – bureaucratic, political and organizational.

Understanding the new public management and what it means in practical terms is difficult, not from any simple understanding of the concepts, but rather their applicability in particular local settings. The mature Western democracies and all the different sectors present a very different picture to perhaps some of the new emerging democracies, both in the southern hemisphere and indeed Eastern Europe. There is an argument, though, that the new public management approaches can be more quickly implemented in the emerging democracies, because the huge leap of thinking and changing practice can be implemented more easily in less resistant situations.

What are the essentials of the new public management? Perhaps a good way to illustrate this issue is to talk in terms of style and then to consider some particular aspects of the new public management which illustrate the quite significant changes and differences in approach. New public management brings a whole new contrasting style to the bureaucratic approach which has held sway for so many decades. Set out below is a list of the characteristics of two contrasting styles that illustrate differences. In the left column is the bureaucratic style and in the right, the new public management style.

efficiency	effectiveness
today	tomorrow
reactive	proactive
internal	external
inputs	quality
control	accountability
tradition	innovation
detail	pattern
directing	guiding
procedure	principle
authority	responsibility
risk avoider	risk taker
uniformity	flexibility

But there are also spectrums with styles varying to different degrees and different intensities in different organisations. For example, there might be an organization that is midway in the spectrum where there is a joint focus on both efficiency and effectiveness. Indeed, in illustrating the extremes it is not to suggest that there needs to be one and not the other. For example, there is a balance to be struck between accountability and control, but perhaps the illustration would be that the emphasis on the new public management would be on accountability as opposed to a control agenda set by the organization.

What, then, would be some key elements of the new public management that would illustrate some of the quite distinct differences of approach? These are many and varied, but the following may illustrate where major steps away from the bureaucratic model have been taken in moving towards the new public management.

Strategic management

In illustrating contrasting styles there was a counter-pointing of today and tomorrow. Strategic management has been the major force of change in many of these changing organizations. The essence of strategic management in the public sector is, put simply, drawn from the best of the private sector experience, but given a broader cast. Strategic management is about developing, adopting and implementing an overall approach to the aims and vision of the organization in respect of the environment it is dealing with. Strategic management is about painting a broad picture of where the organization wishes to go with the environment within which it deals, and at its best using processes of strategic management that enable the widest perspective to be adopted in developing the end outcomes that are required. So, the emphasis is on looking at the picture overall, thinking outside the organizational structures which are often a way of simplifying the problem for organizational convenience' sake and more importantly developing a holistic approach which may – and usually does – involve other partners and players who are not necessarily within the gift and control of the organization concerned. At the local authority level – and in Knowsley's particular case in developing a strategic management agenda – there were some very simple questions to be asked at the outset by the council. The questions that were asked were as follows:

- Where do you want the place to be by the year 2000?
- What sort of balance do we want in jobs, environment and housing?
- What resource base do we have at our disposal?
- Can we agree and support a vision?

The developing of this approach took some eighteen months, but illustrates that the process of the work was as important as the outcomes reached. In the end a strategic management agenda that was fully empowered was set out as below:

The sole purpose of Knowsley Council is to provide services of high quality to all who live and work in the borough and to local employers and visitors.

In providing these services the following priorities have been identified:

- the environment is attractive, safe and healthy and that every effort is made to reduce crime and vandalism; people in the community feel a sense of belonging and pride and the disadvantaged and vulnerable are supported and represented;
- housing available is affordable, well built and maintained and attractive to a range of income groups;
- education and training opportunities are available to local people and the developing partnership with industry and commerce attracts and retains a continuing commitment to Knowsley from the private sector;
- there is access to good shopping and leisure facilities and health services and transport links enable people to take advantage of these;
- opportunities are available for all Knowsley's citizens to contribute to, thus fostering a sense of belonging, responsibility and pride in, the borough and its people.

As can be seen, this is a very simple – and some might say 'an apple pie' – sort of statement, but behind these strategic aims lie a whole host and wealth of implementation plans which act as the building blocks for operational achievement of the aims. The actual strategic agenda is very simple, but it took some getting there. The phrase 'I'm sorry this letter is so long, I didn't have time to write you a shorter one' is very appropriate here.

Strategic management in itself is worth some extended study, as it can act as the cornerstone or building block for the re-engineering of change in bureaucratic public sector organizations in adopting the new public management. But it is not the only building block; indeed, the whole process of strategic management illustrates the point that there are a series of building blocks, which all need to be in place to achieve the overall change in organizational focus and direction.

From client and user to customer

Another important element, which illustrates the new public management, is the change in focus on the approach to the people who are served by the activities of the organization concerned. In the past the tendency would be to see the people who are recipients of services very much in terms of clients or users of services, with an organizational relationship defined more in terms of the organization above the users or clients, in doing to them rather than providing services for them.

The word 'customer', though, has many negative connotations and indeed has been the subject of much criticism in some of the comment on the new public management. Much of this criticism is misplaced as it tends to focus on the imagery and resonance that the word 'customer' suggests. In my terms the new public management's use of the word customer is not seeking to overlay a private sector approach – with all the assumptions of multiple choice that the customer has – nor to focus on service and profit. Indeed, there is a certain logic about using 'customer' to describe the users and recipients of services that are usually provided by a monopoly or certainly in a semi-monopoly situation. But, in terms of organizational change, the use of the word customer is potent in illustrating to employees that there is a new way of appreciating the importance of those who are in receipt of our services. What will be seen from the above strategic management statement is that one of the first issues to be settled was to assert the sole purpose of Knowsley Metropolitan Council, which was to provide services of high quality to all who live and work in the borough and to local employers and visitors. It was a recognition that the only reason that the council existed was to serve those people out there in all their forms. Previously the culture of the organization suggested that the people we provided services to were the biggest problem. Indeed, the half humorous comment of 'these councils would be wonderful to run without the people we have to provide services to' or 'these schools would be excellent without the pupils', reminds us with just a grain of truth about how disruptive those who receive services are within the rational process of service provision.

Organising around the customer

As pointed out above, one of the key problems in public service provision in recent years (and not so recent years) has been the abilities of bureaucracies to organize to suit themselves in neat organizational boxes and sometimes make it as difficult as possible for service users to access services. At its simplest level this has meant making offices inaccessible, not providing any coherence in accessing services and indeed making sure that users really had to work very hard to gain services. Illustrations of this include closing offices for lunch when most people would be wanting to access services, and also closing at times when most people want services to be available. In Knowsley, as well as changing towards a programme of one-stop shops, which are a single service point for all services to be accessed, moving towards 24-hour call centres, we have also taken to using marketing techniques – to develop a whole new range of approach to service provision – which at the core are about providing the service when the customer wants it, where he or she wants it, at the level he or she wants it. For example, nowadays, if you are renting a council house from Knowsley, you could ring up until 10 pm seeking services and indeed our own housing officers ring tenants until quite late in the evening, enquiring about rent arrears and seeing whether there is a possibility of settling the debt! The simple theme is organizing around the customer, as most of the private sector does if it is to be successful.

The most poignant demonstration of this is in the field of economic development. Local authorities are in many ways the worst barriers to economic development and inward investment success. Bureaucratic approaches to provision of service have so often been the subject of complaint and criticism from the private sector. Inward investment, economic development, people interested in developing and expanding businesses into new areas of countries, are interested in a number of basic things. They are interested in the costs of establishment, the quality of what they can get in terms of land, buildings, employees but most importantly they want a simplicity, clarity and ease of approach in dealing with the public sector muddle, as they perceive it, of regulation and control. In Knowsley's terms we have followed the principle of organizing around the customer in the business arena as well. We have a one-stop business resource centre where any private sector business, or any organization for that matter, wanting to gain access to our services is dealt with. There is one single point of contact and that contact then deals with the bureaucracy on behalf of the customer. It isn't just cosmetic either. It's about improving real service at a cost and quality which means there is a real sized change in inward investment. One of my favourite anecdotes is the story of the American company who have now invested in Knowsley. From the day they saw the site they wished to buy – with the processes of acquisition, planning permission, building regulation control, to the day the bulldozers started – took only seven and a half weeks. The American senior executives still talk about the pace and speed and quality of the public sector response to their demands: they are the best advertisement for our inward investment ability.

Performance management

Underpinning the changes in new public management – as illustrated in the contrasting styles list – is a great emphasis on the specific performance achieved by the organization, with measurement being focused on real identifiable outputs as opposed to meaningless input measures. Performance management, without being too detailed in description, is about making sure that the task that is focused on through the process of strategic management is undertaken with a view to looking for the highest levels of success in achieving the objectives; it is being in a position with appropriate monitoring; and it is being responsive to changes required to achieve the best performance possible. Performance management is often misunderstood. It is not simply about control, statistics or performance indicators, which are useful tools in the process. It is the process by which, in many public sector organizations, the new public management can be both monitored and focused in terms of outputs. It lays emphasis on accountability, quality, innovation even and perhaps, more importantly, measurement of success and flexible responsive systems which enable small changes, through slight touches of the tiller, to gain appropriate changes in operation. Again, performance management in line with strategic management is an area which needs exploring in full to realize the benefits that can be gained as part of an overall approach to the new public management.

There are many other areas where the new public management and its approach can be illustrated in contrast to the bureaucratic models that we know so well in the public sector. These range and vary and are just as important as others described above but include, in terms of accountability, a cost centre or business unit approach to organizing the bureaucracy so that there is a marrying of operational responsibilities, together with financial accountability and a clarity and knowledge about levels of responsibility and requirements of individuals. Performance appraisal and performance-related pay are important tools in this process in developing an employee structure which is focused, accountable, effective, but at the same time one which has high levels of capacity for innovation, high levels of acceptance of responsibility and where the workforce shares an overwhelming commitment to the strategic vision and aims of the organization involved. Decentralization is an element of such approaches, although again there are examples of public sector organizations that remain highly centralized in terms of policy direction for all sorts of good reasons, but at the same time have, through service provision, provided a flexible, focused, empowered employee group who provide high quality effective services.

There is one final note which it is important to stress, particularly in the context of a discussion on the new public management in the context of British local government. In the UK the new public management has not simply been a response to the compulsory competition and other pressures brought in by the previous Thatcher government and successive conservative government of later years. Indeed, there is a strong argument to suggest that the new public management had its groundings in a period earlier than the Thatcher government when there was a growing appreciation that the comprehensive blueprint planning of Programme Planning Budgeting Systems (PBBS) and the rest have proved to be yet again another failed initiative in improving the quality and capacity of public administration. All these other approaches, such as PBBS, have had limited success and this was increasingly recognized as being because of the lack of overall connection with the holistic style and culture of management of public sector organizations. If public sector organizations are to be transformed they require an integration and a holistic approach, in many ways far greater than any other private sector comparable organizations. The reasons? Well, put very simply, the private sector has a clarity of purpose which is centred around service, profit, customers, and so on. This is a gross oversimplification but it is to illustrate the point: the public sector, particularly local authorities in the UK experience, have first a whole set of responsibilities and a disparate range of services which in a private sector analogy you would never find in a single company, as many of the services provided have the remotest connections with each other, except that they are within terms of public provision of service. Secondly, as well as having this multiplicity of services, there is the overlaying of political control which in the best of local government in the UK has asserted its remit and responsibility and legitimacy in the field of strategic management and policy aims and development, rather than detailed political involvement in service provision on the ground. All of these factors demonstrate the need for a higher quality holistic approach to the re-engineering and re-focusing of many of our public sector organisations, with single type initiatives or system initiatives like PPBS, proving not to be sufficient to make the change.

For the future, though, there are continuing changes. The whole area of government service, be it at central or local level, together with the new emerging managerialism, is leading to new tensions. There will, in my judgement, be a continuing and growing tension between the needs of politicians, at whatever levels, to re-assert what they feel to be 'control' over these bureaucracies which at the same time as becoming re-focused or energetic, sensitive, adaptable and flexible, appear to be in some cases to be out of touch with the political directive. There are illusions here, and put again with stark simplicity, the issue here is not a system problem or structure problem, it is about leadership issues which have to be resolved between the conflicting and sometimes competing players in the political, managerial and administrative groupings.

4

Learning from charities

CHRISTOPHER BEMROSE

Introduction: 'To be true to their name, charities need to be inspired by love'

The sense of love is often easiest to find in a charity's early days. There is the sense of overwhelming commitment to a particular group of people, responding and maybe identifying with needs in a particular way. There is a sense of creativity which provides the energy to overcome initial obstacles. There is a sense of excitement, moving into uncharted waters.

Over time, however, commitment cools and creativity can turn to crisis. Excitement seems to be elsewhere. In some cases the organization becomes increasingly irrelevant, entrenched in a conservative mind-set in which any changes are seen as a betrayal of the founder's beliefs and practices. In other cases the sense of the special and distinctive is watered down as the organization follows the norms of the world. Once lost, it becomes difficult – if not impossible – to recover the original spirit of charity and love. As Christ said, 'Salt is good, but if it loses its saltiness, how can you make it salty again?' (Mark 9:50).

This chapter seeks to explore some of the temptations that charities face as they try to retain their 'saltiness' – the particular values that make them distinctive. In so doing, I have used the temptations that Christ faced in the desert as a guide. I believe that the temptations themselves and the responses of Christ have lessons both for charities in general and their leaders in particular

The article draws heavily on examples from L'Arche. It is an organization I have come to know well over the last two years. It provides an example of an organization which, thirty-five years after its foundation, still seeks to be guided in the spirit of the gospel. L'Arche (French for The Ark) began when Jean Vanier, a Canadian, felt called to share his life with two people with learning disabilities (mental handicaps). From the initial two people, Raphael Simi and Philippe Seux, L'Arche has grown into an organization with 4000 people in 100 communities around the world.

L'Arche implicitly follows the family model in the way it organizes itself. As such, it provides something of an alternative. Assistants live with people with learning difficulties, not as service providers with clients, but as people sitting around the same table – each giving and receiving from each other in different ways. There is an emphasis on a simple lifestyle which emphasizes relationships. There is a belief in the importance of welcome, especially of those who are weak or rejected.

L'Arche is limited in many ways, It is, as one person put it, like a leaking boat in a raging sea. Numerically, it is insignificant against the millions of people with learning difficulties world wide. Organizationally, it has the same questions and problems as any other organization of the same size and stage of development. Spiritually, trying to discern the organization's call and direction is seldom simple. But as I look at the temptations of Christ in the desert and the temptations that face value-based organizations such as L'Arche, the similarities seem considerable. I want to explore and compare our experience in L'Arche and Christ's temptations in the wilderness. It is possible that there may be similarities which can be seen in other organizations.

1. The temptation of efficiency: stones into bread

Jesus, we are told in Luke 4:1, was full of the Holy Spirit when he was led into the desert for forty days. It was the start of his ministry, a time when we can imagine that he was full of hopes and expectations, as well as fears – not dissimilar to those involved in starting out on any new charitable venture. He was presented with his first temptation.

> Jesus was hungry. The devil taunted him: 'If you are the Son of God, tell these stones to become bread.' Jesus answered, 'It is written: "Man does not live by bread alone but on every word that comes from the mouth of God."' (Matthew 4:3-4).

This temptation is like the organization which seeks to be driven only by the three Es of efficiency, effectiveness and economy.

I doubt that there is any organization that could not benefit in some way from becoming more efficient, effective or economic. There is always scope for improvement, and charities need to avoid waste and inefficiency as much as any other business. To be truly inspired by the spirit of love, however, this must not become a soulless functionalism.

In this context, I see the 'stones' in the temptation as things which, at a material level are unnecessary to basic functioning of organizations, but which at another level help to give purpose and meaning. Let me give a few examples from the L'Arche community in which I live.

One 'stone' is the focus on the home. There are nine houses in the community, each with around six people with learning difficulties and six assistants. There is much focus on developing the life of each home. Each home has its own identity and customs, which creates a sense of belonging. This is important not just for the people with handicaps, but also for the assistants, many of whom have never had a real sense of 'home'.

It is often said that cooking centrally and then distributing the food to each house, or having a canteen would be both more economic and efficient. But often the process of preparing the meal – deciding the menu and involving people in its preparation – is as important as eating the meal in building up and sustaining the sense of 'home'.

Or take the example of offices. In my community the offices are scattered around the village of Trosly: the director in one building, the person responsible for assistants in another, the head of the workshops in another and the accountant in yet another. It's madness – in one way it doesn't lend itself to efficient working but at another it's a treasure. In walking from one office to another, you are brought back to the reality of what L'Arche is all about: sharing lives with people with mental handicaps. You never know whom you will meet en route, but there is nearly always an enlivening encounter somewhere along the way. Cooped up in an office together, there would be no need to go outside and a division between the 'bureaucrats' and the rest of the community would soon form.

A second 'stone' is the simple passing of time with people, with no other objective but to enjoy their company or share their sorrows. In the chase for efficiency it is easy to reduce the time that one spends with people – whether, in the case of L'Arche, be they other assistants or people with learning difficulties. It is easy to think that 'getting the job done' is the most important thing, and to therefore close yourself off to interruptions. But when I reflect on the day's events, I am often struck by the fact that it is so often the interruptions – the unexpected personal encounters – which give more sense and meaning to the day than anything else.

Time is the most scarce resource. It is interesting to see the different ways in which it is perceived in different countries. In Europe and North America, time is money. In Africa and Central America, time is the key ingredient in developing relationships.

In most L'Arche homes in Europe one assistant cooks while another cleans the house. In Haiti they think that very odd; there both of them would do the cleaning together room by room, and then go onto the cooking, talking and laughing all the while. Maybe it takes longer and maybe it's less efficient, but at the end of the day I have little doubt that the Haitian assistants feel more satisfied.

Celebrations are another 'stone'. In the house where I live there was recently a celebration to mark the departure of one of the assistants. The theme was taken from the passage in Exupery's *The Little Prince*, in which a fox talks to the little prince about what it means to be tamed: to move from a state of fear and distance to a relationship of love and respect. There was much laughter as sketches were acted out, showing how the assistant had been 'tamed' by everyone in the house, as well as how the people in the house had appreciated her presence. It helped to mark the end of her stay in the house in a positive way both for her and the people staying on. It required considerable thought and preparation – and in one sense was unnecessary – a short appreciation during a meal would have been perfectly acceptable. But for all the energy it required, it was a source of life and joy and helped to give meaning to the time she had spent there.

Prayer is another 'stone'. How could anyone make an effective evaluation of the effectiveness or efficiency of prayer? How, on an economic level, can you justify the time that people spend in church? It should be an obvious candidate for removal by the efficiency brush. But I am struck when I talk to many of the older assistants at L'Arche, to discover it is often prayer which keeps them going.

What is the lesson of all this for the charity leader? It is, I think, to operate not just in the functional dimension – the dimension of efficiency, economy and effectiveness – but also to recognize the importance of the spiritual dimension: the word of God.

This was appreciated by the founder of the Ford Motor Company:

I know there are reservoirs of spiritual strength from which we

human beings thoughtlessly cut ourselves off .. I believe we
shall someday be able to know enough about the source of
power and the realm of the spirit to create something ourselves
... I firmly believe that mankind was once wiser about spiritual
things than we are today. What we now only believe, they
knew.*

We can try to reduce our lives – and the organizations we work
for – into dry, well-functioning machines. But without the spiritual
dimension, it is unlikely that we will find the sense of life and
fulfilment we seek. It is like living a life in black and white rather
than colour; a life of prose rather than poetry. It is at this point
that the spiritual – the non-functional – comes into its own. If a
fundamental human need is to love and to be loved, the challenge
for the Christian organization is to develop this in practice.

This can mean many things. It means valuing people not for
what they can do, but for who they are. This is one of the main
things assistants find at L'Arche: coming to appreciate and regard
people simply for their presence, regardless of how able or disabled
they may be.

It means being willing to spend time with people. Reading the
Gospels you are not inclined to think that Christ had a rigid
regard for the three Es (efficiency, empire building and evasion
of responsibility). He passed a considerable part of the day with
the Samaritan woman by the well (John 4:1–26); he approved
the actions of the woman who poured perfume on his feet (Luke
7:36–38); he endorsed Mary for passing time with him while
admonishing Martha for busying herself in household chores
(John 10:38–42). He would have exasperated any time and motion
expert.

Developing the spirit of an organization means constantly
finding creative ways to nourish its values. For leaders of L'Arche

---

* Henry Ford, quoted in Peter M. Senge, *The Fifth Discipline: the
Art and Practice of the Learning Organisation* (Doubleday, 1990).

communities it means enhancing the sense of community life. It is this, above all, that attracts and builds up people. It means building and developing the traditions and customs of the community. Whether it be major celebrations or simple acts (such as holding hands during grace as a gesture of unity) they all help to preserve the spirit of the community. Such traditions need to evolve if they are to continue to have meaning – but the real danger is rejecting them entirely in a ruthless quest for greater efficiency.

Perhaps, above all, it means spending time in prayer and contemplation, as Christ did. I am increasingly struck by the number of leaders, both within and outside L'Arche who attribute what they are able to do to prayer. The sense of being open to the Spirit of God to direct their lives – and the lives of the organizations they lead – seems to create a peace and adventure which is not easily found elsewhere. Prayer becomes a way in which God's spirit helps to rekindle their deepest thoughts and creativity. It becomes the place in which personal judgement develops, cutting through superficial and changing emotions.

What is true for individuals is also true for organizations. Again, I am struck by the unity and commitment that is often evident when a community (or a church) has prayed collectively for guidance over a particular issue. Perhaps we are naturally suspicious of approaches which are not fully cerebral – but we need to learn to overcome our fears and suspicions.

2. The temptation of empire: possessing the kingdoms of the world

Having resisted the temptation to turn stones into bread, Jesus was led to the top of a mountain and shown all the kingdoms of the world. The devil said to Him,

'I will give you all their authority and splendour, for it has been given to me and I can give it to anyone I want to. So if you worship me, it will all be yours.' Jesus answered, 'It is written: "Worship the Lord your God and serve him only."' (Luke 4:5–8).

This temptation is epitomized by the militaristic strategy plan which depicts the future solely in terms of size. The target is to become number one and to achieve this other organizations are seen as competitors or (more rarely) tactical allies. People (clients and supporters) are prizes in a battle of one upmanship. Winning contracts is more important than delivering on them. Organizational weaknesses are ruthlessly excised; exposure to strategic threats eliminated. There is an emphasis on uniformity – difference is not encouraged.

At one level, there is nothing wrong with any of this. For an organization to grow in size is not unreasonable. Given the needs of the world, anything more that an organization can do is to be welcomed. An organization which does not want more people to know about it probably has something to hide. Similarly, organizations that are delicate and about to collapse help no one. Uniform standards can help to guarantee minimum levels of service.

The difficulty comes when these factors lead an organization into empire building for its own sake. Empire building is when growth becomes the sole or overriding objective; when how much an organization does is seen as more important than how it does it; when central control and imposition of organizational norms stifles individual creativity and freedom. In sum, it is when an organization's values are sacrificed on the altar of growth.

The empire-building organization overemphasizes the role of measurement. This is not surprising. Empires lend themselves to empirical measures. They are concerned with power and might: how much of the world is painted pink, red or yellow. Growth is not something that comes naturally, but is forced and fought for – often driven by the need to recognized, admired and feared. But what Christ said about people, 'what good will it be for a man if he gains the whole world, yet forfeits his own soul' (Matthew 16:26), could equally apply to organizations.

It is a very real temptation for L'Arche. With 100 communities in twenty-eight countries, it is easy to think that the target should be to have, say, 140 communities in thirty-five countries in three years' time. But that would be like parents concluding that a family with six children is intrinsically better than one with two children. In both organizations and families, it is not primarily numbers which count, but the quality of the relationships. Building up those relationships, ensuring that values are shared and that each community is becoming more mature and feels fully part of the organization as a whole, is much more important.

Numerical growth has not been an explicit objective in L'Arche. When Jean Vanier started L'Arche he had no vision of what it would turn into. He firmly believed that it should never be bigger than five people; in this way everyone could fit into one car. Growth came about more despite than because of his original intentions. Even now, while the development of new communities is celebrated and welcomed, it is never a target in itself.

The same thing is apparent in the Gospels. Jesus was not impelled by numbers, even though others wanted him to become leader of a large nationalist force. When he was attracting more disciples than John the Baptist (John 4:1–3) He deliberately moved to another part of the country. When his supporters ran away in droves (John 6:66), he did not give the impression of being unduly concerned. His overriding strategy, if you can call it that, was not to build up numbers, but to remain true to his vocation. When that came to fulfilment on the cross, he was accompanied by just a handful of people.

The empire-building charity responds ruthlessly to weakness. It cuts out weak parts of its own organization rather than nurse it back to health. Weaknesses in other organizations are exploited as a source of competitive advantage; weak parts of its own organization are ruthlessly cut out rather than nursed back to health.

But how organizations respond to weakness provides a key test of their humanity. A key difference between humans and other animals is that humans seek to care and protect their weaker members, whereas animals leave the elderly and weak to die.

In L'Arche there are always a number of communities facing difficult times. At one level, it would be relatively easy to allow them to fend for themselves and – if necessary – to die. After all, there are many new communities waiting to be formed which could take their place. It is not always easy to find the patience and other emotional, human and financial resources to nurse communities back to health. Nevertheless, the sense of love and commitment help to make this a priority, even though it may be impossible to do all that might be desired.

It is not, however, just a question of duty. There is also the belief that God is revealed through weakness. As St Paul said, God's power is made perfect in weakness (2 Corinthians 12:9). Weakness is linked to fragility, and often the most creative people are also the most fragile (Beethoven and Van Gogh are prime examples). Within L'Arche, working with people with limited intellectual capacities, one is often struck by their gift for relationship.

It is much the same in L'Arche with weaker communities. You never wish for a weak community. It is difficult, depressing and disappointing for all involved. But it is often communities facing the hardest difficulties that come up with the most innovative solutions. It is the communities going through the most severe shortages of assistants or money which pull in support from other communities, strengthening the sense of common interest amongst L'Arche as a whole. It is the communities that endure conflicts that often emerge with the greatest sense of unity and maturity.

A compassionate response to weakness goes hand in hand with being open to insecurity. Empires resist insecurity and protect themselves behind high defensive walls. Charities can be the same: building up huge financial resources to provide for difficult times, binding people into onerous contracts, or turning inwards, oblivious to what is going on in the rest of the world. The result is that they become staid and unresponsive, too comfortable and set in their own ways. To retain their vitality and responsiveness, they need to learn to become vulnerable.

In the case of L'Arche, vulnerability is ensured by its need to find 900 young people wanting to come to spend a year or more in one of its communities for little more than pocket money. There is no guarantee that they will come, and there is always a degree of uncertainty and worry as each new year comes along. But each year people do come and this gives a renewed sense of trust and confidence in God's providence. There is often talk that L'Arche should seek to offer competitive salaries to attract and retain the people it needs. This would, at a stroke, reduce vulnerability. But it is also felt that the need to attract and retain assistants every year sharpens what L'Arche needs to offer.

Empire-building charities also seek to impose their own particular cultural norms: the use of a particular language, customs and practices. This is a particular issue for L'Arche. Founded as a strongly Christian (and, moreover, Catholic) organization, it is now ecumenical and – especially in India – inter-faith. There is increasing recognition of the need to adapt the 'L'Arche model' to the needs and culture of each country. But this process will not, I suspect, be easy. In adapting the particular practices and values of L'Arche to the prevailing culture and norms of each country there is a risk it begins to lose its own identity. It is an issue for many organizations (not least the churches) and it is not clear how this can best be resolved. Perhaps the answer lies in seeing it as a process, rather than a once-and-for-all step, of defining what is core to each organization in terms of values and practices and what should be adapted to particular situations.

What then, are the lessons for the charity leader who wants to avoid becoming an emperor? The answer Christ gives is to worship and serve God alone.

This means examining our own motives for leadership. Are we seeking it for what we can get out of it in terms of money, power or reputation – or because we feel, in a profound sense, that it is the best way in which we can serve? As Christ said, 'Whoever wants to be first must be slave of all. For even the Son of Man did not come to be served but to serve and to give his life as a ransom for many.' (Mark 10:43–45).

As it is for us individually, so it is for the organizations we work for. If our organization seeks to become a leader in its field, what is the underlying motive and rationale? What needs to be done to protect against the danger of building an empire for our own glory?

It means listening attentively as much to the weak as to the strong. In L'Arche that means listening especially to what the weaker communities are saying – it is often they who feel the changes in policies and practices the most; it is often they who come up with the most innovative solution to problems. Similarly, it means listening particularly closely to people with learning difficulties not just because it is politically correct, but also because they have something important to contribute. Their presence in the discernment of new community leaders can give a focus on the fruits of the spirit – love, joy, peace, patience, kindness, goodness, faithfulness, gentleness and self-control – to a degree that might otherwise be lacking.

It also means humility. Even the Roman emperors had someone to remind them of their mortality, particularly when glorying in success. We similarly need to recognize our powerlessness, believing in the Almighty more than in our own might. It is this which enables us as individuals and organizations to allow ourselves to face the unknown, even when it feels vulnerable. Christ provides an example: born into a poor family and leading a simple life. He sent out his disciples as 'lambs amongst wolves, without a purse or bag or sandals' – let alone a sure place to live (Luke 10:1–12). This implies a strong focus on living the present moment to the full rather than living in nostalgia of the past or plans for the future.

There is also a need to trust the judgement and capacity of others. God does not work through leaders alone. A very directive approach may be necessary in some situations – in a crisis, for example. In general, however, the leader needs to allow and encourage individual flexibility and creativity if the organization is to flourish. The analogy might be that of a gardener – providing the right conditions for growth, but allowing each plant to grow in its own particular way.

3. The temptation of evasion: throwing yourself off the top of the temple

> The devil then led Christ to Jerusalem and had him stand on the highest point of the temple. 'If you are the son of God', he said, 'throw yourself down from here. For it is written: "He will command his angels concerning you to guard you carefully: they will lift you up in their hands, so that you will not strike your foot against a stone."' Jesus answered, 'It says: "Do not put the Lord your God to the test."' (Luke 4:9–11).

If the previous temptation was about seeking power, this one is about giving up responsibility. It can be epitomized by the organization that wants to do everything, but avoids a decision to do anything. It tries to evade its responsibility in its chosen field by seeking roles in other fields, especially those which appear new and exciting. Faced with an organizational problem, it either ignores it, hoping God will sort it out alone, or goes for a 'quick fix' which simply deals with the symptoms. Either way, it evades going to the root of the problem.

Evasion is often linked to trying to do something spectacular with minimum effort. Being overtaken by others in some field, the organization heralds in a new revolutionary approach which it has not fully developed, let alone tested. Faced with a problem in one area it is immediately closed down, rather than looking for solutions. Faced with a financial crisis the organization 'goes for bust' with a new fund-raising technique which seems simple and bound to succeed, but which has never been tried out.

These temptations are felt most by organizations that have lost their identity and sense of direction. They are 'bored' with what they currently do and seek greater excitement in other fields or activities – particularly if they believe that they will then be more successful. The temptations are also felt by organizations that cannot choose: unable to establish priorities they try having a go at everything, dissipating their energies in the process.

In L'Arche, as in any other organization, there is the temptation to be all things to all people. A Board discussion in one L'Arche community touched on the question as to whether it was primarily a community of faith, or a social concern. 'We are both', said one Board member. 'No', replied another, 'we need to be clear about our identity and unless we make a clear decision that one or the other is most important, we will be lost for ever.'

There is also always the temptation to avoid responsibility for the day to day and go for the more spectacular. Much of the work in L'Arche involves cooking, eating and cleaning and it is not, in itself, particularly glamourous. Inevitably there are times when you want to do something grander and more exciting. The key, however, is in finding meaning in the everyday – particularly in the relations between each other – rather than in the exceptional.

Moves into new fields and activities are not always wrong and are often signs of an organization that is brimming with life and activity. Many L'Arche communities are moving into providing domiciliary care, and particularly in developing countries, there is much work with children. Work with people who are mentally ill is a possibility. But in each case the motivation needs to be closely examined: is it being done to impress and escape problems in existing activities, or is there a clear rationale and sense of vocation?

There is also the question of trusting in God's providence, especially for money. At what point does this become a matter of testing God? The answer is not always clear, but it does help to develop a sense of God's providence not just in providing funds, but in providing people with particular skills, including fund-raising.

What are the lessons for the leader tempted to evade responsibility by metaphorically throwing himself or herself off the top of the temple? Overall, it is to ensure that decisions and actions are not taken in a spirit of evasion of responsibility, trusting that God will somehow fill the gap, but that they are firmly based on a strong sense of what is God's will.

First, there is the need for the leader to develop the courage and confidence to take difficult decisions. It needs courage to cut, prune and, in some cases, replant ideas and people. It requires confidence to allow different views to be expressed, knowing that only if this happens will a real sense of unity be achieved. It requires trust to let go of the reins a little, helping each person to give of their best. It is a question not simply of giving life, but of trying to channel it – helping each person to play their part and bear fruit in the long term.

Secondly, there is the need for consistency and faithfulness; living through the difficult patches where, despite everything, life seems dry and unfruitful. It means both preaching and practising the same message. It is not easy: there is the temptation to cut and run, or to try to change others rather than yourself.

Christ does not give the impression of being scared of conflict or of making decisions. One of his first actions in his ministry was to throw the money changers out of the temple (John 2:13–16). He pulled no punches in his advice to the rich young ruler (Luke 18:18–30). He put Peter in his place, calling him Satan and a stumbling block (Matthew 16:23). Neither did Christ give up, even when tempted to do so. In the Garden of Gethsemane, he asked God to 'take this cup from me' (Luke 22:42), but nonetheless recognized that it was God's will that was paramount.

Conclusion

Over-emphasis on efficiency, empire building and evasion of responsibility: these are three temptations which rob charities of their saltiness – the distinctive values for which they stand.

I have tried to suggest some of the ways in which charities and their leaders can avoid giving in to these temptations. In each case the example of Christ is paramount: coming in weakness and poverty to serve the weak and the poor, exhibiting courage, confidence and constancy, seeking to serve rather than to be served; showing love and compassion in little things; being true to his own inner calling rather than the call of those who shouted loudest.

The key, I think, is in Christ's relationship with God: the time he spent in prayer, understanding God's will. The same is true for us too. It is ultimately only through listening to the still, small voice within us that we – and the organizations we work for – can develop the confidence to trust him more than we trust ourselves.

Learning to do so is not easy, however, and the temptations do not go away. Having tried to tempt Christ three times, the devil did not go away forever. He simply 'left him until an opportune time' (Luke 4:13). We need to be on our guard continually.

The seven deadly sins

Gluttony: Focusing on growth in the belief that bigger means better. Thus, an organization that has lost its sense of direction or 'vocation' simply concentrates on growth in size. While such growth is not wrong in itself, it should not be a substitute for growth in learning and understanding.

Sloth: Feeling so comfortable with the status quo that an organization is too scared to respond to a new sense of mission – especially if it challenges some of the established principles and practices.

Pride: (1) Believing in the superiority of your own organization to the extent that others are seen as inherently inferior. (2) Knowing your organization is not superior – but acting as though it is.

Envy: The opposite to pride. Believing that what other organizations do – or how they do it – is inevitably superior to your own. This leads to the organization following the lead of others, becoming a 'me too' rather than taking the risk of following its own vocation.

Lust: Longing to possess something which belongs to another organization (e.g. its name, funds, staff, style, etc.) without taking the effort to look below the surface.

Avarice: Seeking to pursue efficiency and economy to the point of soullessness. People are valued more for what they do than for who they are. Everything is so planned that spontaneity is eliminated.

Anger: Lacking the internal peace and contentment such that a slight external provocation or set-back produces a reaction which is out of all proportion.

5

Transformational leadership

JAYME ROLLS

All organizations, secular and sacred, are finding limitations in their current way of conducting business. Both church and business are faced with their stakeholders having a crisis of faith and hope in their institutions: low commitment, disbelief, disenfranchisement and disengagement.

The church has been called 'culturally light years behind the rest of society because of its innate conservatism and resistance to change' by one of the General Synod's most senior policy makers. 'It has become terminally tedious and in danger of consigning the institution to irrelevance,' he wrote. 'A refuge of the pedant, bureaucrat and the bore.' 'A bureaucracy modelled on the civil service.' Other church leaders have expressed concerns for democracy and accountability and have called urgently for the development of a new culture.

In many corporations, there is widespread poor morale and lack of productivity. In the US there is less than 5% unemployment but 70% of employees say they have less job security and more job stress than ever. Business urgently needs human renewal and re-inspiriting to engender the engagement vital to successful change and commitment in a beleaguered, battle-weary workforce.

Charles Handy comments on this, claiming: 'A business could and should he more than a wealth-creating instrument for its owners. It could and should be a community with a purpose beyond itself, because if we are honest with ourselves, it is only that sort of purpose that can justify our existence. Business is, in the end, a moral matter.' Handy has his doubts. 'I am not optimistic. Old ways and habits die hard before they change. Organisations will persevere with their attempts to command and control, to see themselves as the instruments of their owners and their people as the instruments of their purposes. They wolf overwork and often overpay the best of these instruments, wearing them out before their time.'

Corporations are still predominantly spiritually bankrupt with inhabitants experiencing anything but a soulful, rewarding worklife. According to Handy, 'Instrumentalism and reductionism have been the besetting sins of business in modern times. Between them, they have turned the organization into a prison for the human spirit.'

Widespread pain

People in our communities today are in significant pain. There is detachment and depression. All too often they are relegated to being driven only by survival needs, feeling cornered by the loss of security in environments of secrecy, fear, stifled feelings and loss of work identity:

- they are living through the chaos of upheaval as the very foundations of their worklives and self esteem are being rocked;
- they are embroiled in self preservation proving that the way they have always done it does work;
- they are experiencing the havoc of change with its demands to re-evaluate everything they've counted on as truth, coupled with the risk of stepping into the unknown;
- they are carrying the malaise of the epidemic plague of post-downsizing disease from company to company as workers move with feelings of violated dependency.

Work environments can be demanding and draining, and workers are called upon for nothing less than heroic action, often to the point of depletion when the soulfulness of their livelihood becomes elusive. There is a growing resistance to environments devoid of meaning, and institutions are shifting their focus from self interest to seeking meaning in the broader context of relationship and community making. How can we restore the sense of meaning in our own institutions?

We move in our society to rushed and staccato rhythms, anxious, burdened, beleaguered. Soulfelt joys of connecting with others have been lost in the undertow of fleeting purposes. Making life sacred once again and restoring ourselves to our deepest most authentic ways releases our natural creativity and amplifies our life force.

Significant and substantial healing is needed at a deep level. Recovery is elusive. Institutions cannot answer fully the need for renewal of the human spirit. Churches are not experiencing the attendance they once enjoyed. When countless efforts are made in organizations to work with employees, many find themselves addressing a battered workforce who cannot be fully present and engaged.

This profound need for healing has gone unmet and has far reaching implications for families and communities. It is a time for a dramatic revolutionary shift from the past ways of thinking to solve this pervasive problem.

Ours is a critical time for institutions to attempt to renew themselves, for inhabitants to be re-inspirited and revitalized, to reclaim their hope and realize their deepest yearnings. Changing our work experience is about re-envisioning relationships, creative engagement, friendship and fellowship. Liberation from joylessness comes from self-repurposing, recalibrating through a sense of relationship and self-awareness in community; to reconnecting with our birthright to express fundamental values and fulfil potential.

Institutional renewal comes from listening one by one and

responding to stakeholders; redefining voice and partnership, power and information; and re-inventing institutions around the dramatically changing needs of inhabitants.

The need for human renewal

The largest organizations and consulting firms acknowledge that they do not fully understand how to bring human renewal into a workplace that is in dire need. There are limits on what organizations are achieving with interventions in the workplace. We need information in pioneering and developing new ways of thinking about traditional models which can he achieved through a new spirituality of work and community.

What will spur organizational change is an intersection of the values of the secular and sacred. This will involve developing a workplace spirituality characterized by service, authenticity, compassion, heroic action, courage and daring. It will require risk taking, readiness, change agility, innovation, a broadened context of commitment to the greater good, connecting to stakeholder voice and transformational leadership.

The new principles

Organizational transformation requires questioning the prevailing thought, dealing with the art of the possible, experimenting and continual re-invention of the self and the organization. The new principles are stakeholder voice, co-development and inclusion, inspiring trust, faith and hope, creating mutually supportive alliances which treat all constituents like partners.

The key tenets of the change needed for all organizations are:

- constituency-focused, driven and responsive models;
- constituency-service and satisfaction-driven organizations;
- decentralized power; empowerment on an individual level;
- shared communication and power;

- acceptance of contrary views, other cultures and beliefs;
- continuous innovation;
- commitment to new learning;
- commitment to the 'emergent view'.

Co-development means the creation of an emergent point of view, not 'yours or mine', but through generative dialogue, a third point of view. Initiatives undertaken consequently enjoy shared ownership, the result of hearing all voices and benefiting from the best thinking of all parties, ensuring all needs are met. Co-development brings the joy of creation to all stakeholders, a sense of contribution and meaning and collapses resistance to new initiatives.

The shape of the alternative church?

The twenty-first century is being called the 'age of choice' as people move from authoritarian to libertarian values. The shift is dramatic and evident globally: in politics, in religion and in corporations. People are no longer willing to accept a belief unless it is of their own experience. Self-determination is a dominant trend and institutions are being widely impacted. People favour experimenting and experiencing over adhering to rules. There is a move away from direct information transfer to a process of guided self discovery, of action and reflection.

The new alternative church services often incorporate forms of worship that take into account new sociological factors such as the demand for self governance and self expression. They are mapped to seekers' needs and feature a high level of adaptation to cultures, desires and perceived needs within some context of speaking about God. They balance old and new; varying forms and formats of worship are made more relevant, with styles influenced by the culture of the congregation.

The alternative seeker service in the Willow Creek Community Church located in South Barrington, Illinois, near Chicago, draws

15,000 people each weekend. The new worship style is a result of feedback from surveys which asked unchurched people why they didn't attend church. The surveys revealed that many people consider churches boring, money hungry, irrelevant to their lives, unfriendly, and alien in both music and dress. The new service is intentionally designed to map the responses of this constituency and addresses the 'cringe factor', how younger generations feel about bringing a friend to a traditional service.

These churches follow the example of the early church in adapting to the culture of the people they are trying to convert. They excel in drawing large numbers of unchurched people. Seeker services are congregant-centric; they use the language and the music of the people rather than that of their traditions. These institutions offer worship services that are on the periphery of their denominations or they proffer no denominational attachments. Their attendance, vibrancy and financial strength is enviable.

There are other forces that are also becoming more evident in emerging liturgy. These include empowerment, first-hand experience and the blurring of boundaries. We see this manifested in the increase of lay persons co-leading and participating in services. The need for experimentation and variety is resulting in more types of services, meditation, length, music and so on.

We see self-governance needs represented in moving the power and control of worship from clergy to congregations. The move to greater speed for self expression is resulting in increased numbers of guest speakers.

'Market of one' impactors result in a service being marketed virtually one by one to the needs of their constituencies, connecting the dynamics between worship and culture, maintaining close connection and responsiveness to changing cultures and 'audiences'.

Today's new forms of learning are characterized by more performance and event worship which I like to call 'edu-tainment'!

The impact of search for meaning

People are making the choices that are creating richer, more meaningful lives. People have begun consciously caring for soulful needs. The new values are resulting in lifestyle downscaling, the rising value of home life over the workplace, deeper relationships, workplace democracy, flex firms responding to employees who want to adjust and shrink worklives around other needs, and home offices that offer improved quality of worklife and increased freedom.

The work environment that corporations provide needs to be meaning-rich in order to acknowledge the values of an increasingly soul-conscious workforce – and not just out of altruism. What motivates employees has changed from receiving a pay cheque to an opportunity for fulfilment. Identifying and fostering soul in business is likely to result in some very big wins for corporations.

For example, a very fundamental tenet of soul is that it seeks relationship. Power in organizations is generated by relationships; and what is important is how an organization organizes its relationships, not its tasks, functions or hierarchies. Power is energy and needs to flow through an organization. What gives power its charge – negative or positive – is the quality of its relationships.

All organizations are in transformation. Transformation is about changing relationships. Transforming cultures is about changing relationships – with the customer, with the employee, with the manager, with work, with each other. Rethinking work to allow for the emergence of the soul may well provide an impetus to transformation.

Business can unwittingly starve the soul and taste the consequences, or celebrate it and profit from it. Where soul is neglected, it doesn't just go away. It can appear symptomatically in emptiness, meaninglessness, vague depression, lack of connection to the company and its purpose, a lacklustre, just-enough performance, absenteeism, poor morale, drug abuse and lack of fulfilment. Distress seems widespread today and may be responsible for the movement we are witnessing in people's search for meaning. Because we have lost touch with ourselves, we can take the temperature of our souls only as it manifests itself in problems.

A true harmony of interests

Needs of business to remain competitive	Employees' soul needs
learning	learning, exploration
change agile	experimentation
creativity, innovation	creativity, innovation
partnering	relationship
continuous training	discovery
teaming	connection
dialogue	dialogue, expression
participation	engagement
risk taking	space to make mistakes
proactive	empowerment
peer assessment mentoring	reaching out, friendship, closeness
vision	meaning
large context	complexity, depth
alternating roles	experience
invention	possibilities
imagination	imagination, reflection
communication	communication
integration, end of silos	wholeness
broadening of boundaries	expansiveness
employee growth	growth
communal sense of self	attachment
community	community, neighbourhood
stewardship	family

How can the church, long the steward of the soul, learn from this model to create transformative, constituent-focused change in its institutions?

Moral development and transformational readership

(1) Moral development as a precursor of organisational change

A corporate culture that is characterized by unwavering commitment to higher values and holds them regardless of the consequences is highly change agile. An organization that engages heavily in groupthink, filtering out critical information and resistant to criticism from without or from within is change fragile and is at risk. The latter is in part a consequence of the incomplete moral development of its inhabitants. There are various levels of maturity involved in the development of moral awareness from childhood to adulthood, and people only gradually and sometimes with great difficulty arrive at the point of mature moral existence.

(2) Stages of development in moral understanding

There are three stages of development: pre-conventional morality, conventional morality and post-conventional morality.

In pre-conventional morality, people see their world as a system of rewards and punishments. This is the immature state where they appear to be acting very ethically, but inside they are not responding from a sense of the universal good, but rather to avoid pain.

A second phase of moral development is conventional morality. People in this stage have a strong need for affiliation and want to belong to and have the acceptance of a group. While people in this phase are no longer motivated by reward and punishment, the group's opinions and decisions on what is crucial for survival are the deciding factor in their behaviour.

People in this phase allow right and wrong to be determined more by the group than by the merits of a course of action and do not question group judgement. In organizations this provides a strong undertow and there is a great deal of energy being expended to get stakeholders to comply with the prevailing thought. What is critical is to preserve group identity and repudiate those who question it.

The implications for the transformational leader, sponsor of change or change agent, are dramatic since some moral theorists feel that the majority of people remain in this conventional phase of moral development, which is resistant to criticism from without or from within the organization.

There is a higher phase of moral development – post-conventional morality – in which one does what is right for no other reason than that it seems intrinsically and unconditionally good, and stems from universal values. People in this phase feel an unwavering commitment to these higher values and hold to them regardless of the consequences.

True transformational leaders exist at the post-conventional stage of morality and this is why they are a rare breed. People in this phase are strongly inner-referenced, living from a sense of inner values. They invariably say that this is the hardest work they have ever done, since the pressures to conform are enormous and, perhaps more importantly, they will inevitably come into conflict with those who reside in the first two levels. In the face of all this, they must maintain their conviction to operate by intrinsic goodness. The sense of being embraced by this goodness can provide the courage to pursue an ethical ideal even when one is being assailed from all sides by those who have refused to go beyond levels one and two.

Change in organizations means moving from narrow self-interest to the greater good and questioning the prevailing judgement of the existing groupthink. Transformational leaders have the charter to lead change and this very often requires followers to operate from a higher level of moral development. Since most inhabitants exist in the conventional morality stage, employees often fortify the boundaries and heighten resistance until the leader feels not-so-subtle pressure to live by the prevailing rules of the group. If the leader does not heed these messages, ostracizing fellows in a later stage, then finally the group works overtime to excise the leader from the environment.

We have thought of cultures as advanced and change agile that are dignified and respectful of cohabitants. A more meaningful measure of an advanced corporate culture poised for success and able to demonstrate healthy and frequent change would be rather the preponderance of stakeholders who exist at a higher level of moral development.

A new transformational leadership

The successful change leader supports growth, and helps employees orient and transition. These are leaders who allow employees to free energy from protecting themselves, to show that sharing feelings is encouraged and that the company supports people who want to learn. Organizational transformation deals with the deep issues of cultivating organizational and individual spirit, vision, trust, personal growth and sensitivity. Today's leaders are charged with 'creating the conditions' that foster growth and can effectively lead cultural change.

Deep reflection is required for leaders to make a personal transformation themselves that is a prerequisite to move 'from commandos to coaches', from remote to accessible, from power and information withholding to sharing. Today, leadership is administered one by one, connecting deeply with each stakeholder, helping him or her to do the interior work necessary to navigate change.

These leaders are coaches, facilitators, stewards, relationship builders, mentors, teachers or role models who can help others navigate their transformation as they live through change. They help them find meaning and fulfilment, to develop, to align their values with the organization's values and mission.

In their own lives, these leaders are on a continuous road of becoming; they are powerful, active, courageous doers and change agents who don't settle, who believe strongly in doing good and in the common good. They believe in integration between the personal self and the employed self, and they work to nourish the soul and the human spirit.

They are 'spiritual entrepreneurs', inner-referenced and other-directed. These change agents have the spiritual values of other-directedness in the way they value relationship and honour and respect others, feel responsible for others and have a sense of mission and duty to them. Human nurturing is a guiding principle to them. They enjoy others' achievements, provide hope and meaning, and help employees trust each other and feel needed.

They are inner-referenced in many of their qualities: they are true to their inner self and inner values, typically challenge the establishment, are change agents, have a personal drive for growth and learning, are risk takers and are willing to undergo the self-examination that personal transformation requires.

Unfailingly, they describe their work as the hardest they have ever done. They are intertwined in a web of change with endless variables and constant pressure to learn and improve, to build relationships and to honour each person's development. Leaders need compassion and patience when subordinates don't have vision or are afraid, when they have to help employees look at things differently, and encourage risk when employees have a wait-and-see approach and don't believe 'this place can change'. The work is difficult and tiresome, with untold pressure from above and below. It often feels like three steps forward and two steps back; the results are slow and barely visible.

They are depleted from above and depleted from below. Subordinates and superiors are often slow to risk and to believe, and the leader is trail-blazing with management and employees at the same time, fighting battles in both arenas. As leaders, they must promote a vision, be stalwart believers and undaunted, inexhaustible pioneers.

An enormous amount of energy is required to create momentum, greater still because it is often against resistant forces. They are blazing the unknown territory of change, understanding people's psychological reactions, and living with their inevitable, growing frustration and draining energy.

If an institution is fortunate enough to find a leader who is a skilled change agent and can effect transition in the organization, that leader is someone to hear and endorse. It is the obligation of both those above and below to keep that leader in place.

People within an organization have the obligation to risk, to support the leader's courage and advocacy for them, to take a chance, to follow the lead, to suspend disbelief and self interest, to commit to the vision, to feed back to the leader the energy he or she is giving, to help the leader see the results of this work, and to see change, which is a prime motivator for the change leader. People with responsibility have an obligation to give the leader space, to believe, to risk, to endorse change efforts, to be open to dramatic new ways of thinking, and to be willing to support the leader to their superiors.

That is easier said than done. The values of this leader are different from the values of a traditional corporation. Management's exclusivity in power, information and communication is not consistent with how a change leader operates day to day. Since relationships and connection are critical to transformation, the leader will be inclusive and share information and power.

To help a change leader flourish, superiors need to listen, accept and learn about cultural change from him or her. This kind of leader dedicates him or herself to something larger than himself or herself. Retention of that leader can come with hard won results, from seeing the effects of change.

There are other obstacles to retention. The transformational leader's growth is fast paced because they are change agents, are change eager and are driven by upward evolution. Since individuals change faster than cultures, as the leaders spiral upward in their own growth, they will need a culture which is continually more advanced in its change readiness. Also, they experience loss of fulfilment because of the reticence in management and in stake-holders, and so need a fresh environment.

The way to get results is to assure the leader's subordinates that the leader has the full endorsement of management and to provide unbridled support to the leader, or a rare opportunity will be squandered. It is essential to understand that regardless of duration, a change leader will have a decided impact on the environment and leave a legacy. Employees need a sense of meaning, contribution, self-esteem and dignity; to create, to be listened to and feel cared for, to respond to a call to adventure, to risk in an environment of safety. The characteristics of the new leaders are the qualities that as we all become leaders and all become followers we will each need to cultivate, as the organization becomes increasingly interdependent. Creating an organizational understanding, resolve and commitment to identifying, attracting, retaining and developing these leaders is key to successful organizational change.

A new role for clergy as change agents

Clergy have from the early days of the church played a vital societal role as change agent, interpreter and translator. The expertise and skills of their profession are about to be called upon in profound and new ways. It is a profession that is embarking on an unprecedented challenge as it runs headlong into its destiny to lead a global society in nothing less than the reinterpretation of organizational values. Globalization has created questions of cross-border ethics, moral imperialism and ethical relativism for which business has yet to find solutions.

Increasingly, the sociological context of theology is shaping society. It is helping a seeking populace find wholeness and meaning. Clergy construct a sheltering world-view fabric of meaning, and the profession will be the architect of spiritual meaning-making, acting as moral steward and Edgar Schein's 'culture creator and carrier'. Clergy will be called upon to be the artisans who weave the fabric of the emergent *nomos*, a new meaningful order.

The profession will he called upon to reshape, reinvent and reconnect society globally. According to *Christ of the 21st century*, Ewert H. Cousins claims society will move into the complex global consciousness of the future by entering into the spiritual process of inter-religious dialogue.

He claims that, traditionally, religion has focused on the transcendent, the divine realm, and has been the dominant force in culture. Yet culture grounds itself in the concrete and the material. The profession will translate and reinterpret the former transcendent realm of religion into theology applied in new ways to social, political and economic foundations. The profession will lead the way in showing how the sociological components of religion will be the tools used to shape an emergent global culture.

The demand is already present and pressing. There is a burgeoning need for examination and review of the moral and social contemporary issues in society. The application of theological ethics to establish new worldwide standards of moral governance will be critical. One example is the four US clergy who recently travelled to Switzerland to help religious and civic leaders face their history, having recently discovered that Switzerland provided a haven for gold stolen by the Nazis.

The blurring of cultural boundaries inherent in multinational alliances is even now surfacing grey areas in cross-border ethics. Raising questions about a new politic of morality are cross-border workers' rights and employment practices. Issues like these are creating a moral structure under review where ethical imperialism and relativism are being sharply debated. Clergy will be called upon to help a struggling society achieve what is now an elusive moral interdependency.

Work and meaning

The heart of work concerns itself with relationship, humanity, meaning-making; and infusing spirituality into business helps people to listen, to co-develop, to share power and information and create meaning, commitment and community. It serves to help workers broaden and elevate their self-interest to the larger good of the group, encourage self-awareness, invite collaborative meaning, embrace personal growth, applaud others' growth and value each other to create caring, humane working environments and empower workforce communities.

Spiritual leaders can serve the interests of this greater good by helping to build organizations that will unleash the human spirit and foster faith, truth, connection, respect, tolerance and charity, rather than encouraging fear, hopelessness, dishonesty, conflict and distance between people. People are naturally meaning-makers at their core, wanting to make a contribution, and are natural learners. Humane, fostering leaders adept at removing artificial structures and barriers to spiritual values in the workplace can liberate the life-affirming, implicate organization, soaring spirits, productivity and profits.

Stakeholders need a sense of meaning, contribution, self-esteem, connection, dignity and security. In the chaos of today's global transformation, we are grappling with how to effect meaningful change. Clergy could become the moral stewards leading a bewildered society into the new millennium – the visionary moral architects who design and raise a new spiritual canopy and create the emergent sociological and organizational *nomos*.

A new partnership for church and business

'A period of unrest precedes a revolution', according to Thomas Kuhn; and it may be a time for revolutionizing new thinking in the business/industrial mission partnership. *Unemployment and the Future of Work* claims, 'There have been experiments in sponsorships by business'. Business urgently needs the skills of industrial mission to connect people to their sense of worklife meaning and identity to achieve personal and organizational goals, and business is willing to pay handsomely for the abilities of those who can promote improved morale and productivity.

The church can help take today's industrial mission model into organizations. Business very much needs the knowledge, perspectives, skills, numinance and abilities of industrial mission, but in new ways. Industrial mission and business can both reinvent themselves to work together in new ways in today's organizational model. The church needs to deploy a valuable asset whose gifts are under-utilized and facing extinction. Business needs its workforce to be uplifted, re-inspirited and revitalized. To meet these needs, industrial mission has to work with companies and host churches in more sophisticated ways. They have to meet new business-critical needs by first, connecting with the organization's strategy; and secondly, by coming to the table with neutrality of objective, of creating win-win partnerships, engendering the 'emergent point of view', not to pre-assume an advocacy position for the downtrodden.

When industrial mission is an advocate for creating a co-development for the emergent point of view, the debate over 'on what agenda are we working?' – church or employer – because of who pays, disappears. It is neither church nor employer. It is capturing the composite, the collective needs of *all* stakeholders. That is the view of the new organization and how authentic commitment is achieved.

Industrial mission needs to disabuse itself of the traditional view encapsulated by one industrial missioner, 'I want to be free to leave an organization if it is acting unethically and would rather be sponsored by the church.' This is contrary to the notion of co-development of views and developing a collective consciousness, a key tenet of all new institutions. Further and not incidentally, courage is one of the key competencies required in today's organizations. Where is the heroism in being insulated by the church? Who provided insulation for the employee? On a more practical level, the church simply cannot afford to fund IM on the level commensurate with the burgeoning organizational needs.

Corporations face the challenge of being open to an entirely new mental model that welcomes input from informants traditionally not considered full partners to providing input on core organizational issues, welcoming new philosophies, viewpoints and potential new solutions.

There is a need for professional collaboration between the secular and the sacred to fill new organizational positions such as Chief Officers of Human Renewal, Chief Officers of Moral Governance and others, to foster the conditions under which we can live in globalized institutions, connect deeply to constituencies whose needs are ever changing, to help people change one by one, to be in places of most pain, to live a life characterized by ambiguity and change.

The goal is to connect church and business more closely by aligning them with their shared constituency voice, to connect business and church in the contextual framework of dramatically changing business needs, to secure commitment to new partnerships founded on mutually beneficial principles, to help business and church re-position their work to create pathbreaking linkages that unite work and spirituality in new and more profound ways, to think boldly, imaginatively and innovatively about spirituality and organizations and about how they might forge new partnerships that will take them into and beyond the next millenium as we usher in the twenty-first century.

When the tallest buildings in the town are the spire of the cathedral and the skyscraper, business and the church need to join together to accept responsibility for their joint role in human welfare, to become partners in fostering human renewal and bonding, interdependency, compassion, service and authenticity, and effectively blur the boundaries of that which separates us in the human condition.

Bibliography

Chris Argyris, *Integrating the Individual and the Organization* (New Brunswck: Transaction, 1990).

Peter Block, *Stewardship* (San Francisco: Berrett Koehler, 1993).

Ian Bunting, *Celebrating the Anglican Way* (London: Hodder & Stoughton, 1996).

Madeleine Bunting, 'Our Irrelevant Church', *The Guardian* (20 March 1998).

CCBI, *Unemployment and the Future of Work: An Enquiry for the Churches* (London: CCBI, 1997).

Tom Chappell, *The Soul of a Business* (New York: Bantam Books, 1993).

David J. Cherrington and Laura Zaugg Middleton, 'An Introduction to Global Business Issues,' *HR Magazine* (June 1995).

Ken Cottrill, 'Global Codes of Conduct', *Journal of Business Strategy* (May/June 1996).

Council of Churches Britain and Ireland (CCBI), *Unemployment and the Future of Work: An Enquiry for the Churches* (1997).

Ewert H. Cousins, *Christ of the 21st Century* (Rockport: Element, 1992).

Bill DeFoore, *Rediscovering the Soul of Business* (San Francisco: Sterling and Stone, 1995).

Thomas Donaldson, 'Values in Tension: Ethics Away from Home', *Harvard Business Review* (September/October 1996).

MaryEllen Fillo, 'Churches Adjust Schedule to Fit into Today's Lifestyle, Changing Times and Days', *The Hartford Courant* (15 February, 1997).

Howard Gardner, 'When Leaders Set Out to Conquer the Word', *The Independent* (23 January, 1995).

Charles Handy, *The Age of Paradox* (Boston: Harvard Business School Press, 1994).

John F. Haught, *What is Religion* (New York: Paulist Press, 1990).

Thomas Howard, *The Liturgy Explained* (Harrisburg, PA: Morehouse, 1981)

Urban T. Holmes III, *What is Anglicanism?* (Harrisburg, PA: Morehouse, 1982).

Mike Johnson, *Managing in the Next Millennium* (Oxford: Butterworth Heinemann, 1995).

James L. Kidd, 'Megachurch Methods', *Christian Century* (14 May 1997).

Gordon Legge, 'Religion, Faith and Values', *Calgary Herald* (21 May 1994).

David S. Luecke, 'Is Willow Creek the Way of the Future?' Willow Creek Seeker Services, Evaluating a New Way of Doing Church', *Christian Century* (14 May 1997).

John McClenanen, 'Working the World', *Industry Week* (1996).

Thomas Moore, *Care of the Soul* (New York: HarperCollins, 1992).

Rolf Osterberg, *Corporate Renaissance* (Mill Valley: Nataraj Publishing, 1993).

Mike Pedler, John Burgoyne, and Tom Boydell, *The Learning Company* (London: McGraw-Hill, 1991).

Patricia Rice Post, 'A New Day: Churches Offer Alternatives to Sunday Services', *St Louis Post Dispatch* (11 August 1996).

Jayme Rolls, 'Seven Drivers Predict the Future' (1996).

James M. Rosenthal, Nicola Currie, *Being Anglican in the Third Millennium* (Harrisburg, PA: Morehouse, 1997).

Edgar H. Schein, 'Coming to a New Awareness of Organizational Culture', *Sloan Management Review* (Winter 1984).

Edgar H. Schein, *Organizational Culture and Leadership* (San Francisco: Jossey Bass, 1985).

Peter M. Senge, *The Fifth Discipline* (San Francisco: Doubleday, 1990).

Noel M. Tichy, *The Transformational Leader* (New York: John Wiley, 1986).

Nick Wagner, *The 101 Most Asked Questions about Liturgy* (San Jose: Resource Publications, 1996).

Meg Wheatley, *Leadership and the New Science* (San Francisco: Berrett Koehler, 1992).

William J. Wolf, *Anglican Spirituality* (London: Episcopal Divinity School, 1982).

6

Christian leadership in a
postmodern society

PETER BRIERLEY AND HEATHER WRAIGHT

Most of us had hardly heard the word 'postmodern' until a few years ago. Now it is used as a 'catch all' to explain the good, the bad and the ugly. It is seen as the underlying reason for things as diverse as the loss of a sense of community, and why some advertising hoardings seem to need a translation before we can understand what they mean. Postmodernism is especially likely to be blamed for any change in society which individuals don't like!

Peter Drucker, the American management guru, has written:

> Every few hundred years throughout Western history, a sharp transformation has occurred. In a matter of decades society altogether rearranges itself – its worldview, its basic values, its social and political structures, its art, its key institutions. Fifty years later a new world exists. And the people born into that world cannot even imagine the world in which their grandparents lived and into which their own parents were born. Our age is such a transformation.[1]

Analysing these changes in detail, or describing the components of postmodernism, is beyond the scope of this chapter and has been done expertly by others.[2] What none of us can escape is the impact of postmodernism and the challenges and opportunities it creates. Even if they want to, leaders cannot bury their heads in the sand and hope postmodernism will go away. This is one of the reasons why it is so important, having gathered qualitative and quantitative data, to interpret that data correctly. 'Reading the signs of the times' means not only understanding the current situation, but also identifying the trends revealed and, perhaps most significantly, thinking through their meaning both now and for the future.

We have not undertaken any research specifically into postmodernism, but evidence of it crops up in various ways in the research commissions that Christian research undertakes. There are not many statistics in this chapter, but those that are used have been culled from various recent projects, to illustrate the effects of postmodernism on churchgoing people and so to help us in our thinking about the meaning of leadership.

We therefore propose to tackle the interaction between postmodernism and leadership from two directions: by taking seven characteristics of successful leadership and looking at how they apply in a postmodern society and interweaving them with seven characteristics of postmodernism and what implications they have for leaders. Most of these can be paired or grouped in the following way:

Seven characteristics	
. . . for successful leadership today	*. . . of post-modernism*
I	personal choice is king
2 identified values; applied worldview	changing values
3 wise decisions	spirituality without christianity
4 understood communication	language valued for impact more than meaning; the book giving way to the screen
5 good relationships	loss of confidence in institutions
6 clarity of vision	the future is irrelevant
7 high energy	

1. Personal choice is king

We live in a society where it isn't only the sweets in Woolworths that are 'Pick 'n' mix'. It has become acceptable to make our own choices about a wide variety of aspects of life that were not options for previous generations. This is expressed in all sorts of ways, from the consumerism that has spawned the phrase 'I shop, therefore I am', to changing sexual mores which result in over half of under 25s (53%) finding co-habitation acceptable compared with only 11% of over 75s[3].

Also, the changing pattern of church attendance is probably at least partly to do with personal choice. *Finding Faith in 1994*[4] found that two in five regular churchgoers are likely to stop attending church for at least one year. This is after an average of fourteen years' attendance (less for younger people, more for older). In the past that pattern of behaviour would have been questioned or even considered as 'backsliding'. Nowadays it appears to be part of the spiritual journey for many. Another change that has yet to be measured nationally is decreasing frequency of attendance. One vicar said, 'Those who used to come twice on Sunday now only come twice a month.' People still consider themselves as regular attenders and as belonging to such-and-such a church, but on some Sundays they choose to do other things, whether that be visiting family, going shopping, or watching little Johnny play football.

Teenagers are particularly prone to express their choice – or not – of Christianity by dropping out of church. Every national Church Census[5] in the UK has shown a haemorrhage of young people, while only 48% of churchgoing teenagers say they are very likely to still be attending church as an adult[6].

People within the church are also exercising choice – about what to believe, who to follow, which church to attend. We have all played musical chairs as children; people now play musical churches as adults. Even church leaders have choices to make. For example, Anglicans have to decide whether to accept the ordination of women, or join up with Reform, Forward in Faith or the Modern Churchpeople's Union.

This consumerist approach means that the whole culture in which the church and Christian organizations exercise their ministry is changing radically. As the poet Pam Ayres has put it in 'Nowadays we worship at Saint Tesco',[7] the church is facing competition of a kind it has not had to wrestle with before. Choice in itself is, of course, neither right nor wrong, but this consumerist culture impacts leadership in a huge number of ways including:

- how to view people who drop in and out of church;
- finding strategies to keep young people;
- helping Christians to make informed choices rather than be driven by circumstance.

The key question is surely how we make those choices. What moral, ethical and spiritual values remain in society to guide people?

2a. Identified values

Christian leaders need to know not only what they stand for but also must be able to identify the relevance of those values to their work. What's more, they need to be able to do so unambiguously in a postmodern society which changes values according to the situation in which they have to be expressed.

Values are part of our culture, as are our standards, expectations and image. Walter Wink, Professor of Biblical Interpretation at Auburn Theological Seminary, New York, in the third volume of his trilogy on the 'Powers', describes culture as that which:[8]

- teaches us what to believe;
- teaches us what to value;
- teaches us what to see.

Whilst this definition almost attributes biblical authority to culture, it unambiguously roots values to culture. What does this mean in practice in a postmodern culture? It means identifying what are the values we have now in our organizations, our churches and our institutions. One way of identifying our values is to answer questions such as the following:

- Why does your organization exist?
- If you didn't exist, who would miss you and why?[9]
- If you re-invented yourself, what would you look like?[10]
- What do you have to do to stay in business?[11]
- What do you want to have become in, say, five years time?

Such questions are usually best answered by the organization's leaders spending time apart, for a day or two, often helped by a facilitator. Identifying your values helps provide the motivational energy for leadership.

2b. Changing values

Young people have a tendency to think that their parents are old-fashioned and out of touch; in other words, they have different values. The *European Values Study* showed unequivocally that the values we acquire as young adults stay with us.[12] This is clearly seen in the varying values of the current generations: Generation X, Baby Busters, Baby Boomers and the Maturity Generation.

A postmodern trend is that values change not only in the long-term, from generation to generation, but also on a daily basis, from one circumstance to another. Truth is relative rather than absolute and so one finds that even one in four (23%) of churchgoing teenagers agree that, 'the only sensible way to live is to make the best choice you can, based on your gut feeling at the time'. Only 40% actually disagreed with this statement.[13]

Changing values means the moral basis for action is shaky and yet, presented with moral absolutes, fewer people are willing to accept them. For two in five church teenagers in the *Right from Wrong* survey, sexual intercourse between two consenting adults who are unmarried is morally acceptable. Yet church teaching in all denominations continues to be clear that such behaviour is not acceptable.[14]

The loss of shared values is part of the postmodern disbelief in meat-narratives or grand stories (including the gospel) that seek to explain everything. No longer can ministers assume that their congregations know – or if they do know, believe – Bible stories. It is something of a cliché that 'the only thing we learn from history is that we don't learn from history', but these days even a Christian perspective of history as *his* story is dismissed. Similarly, churchgoers are unlikely automatically to accept propositional preaching or carefully argued moral reasoning, even if it is based on biblical and church teaching. This presents leaders with challenges such as:

- not to make assumptions in their preaching and teaching;
- the need to help people identify key values;
- to have the courage to act on these values – all the time, not only when they feel like it.

Which, of course, means that leaders themselves need to have put the time and effort into thinking through their own values. 'Don't do what I do, do what I say' was never a very credible way to lead, and it's even less so in today's world.

2c. Applied worldview

Our worldview impinges on our personal culture. Tom Wright, Dean of Lichfield Cathedral, has articulated the elements of a Christian worldview very helpfully:[15]

A worldview has to be able *to answer life's key questions*. These are postulated as:

- *Who are we?* Why are human beings on this planet? What are we supposed to be doing? What kind of being are we really?
- *Where are we?* What is the nature of the world and the universe in which it is placed? How did they get here? Where are they going? Is the scientific answer the only one? If we believe God made the world, does that mean he is the supreme Governor of it?
- *What went wrong?* Why is there so much evil and suffering everywhere? Why do I face so many obstacles and problems?
- *What is the solution?* Is there a way out? Christianity has a specific answer on this, but so do many non-Trinitarian churches, cults and other religions. What needs to be done? What do I have to do?
- *What time is it?* Where are we in the global pattern of time? How does 'now' fit into the picture?
- *The key questions of the day*. These will naturally vary with time. One of the current questions is why the life and death of Diana, Princess of Wales, attracted such enormous attention. Also, did the reaction to her death reveal a spiritual need?[16]

A second element of a worldview is *the story by which we interpret life*. For Christians this is essentially the scriptural view with creation, redemption and ultimate destiny in heaven. Others assume that this life ends with death; there is nothing more. Others believe in conditional immortality. But whatever view we hold, it affects our thinking and possibly our motivation and actions.

Bishop Lesslie Newbigin, the brilliant ex-Indian missionary who could keep audiences captivated right up to a few weeks before his death in January 1998 at the age of eighty-eight, explained the key elements of the Christian story:[17]

- the Bible gives a unique interpretation of history;
- the Bible gives us the meaning of history;
- it is the story of God not of this world;[18]

- it is the story of a people God has chosen to be the bearer of his blessing for the whole of his creation.

This leads to the third element. A worldview helps to decide *the way we choose to live*. So, for example, a Christian worldview takes seriously Jesus' words, 'By this all men shall know you are my disciples, if you have love for one another (John 13:35).[19]

The fourth and final element of a worldview is *the symbols that represent our culture*. Christians use the cross constantly as their symbol. In Britain, the National Lottery's crossed-finger logo is a symbol of chance and luck. Across the world, wherever you go, is the big M for McDonald's, with stores and menus the same. These symbols do not just represent our culture, they actually shape it by the image they represent. They are literally a sign. How, then, should Christians use the Cross? At one time people would have dismissed the church as dull, boring or irrelevant. Today, they are more likely to complain that it is 'unspiritual'. And while they may be unclear as to what 'spirituality' really is, a central part of it is undoubtedly this concern to find a new, all-embracing way of understanding and making sense out of the reality that is modern life.[19] People want authenticity,[20] or, perhaps more accurately, an authentic worldview in which they can trust.

This suggests that church leaders need to recapture the power of story-telling and to explain the significance of Christianity in cosmic terms – creation of the universe, the fall, redemption, the return of Christ and coming judgement. They need to root the history of the Bible in our own history, even though many are not interested in history today. And they need to explain what Christianity means in terms of the values by which I should live.

3a. Wise decisions

Leadership requires the ability to judge between different factors, to sift them, identify the pros and cons of each and to decide which path the individual or organization will follow. In a postmodern society, awash with information constantly being updated, the opportunity to view the total picture is more difficult – sometimes impossible – and makes the decision-making process a blur over a period rather than instant at a moment in time.

The wisdom of our decisions often depends on the way in which we utilise the information before us. The following assumptions underlying valid information gathering are based on George Barna's book *Church Growth without Compromise.*[21]

a. Information is useful if it enhances your decision-making

Information gathering must have a specific purpose in view, an object or goal that will enable you to make a better decision because you are more informed about something. Leaders are swamped with information today and therefore need to select only that which is important to them in their context.

b. Information is only one important element in decision making, but it is one of the most crucial elements

This recognizes that whilst data is something it is not everything. Spiritual elements are also important for Christian people who sense that God is leading them in a particular way. The financial element is also vital in making decisions. When John Kennedy in 1961 said that the Americans wished to put a man on the moon before the end of the decade, he implied that the funds to make it happen would somehow be found. Postmodernity focuses on feelings not facts, and Christian leaders must resist the temptation to act simply 'by their gut sense' or 'as the Lord says' if there is *no* corroborative support.

c. The only thing worse than no information is bad information

'Bad' information has not been properly researched, is not valid in some way, or maybe the method by which it was obtained is dubious or causes bias. If data looks peculiar in one aspect, assume in the first instance that it is wrong. Leaders need to assess the quality of the information that is to hand – a cardinal principle.

d. Get both primary and secondary data if available; use both quantitative and qualitative information if possible

Primary data is the known data, the collected data, the direct quote. Secondary data is derived from that. Quantitative information is often broader in scope, qualitative is often deeper. Leaders need to use both to get the overall picture. But postmodernity frequently focuses on the local without looking at the wider, something Christian leaders need to resist.

e. Collect information that can be meaningfully applied to your ministry context

The data you are using need to be relevant to your purpose, as far as this is possible. It is important to distinguish between 'need-to-know' and 'nice-to-know' data. If you want information to decide whether or not you should plant a church in a certain location, you need to have details of the size and type of population in that area. How many times residents go to the cinema each week may not be very useful. Whether or not they have cars might well be, especially if the new church site is outside the town.

f. Look at both strengths and trends

The basic numbers are, of course, essential, but how are they changing? That is equally important. So ask for the movement in them, which may mean comparing the figures in one survey with those of an earlier study. Postmodernity focuses on the now, not on where the now has come from. Christian leaders need to focus on the now, but in the light of the past and the expected future, if present trends continue. Try to explain why the trends are what they are shown to be. What can be learned from such explorations? Why are the new churches and Pentecostals growing? Because they are planting new churches and frequently emphasising the starting of new churches. This means that they have relatively smaller congregation.

g. Your information base needs to be constantly updated

Any data goes out of date like food that we buy in a supermarket. Each item of data should ideally have a sort of 'use by' date stamped on it. The frequency of update, however, depends on the nature of the material being used and its importance.

h. All data are not created equal

In early 1997 one series of car advertisements had the slogan 'All men are created equal. All cars are not'. Whatever the truth behind that slogan may be, data are like cars – they do not all have the same value. Which is the organization behind the information? Government figures may usually be trusted more than opinion polls. Who are the people behind the data? What kind of reputation do they have? What about the type of data being collected – can it be assumed to be of reasonable reliability? Can you compare it with other data?

i. Research data are not reality; they offer an interpretation of reality

What does '10% of people go to church' mean? What is 'church' – are all denominations included? Do Spiritualist churches count as much as Anglican or Baptist ones? Do you count children in Sunday School taking place at the same time? What does 'go' mean? How frequently do they attend? What about the difference between attenders and attendances? From the way the figure was actually calculated in the *English Church Census* of 1989, it would be more correct to say, 'On 15 October 1989, 10% of the adults in England attended a Trinitarian church service on at least one occasion'. In other words, allowance was made for those who went twice that particular Sunday and the extra attendances were discounted, but morning and evening services were both included. The frequency with which the particular people in church that Sunday attended church was not requested and it might thus have been an exceptional Sunday because there were a large number of visitors – a possibility reduced by choosing a date which did not coincide with holidays, festivals, half-term, and so on. Post-modernists may confuse data with actual reality; leaders must be very careful in their interpretation.

j. The analysis and interpretation of information are two different activities

Analysis can start at the very simple totalling of numbers to the much more sophisticated procedures available through computers. Interpretation, on the other hand, is personal, individual and based on the person's knowledge and experience. It is common to assume that a person skilled in analysis is also skilled in interpretation, but this does not follow. The actual abilities required are different. What does it mean for the people or organization involved? If the growing denominations are planting churches, should other denominations be doing the same? George Carey has encouraged

Anglican churches to consider starting new congregations and in the early 1990s some thirty new Anglican churches were being started every year.[22]

3b. Spirituality without Christianity

Another complication for leaders is that postmodern society has a hunger for spirituality. Some would say this was seen in the massive public response to the death of Diana, Princess of Wales.[23] But the fact that millions either in the streets of London or watching on television joined in the Lord's Prayer doesn't mean that they shared the traditional values and beliefs of a Judaeo-Christian heritage. Within the church there is a growth of alternative spiritualities, such as the interest in Celtic Christianity. One Anglican church that decided to lay on a 1662 service of Morning Prayer once a quarter for its more traditional and older attenders found a growing number of younger people turning up because they liked the spirituality.

This interest in spirituality requires clear thinking about what is essential and non-essential in Christian belief and practice. This is an exercise involving theologians and practitioners, leaders and attenders, national bodies and local churches. Leaders need to be at the forefront of the practical ecumenism which so many churchgoers find stimulating and encouraging.[24] Leadership that is respected for wise decisions will be flexible on the non-essentials, so allowing a range of spiritualities while having the courage to stand firm on the essentials.

4a. Understood Communication

In a postmodern world communication is 'hot', pervasive and persuasive. Christian leaders have to master these elements knowing they cannot command attention simply because of their position. In today's plethora of voices and messages, Christian leaders must be able to:

- communicate well;
- make their message stand out as worth listening to;
- communicate preferably in visual as well as written form;
- use the media, often, wisely and well.

No wonder the Diocese of Lichfield is running a course for clergy on how to communicate better, including making their sermons easier to listen to and understand![25]

4b. Language valued for impact more than meaning

Modes of communication are changing, including even the nature of language. Language has always evolved, with old words changing their meaning (e.g. 'absolutely' to mean simply 'I agree') and new words and phrases coming into every day use (e.g. 'horrendous', 'politically correct'). However, in postmodern communication the very nature of communication has changed. Carefully reasoned argument is rarely respected, let alone understood, and people look for instant understanding of even the most complicated issues. We have developed a 'soundbite' culture which tries to reduce complex issues and problems to a twenty-second explanation.

We are drowning in information, but information is not the same as communication. The world wide web is growing so fast that statistics cannot keep up with it. A British Telecom report listed the time people spend on the telephone worldwide, talking, faxing and sending data:

1985   15 billion minutes
1995   60 billion minutes
2000   95 billion minutes.[26]

'Internet addiction' and 'information fatigue syndrome' are not the stuff of futuristic novels, but reported as fact in newspapers and magazines.[27] Public libraries are going on-line, schools are getting wired for the web and growth in home computers is unabated. The result is that it is possible to obtain information on virtually any subject – and sometimes 'virtually' to be part of it too!

But having access to information and understanding it are not synonymous. There is a desperate need for leaders who can:

- communicate their message in language which is easily understood;
- help people make sense of the mass of information which threatens to engulf them;
- discern the key issues; and
- think through Christian reponses to them.

What effect does this overload of information have, especially on ministry? The former Archbishop of York, the Most Revd John Habgood, wrote, 'To be overloaded with information reinforces the sense that knowledge is just an endless succession of human opinions, that there are no abiding truths and principles by which human beings ought to live.'[28] In a society overloaded with information, the church has to continue to work hard to present the Christian message as an abiding truth rather than just another opinion.

4c. The book giving way to the screen

Added to these and other changes in the means of communication are fundamental changes to the method of communication. No longer do most people get the majority of their information from reading books or newspapers. A 1994 survey for the Religious Books Group of the Publishers' Association[29] found that just over a third of ministers (36%) read twenty or more books a year (about two a month); almost half (47%) read between six and nineteen (about 1 a month). Just over half (52%) also read one or two Christian magazines or journals. However, there is a substantial minority (17%, or one in six) who are effectively non-readers.

The screen – whether TV or computer – provides non-stop entertainment and information, the access to which is controlled by the viewer not the provider. On average, in Britain, people spend twenty-five hours a week watching television. Churchgoers watch about half that (thirteen hours), and ministers even less (nine hours),[30] but nevertheless this is a lot longer than even the most ardent churchgoers spend in church!

When asked which kinds of programmes they watch most frequently, only three attract more than half: news (74%), drama (54%) and documentaries (52%).[31] Churchgoers listen to radio an average of nine hours a week, though one in twelve (8%) does not listen at all. Receiving our information from different sources may well affect what we communicate and how we communicate it. Do we talk the same language when we are trying to communicate the Christian message?

More than that, the media can actually influence our view of reality. One example of this is that no longer do sociologists talk of a 'universal' culture, but of a 'global' culture.[32]

William F. Fore has even gone as far as saying that 'today television is beginning to replace religion as an institution.[33] With multinational corporations (most of which seem to be owned by Rupert Murdoch!) controlling much of the mass media, what chance does the church have of being heard? Perhaps it was prophetic that in the film *Jesus of Montreal* Jesus did not cleanse a temple or a church but a TV studio, knocking over the lights and the cameras in a blaze of righteous anger.

5. Good Relationships and Loss of Confidence in Institutions

At first sight these may seem odd bedfellows! But the key question is, who is trusted in a postmodern society? It used to be said that a gentleman's word was his bond. Underpinning such a statement was an implicit trust in the relationship of one person to another. A postmodern society translates trust into a computer print out and makes personal relationships temporarily useful for as long as they are mutually beneficial. Access may have advertised that 'they take the waiting out of wanting', but postmodern relationships do not wait and so lose the risk of something better.

DHL ran a series of advertising hoardings in 1996–7 based on relationships. Two of them read 'Part of the team' and 'We trust them'. DHL provide a courier delivery service. Now, of course, anyone using their services expects that their parcel will be delivered to the right place, but the trust is hardly of the same degree as one would expect to have in, say, a surgeon who undertakes major surgery on your heart! It is quite a postmodern concept to even feel the need to state trust in relation to services provided. It goes along with the various charters – 'this is what you can expect us to provide and this is what we will do if we don't meet the responsibilities outlined here'.

Relationships, even with the gas board or railway companies, are based on spelling out the reasons why we should trust them. They have to earn our trust by meeting the standards required, and compensating us in some way when they don't. However, this not only applies to such public companies, but is also true of the church, of Christian organizations, and even of individual relationships. Gone are the days when people were trusted because of their status, whether vicar, teacher or policeman. These days someone who is not perceived as worthy of trust is simply not trusted, whoever they are. A leader who is not trusted is unlikely to be followed. In a postmodern society trust is built on relationship rather than on authority, leaders have to earn trust, and earn it repeatedly.

6a. Clarity of vision

Visionary leaders work in tomorrow as well as living in today. They therefore oppose postmodernism when it encourages people to work and live in today. What does it mean to 'work in tomorrow'?

In 1994, the travel guide producers, Frommer's, ran an advertising campaign with the slogan 'Know where you're going before you get there'. Those working in tomorrow have a clear sense of the vision to which they are working, or the set of goals they aim to achieve. One vicar of a large church phoned me one day and said, 'Ten years ago I set myself ten goals for this church. eight have been fulfilled, one has been half done, and I now know the tenth was impossible.' He had a clear sense of where he was going.

Those working in tomorrow have an inner motivation to achieve 'tomorrow'. There is a sense of 'we're getting there' in such people. When Jesus was warned to watch out for Herod, he replied, 'Go tell that fox, "I will drive out demons and heal people today and tomorrow and on the third day I will reach my goal."' (Luke 13:32; NIV). Jesus was not going to be put off by Herod!

Those working in tomorrow believe in what they are doing today. I was so sad to hear of one clergyman who, having taken his final service before retirement, said, 'Now I need never attend church ever again.' Our commitment to our work and plans (or lack of it!) communicates itself not just by what we say but by who we are and by what we do.

Those working in tomorrow not only have these three characteristics, but they also recognize others who have them as well. They tend to gravitate together. Who are they in your church or organization? Can you spot them? If so, how can they best work together?

6b. The Future is irrelevant

The postmodern society lives for 'now'; indeed, it could be said that the slogan of postmodern Britain is 'forget it all for an instant', a slogan of the National Lottery. Many people don't look further ahead than today, or at least next weekend. Is it just a quirk of language that TGFI – Thank God It's Friday – is now a commonly used phrase? We live in the borough of Greenwich and the famous (or infamous) Dome is just down the road. But is there nothing more to look forward to than a big party on 31 December 1999?

7. High energy

The postmodern world is a stimulating, challenging and often exhausting society in which to live and minister. Many leaders, especially in local churches, are tired. They've attended all the conferences (especially in the 1980s), applied church growth principles, wrestled with the demands of pastoral care in a hurting world. And it doesn't seem to have made that much difference:

- there hasn't been a revival – at least not on the scale or in the way many evangelicals have prayed for;
- the numbers attending church continue to decline – unless, of course, we are counting them wrongly because of the frequency issue discussed earlier;
- the Christian heritage of our nation continues to be eroded.

So why bother? Let's just give up and find a job which pays a decent salary so we can afford to enjoy retirement!

True leaders cannot do that. Something drives them on, a something that postmodern society does not question. Leaders have energy: mental, emotional and spiritual energy.[34] They are motivated by a belief that the task is worth doing. They believe their people deserve good leadership.

Janet Cohen occupies a senior position at Charterhouse Bank, for which she works three days a week. She is a governor of the BBC, is on the boards of the Sheffield Development Corporation and of the Yorkshire Building Society. She is married with three children, two of whom were still at home in 1994. And in the years 1988 to 1994 she wrote five crime stories, the first of which won a Crime Writers' Association award, as well as the novel *Children of a Harsh Winter*. One might ask how she does it all! She replies, 'My mother-in-law taught me, "You can shift the world if you do it half an hour at a time". I write for a couple of hours a day.'[35] This is energy.

'Look at a day when you are supremely satisfied at the end,' said Margaret Thatcher. 'It's not a day when you lounge around doing nothing; it's when you've had everything to do, and you've done it.' Whatever else she espoused, she epitomized energy. Winston Churchill once said, 'It is no use saying, "we are doing our best". You have to succeed in doing what is necessary.' That requires energy. May you find the energy to fulfil your vision, have good relationships, with understood communication making for wise decisions, through having identified your values and knowing your worldview in this postmodern culture in which we live!

References

1. Via Rev Graham Cray, Principal, Ridley Hall, Cambridge.
2. Many secular writers have addressed postmodernism from various perspectives: economic, social, educational, architectural, etc. There are a growing number of books from a Christian perspective, of which the following may be found to be helpful: Ian Cundy (ed.), *Tomorrow Is Another Country: Education in a Post Modern World* (London: Church House Publishing, 1996); David Lyon, *Postmodernity* (Open University, 1996); Richard Middleton and Brian Walsh, *Truth Is Stranger Than It Used to Be* (London: SPCK, 1995).
3. Ansvar Survey of English Social Behaviour, Christian Research, 1995.
4. *Finding Faith in 1994*, Christian Research for Inter-Church House, 1994.
5. See, for example, '*Christian' England: the results of the English Church Census in 1989 with comparable figures for 1979*, Peter Brierley (London: MARC Europe, 1991), or *Prospects for Scotland 2000*, the results of the Scottish Church Census in 1994 with comparable figures for 1984, by Fergus Macdonald and Peter Brierley (Edinburgh, National Bible Society of Scotland; London: Christian Research, 1995).
6. *Right from Wrong*, Christian Research for Agapé, 1997.

7. 'Nowadays we Worship at Saint Tesco', in Pam Ayres, *With These Hands* (London: Weidenfeld & Nicolson, 1997).
8. Walter Wink, *Engaging the Powers* (Minneapolis: Fortress Press, 1992), pp. 53, 54.
9. A question from Charles Handy's book, *The Empty Raincoat* (Arrow, 1995).
10. Handy, *The Empty Raincoat*.
11. A question from Robin Gill and Derek Burke, *Strategic Church Leadership* (London: SPCK, 1996).
12. Dr David Barker, *The European Values Study 1981–1990* (Halman and Vloert, 1992).
13. *Right from Wrong*.
14. For example, the 1991 statement by the Bishops of the Church of England affirmed that 'chastity and fidelity' should characterize relationships.
15. Tom Wright, *Jesus and the Victory of God* (London: SPCK, 1995).
16. See the forthcoming booklet being published by the English Lausanne Committee, London, UK, giving the papers presented at a Consultation in February 1998 entitled 'Death of a Princess: Postmodern Spirituality and the Gospel'.
17. Address at the Holy Trinity Brompton Home Focus week, July 1997.
18. Is this why *The Book of God*, by Walter Wangerin, the Bible written like a novel (Oxford: Lion Publishing, 1996), is so popular?
19. John Drane, *Looking at Evangelism from the Inside Out* (St Albans: Administry), Volume 1, Number 5, March 1997.
20. 'The Falseness of Society', looking at the 1990s so far and the fragmentation of society, in the 200th issue of the music magazine, *The Face*, January 1997.
21. George Barne, *Church Growth without Compromise*, 1992.
22. See the Appendix figures supplied by Revd George Lings, Deal, in *Breaking New Ground* (General Synod Report, Church House, 1994).
23. 'Death of a Princess'.
24. For example, *One Voice in York* in 1993 involved over 300 churches including Catholics and almost every Protestant denomination.
25. Reported in *The Daily Telegraph*, 18 March 1998.
26. 'Trends, Analysis, Implications', BT/MCI Global Communications Report, 1996/97.

27. For example, Maryann Bird, 'System Overload', *Time* (9 December 1997), p. 46.
28. John Habgood, 'Culture of Contempt', *Leading Light* (Summer 1996), p. 2.
29. Survey by Christian Research, 1994.
30. Ansvar Survey of English Social Behaviour.
31. Ansvar Survey of English Social Behaviour.
32. 'Modernity once deemed itself universal. It now thinks of itself instead as global ... Universal was to be the rule of reason – the order of things that would replace slavery to passions with the autonomy of rational beings . . . Globality in contrast means merely that everyone everywhere may feed on McDonald's burgers and watch the latest made-for-TV docudrama.' Zygmunt Bauman, *Life in Fragments*, p. 24, quoted by Revd Graham Cray in a lecture, 'Postmodernism and the Gospel'.
33. Quoted by William Biernatzki, Christian Research Trends Vol 15 (1995) No 2.
34. This is worked out in more detail in Chapter 11 of *Management and Ministry*, edited by John Nelson, MODEM (Canterbury Press, 1996).
35. *The Bookseller*, 15 July 1994, p. 5.

7

A new spirit in leadership*

BERNARD KILROY

Leadership has to incarnate value and meaning. In a community of faith, this is to act 'in the place of Christ', as St Benedict suggested almost 1500 years ago in what can be read as a still relevant treatise on community leadership and management. Do twentieth-century ideas fill in some of the detail? When those involved in Christian ministry turn to secular management, they may associate it with the production lines and bureaucracies which are caricatured in Charlie Chaplin's classic film *Modern Times*. That way, to think 'organization' will mean thinking 'machine', not 'organism'. However, these days the dialogue between ministry and its work can be more fruitful; there is a new spirit in thinking about leadership. It turns to the natural if complex world of creation for inspiration, and to the energy and spirit of people themselves. This chapter tries to create an alternative mental association by offering glimpses of how leadership can release and inspire that natural power. It can happen when organizations which are seen as having a culture of 'command and control' listen, build trust and let go.

It's not every day that one has a conversion experience about leadership. After all, something very fresh is needed to soften a natural wariness within the churches about leadership and management 'theories', as if they are foreign to what church is about.

---

* With special consideration of Roman Catholicism in Britain.

Is it that deep down there is a fundamental objection that the orderliness needed for organizations is a violation of the free hand of the Spirit? Or is there simply a more mundane objection that the tools of planning, structures, procedures and monitoring simply don't match the 'messiness' of congregations? To meet such feelings, I offer four examples of creative leadership and then speculate about their message.

1. Manifestations of creative leadership

a. Self-organizing organization: 'boids'

The conversion experience I had was to the idea of the 'self-organizing organization'. This doesn't mean something which would make leadership redundant, but rather concentrate it in the qualities and processes that are vital. The experience was an activity one has to get out of one's chair to take part in. It's called the 'boid' simulation. Yes, seriously. This occasion was a management development seminar of some two dozen people in a large open room.[1]

What we had to do was stand up and select two participants whom each of us would move towards but keep at one arm's length to the left and right of us. The room soon became a throng of slowly swirling bodies before coming to rest, each person standing at one arm's length from everyone else.

What had we done? We had performed a simple experiment which has been simulated on computer with hundreds of 'boids', rather than dozens, to imitate just how a flock of birds behaves. That vital 'Aha!' conversion moment comes when one makes the lateral connection between birds and humans – as the Wright brothers did a century ago in learning the impossible, how to get a human being to fly.

So what is the moral for leadership? The traditional method of air traffic control for humans depends on a centralised guidance system that receives data on each aircraft's position, then maps it against other aircrafts' last known or anticipated positions and then issues instructions to each. Birds are not so endowed. They have developed reliance on each of them having their own sensory patterns so that they keep a safe distance from each other, compare their speeds and re-position, even if parting to pass round an obstacle. If the two systems are compared in operational conditions, *at some level of high volume the centralized system is likely to break down.* Indeed, aircraft are fitted with positioning beacons which allow them to behave like birds and override the central control in an emergency. It is the latter 'Receiver Based Communication' (RBC) which is used in combat by military aircraft. In those situations, a remote and centralized system would risk overload and breakdown or cause collisions.

My readiness to accept this simulation as holding a valuable inspiration for leadership would have to confront a number of instinctive objections from me. The first is that 'it's all very well for birds, but wouldn't work for humans!' just won't wash. Alternatively, I might incline towards technology and suggest that even more expensive software in the central control system would cope. After all, isn't it true that the more complex the question the more complex the answer? The idea that complexity can be matched by simplicity is hard to swallow. Or, I might take refuge in the defence that 'it's only a metaphor!' forgetting that the majority of management terms from 'strategy' to 'span of control' are metaphors having no intrinsic meaning. Alternatively, I might argue that subsidiarity doesn't work below a certain level of responsibility; for instance, that priests in a diocese might self-organize but that for members of a congregation it might somehow present difficulties. Then I read that the principle of self-organization has been used by the maintenance personnel of Xerox photocopiers to improve their effectiveness, through RBC on-the-spot communication.

An even greater challenge may come from the realization that the leader is not the bird in front and that the bird in front is constantly changing. Leadership then becomes the ability to inspire and support a force of agreed values which are drawn *from* the flock as much as they are given *to* it. Gradually, I might start to reverse my initial reluctance about this novelty. Also, there is an immediate attraction in observing and learning from the natural world, with all the simple complexity of its messiness and its apparent anarchy.

b. Self-transforming organization: open space

To inspire its future direction, a self-organising organization might hold an agenda-less meeting, involving (if possible) all its members, using the open space method. This is another example of the kind of idea which could be rejected out of hand as impracticable had it not been so successfully used by secular organizations such as Boeing in order to help revive cohesion in the company in building their new airplane, the 777. Apart from use by hospital trusts facing major upheavals in their organizations, it has also been used most successfully by the (Roman Catholic) Congregation of Religious for their annual general meeting of 190 leaders during three days in 1998.[2]

The numbers involved can be anything from 20 to 2000; large-scale transformations and reviews are thus possible, particularly when the participants have not always met one another before. Above all, it works best *when nothing else looks likely to work*. Only the general theme is set up beforehand (in the case of COR it was 'Creating Space for Naming God'), though a great deal of prior planning is necessary to make sure that the logistics all work. A horizontal mixture of disciplines and a vertical mixture of levels of responsibility is ideal, especially when the issues are complex and imponderable.

The process of each of the (typically three) days begins in the largest space, called the 'market place' with the participants sitting in a big circle of chairs without distinction. A general invitation is made for any participant to announce their intention of hosting a smaller group, naming an issue which they propose to discuss.

The posters for each of the issues are then displayed on a blank wall, each allocated to one of a number of group rooms to be used in parallel during one of the time slots of, say, an hour or more. Other participants may then take part in the group of their choice, with everyone respecting the 'law of two feet' convention that they may stay, or move on between groups as 'bumble-bees' cross-pollinating, or simply observing like 'butterflies'. This free, even chaotic, atmosphere reduces tension and conflict; groups tend to attract enthusiasts or critics who are interested to make their points constructively in order to share.

Each group 'convenor' has the responsibility for ensuring that the discussion is recorded and conclusions printed and posted up, wherever possible incorporating the names and signatures of those who contributed. Therefore, as the event proceeds, the energy level rises and issues will sprout and attract attention and discussion, with numbers attending the groups varying. Each participant is usually given a copy of all the summaries. In the case of the COR event, some forty-five groups convened in thirteen possible rooms during five sessions, with attendances varying between one and forty-two, covering such diverse topics as 'Asylum Seekers and Refugees' and 'Elijah's Cave'.

Responsibility for progressing the issues will lie on those interested and the organization's executive or working group will be able to formulate policy in the light of them. However, it is an explicit understanding of the process that 'whoever comes are the right people', 'whatever happens is the only thing that could have', 'whenever it starts is the right time' and 'when it is over, it is over'. In other words, the agenda drives itself.

It is plain that the sense of ownership and commitment among participants is maximized by such a process. It is also plain that those with overall responsibility for holding such a conference are taking the risk of handing over developments to whoever is invited and attends. However, it is equally certain that decisions made in tune with the meeting will 'stick'. Without such ownership, in my experience as a chief officer of a major service in a London borough (a budget in present terms of some £150 million and staff of some 500), the traditional and 'rational' recipe of corporate planning can grind along on square wheels.

c. Self-implementing organization: networking and dialogue

One might be forgiven for thinking, after an open agenda meeting when all the participants have gone home, that the real business of implementing proposals is left to the hard-headed administrators on Monday morning. In fact, the whole organization can go on being involved in working out how to get things done, including resolving the contradictions and trade-offs. Again, there is a well-documented case study to demonstrate this: the re-organization of a major social service function in one of the UK conurbations. This was no small order since it concerned the daily cross-city transportation of over 2000 children with special needs and disabilities, attending a few hundred schools in a few hundred taxis, cars and minibuses with lifts.[3]

Re-organization conjures up 're-*structuring*', which this wasn't (or only indirectly so). Instead you could call it a 're-culturing'. That was made possible when the service manager had the courage to hand over responsibility for working out implementation to the four parties involved, namely the drivers (the majority in the private sector), the administrative staff, the teachers and school secretaries and the parents and escorts of the children.

The decision to change followed a period when operational failures and hiccups had reached an all time high, accompanied by absenteeism, stress and overspending on the capped budget. This is a familiar tale to those of us who have managed large organizations; the nature of the work involved makes little difference. Very often, as in this case, the breakdown involves a very sophisticated organizational machine, which suffers from 'lock-in' or seizure at several points. *Yet the solution is not mechanical as if requiring, in the jargon, 're-engineering'.*

How did it happen? On the brink of chaos, the threat of complete breakdown acted as a catalyst for the different parties to familiarize themselves with each others' concerns through dialogue: the administrative staff went out to travel with the parents; the parents worked their way through the procedures; and so on. The parties worked in small groups looking at particular problems, by empathizing with each other, probing for the obvious and not-so-obvious solutions. The process was messy, noisy, heated, repetitive, emotional and time consuming – all the very opposite of what most people believe 'rational' management is about. Result: an organism that lives, loves and works; not a machine that functions and breaks down. In the five years since, business has increased by almost 75% with (although not an objective of the exercise) a substantial reduction in average costs, as well as in staff numbers, complaints, queries and sickness.

d. Self-maintaining organization: building cathedrals

What sort of organization would be needed to run its responsibilities day in, day out? Would it be the stereotype pyramid of bureaucracy or would it be like Company XYZ? There, the structure is on three levels, not a dozen. They relate to each other through horizontal rings of project teams and networks, rather than vertical limbs of a hierarchy. Its systems rely on the work-teams to generate and look after their own budgets, for everyone is shown how to read cash-flow statements and balance sheets; all relying on informal and face-to-face communication so that memoranda for the filing cabinets are kept to a minimum. Strategy is the responsibility of the board of 'counsellors' who lead the organization, but all associates (employees) help design their own marketing plans and products as well as having a free vote on where, for instance, to relocate a factory, even though the decision runs counter to that initially recommended. Their financial stake is the 23% of profits that employees decide how to distribute.

Staff are interviewed and appointed by the people who work with them. They set their own salaries in consultation and rotate in their jobs, and decide between them the flexible hours they work. In the offices and factories, women run their own staff development programmes and there are few secretaries and no receptionists. Any job advertisement has hundreds of applicants.

The style is not laid back, even if it relies on informal dress and open floor plans, with machine and desk location as well as decor decided by open agreement. When supplies have been held up, people come in out of hours unpaid in order to meet the production quota they have set themselves. *For the overall mission is not only profit and effectiveness* (hard work is part of the atmosphere; each person is 'building a cathedral', it is said), *but also quality of life, enjoyment and participation at work* (and hence indirectly at home) *as ends in themselves.* Of course, the Company doesn't run itself but has a forceful, mercurial and crusading president. He manages by walking about but he also works regularly from home – only, it must be said, since a 'conversion' following an exhaustion collapse, after originally trying to run the Company on traditional lines.

Many of these features have become more and more common in companies including, among household names in the UK, the John Lewis Partnership dating back to 1929. Actually, Company XYZ is Semco in Brazil. I use Semco because it is the most fully written up and accessible example I know of.[4] I mention it at length because it is also the most extreme antithesis of the classical pyramid which somehow most of us, including clergy and some religious, have imbibed with our mother's milk as *the* norm of organization.

Preconceived ideas from that classical norm may be reinforced in churches because so many volunteers in parishes and congregations have retired or been made redundant from traditional organizations, and perhaps bring their old habits of thought with them. One of the most remarkable features of the Semco story is how many employees, especially middle managers but also trade union officials, felt threatened when confronted with change; *their sense of identity, security and status were inextricably involved with the status quo.* It is a reminder how we too can collude with clericalism.

2. *Problems with traditional approaches*

So far, what I have tried to do is illustrate four different ways in which radical, but nevertheless natural, alternative approaches to leadership can not only work but work brilliantly. It has been, alas, only a whistle-stop tour to create a new impression rather than impart solid information. I offer it in order to free up what is perceived to be an increasing stalemate.

In many church congregations and most especially in my own (Roman Catholic) church, clergy have been increasingly operating heroically as solo bands, but are finding that treadmill becoming impossible, as shortages of priests mean wider responsibilities, such as covering more than one parish. On the other hand when they ask themselves about their role as leaders, many have an instinctive distrust and confusion about what they think the world of management can offer. So, they may be tempted to rely merely on common sense (which goes a long way) or what they are familiar with through conventional wisdom or hearsay (which is not so reliable).

I have some sympathy with their predicament. A great deal of what gets peddled is managerialist, that is management techniques and concepts used inappropriately for their own sake, packaged with jargon.[5] Some appraisal schemes are a case in point. Of course, many of those ideas were in prominence in the mechanistic days of the Henry Ford style of production line manufacturing and have filtered through into common parlance, such as the 'organizational tree' or 'economies of scale' and are far less relevant today, particularly in any kind of voluntary setting. Thus, when many people think 'organization', they think 'machine'; they don't think 'organism'. It has to be remembered that although theories of leadership are as old as Moses and his father-in-law Jethro, the twentieth-century generation of thinking about leadership and management is still in its adolescence and is yet to show maturity in many respects.

For instance, the commonest way in which parish programmes are put together is understandably to start with a local survey or audit in order to produce a strategy ('Where do we want to get to?'; 'Where are we now?'; 'How do we get there?'). Reasonable in itself, this action can be concentrated in the hands of a few parish 'experts' so that the majority feel excluded or disempowered or even talked down to, particularly as the work almost certainly involves the terrible triplets of paper, statistics and jargon and maybe (horrors!) an overhead projector. Before long, I feel I am back at school and longing for the coffee break to begin or the bar to open.

These feelings have to be respected. Leadership means starting where people 'are coming from'. When I have a project at home that involves the carpenter who does work for me, out comes my paper and geometry bits and pieces. He tolerates them, but when he wants to explain to me he gets offcuts of wood to show me in a real model. This way, he knows with his body. It's true. When he saws along a line, it's as straight as a die and the movement is a joy to watch; when I try the same my saw wanders in a slight but infuriating curve. Bodily intelligence is as important as the now heralded emotional intelligence. And the Gospel suits carpenters.

Alternative traditions

Isn't it reassuring that what I am advocating has far more in common with an approach from the sixth century which is still in use, the Rule of St Benedict? The Rule hardly touches on structures, organizational hierarchies or plans and yet can be read as a treatise about leadership and management. It is much more concerned with values, the organizational 'climate', the kind of processes which succeed and above all building mutual trust. Off and on, it has worn well and has been copied or adapted by many other religious congregations up to the present day. It was already

600 years old when, in the twelfth century, it helped shape an agricultural revolution across Europe. Some of its industrial innovations are still visible in Burgundy, France, whether in the gigantic wine presses at Clos de Vougeot or in the smelting forges at the abbey of Fontenay. Eight hundred years later, the 'Rule' still inspires hundreds of religious communities everywhere, my favourite example being the 120 Benedictine sisters who minister to the marginalized in the US city of Erie.[6]

Present predicament in the Roman Catholic dioceses

Formal membership among Roman Catholics as measured by Mass attendance has been falling steadily and steeply for at least the last three decades, long enough to demonstrate that disaffected young people do not generally 'come back' later when they create their own households. Among the general population, the overwhelming majority do claim in opinion surveys to have a spiritual sense, but (equally) the overwhelming majority say they are not attracted by formal religion; witness the Diana phenomenon. There is no reason to suppose that Roman Catholics are different from this general pattern and recently published research on church leavers is in line with this.[7] The reluctant 'limbo' in the weeks after they leave shows an awareness of something missing.

Without the kind of opinion surveys undertaken together by all the mainstream churches in Australia and New Zealand, one cannot be precise about current attitudes.[8] When I look at the Roman Catholic church membership, I am aware (as many others are) of a lot of confusion and fuzziness. Although among Catholics there is a core membership whose faith adherence is strong, there is also a great deal of private disagreement with some church teaching, notably in the sexual field and about the nature of authority. This apparent 'double think' is probably typical throughout the Western world, although the disagreements have become increasingly vocalized in Europe in the 'We Are Church' minority movement. The 'double think' was in strong evidence during the visit of Pope John Paul II to the United States in recent years. Opinion surveys brought out 'cafeteria' attitudes among both young and middle-aged Catholics who have learnt to pick and choose what they want to believe or how they want to live. Nevertheless, the Pope was received by the crowds generally with great warmth, affection and respect. And the same would be said in England and Wales for Cardinal Basil Hume. The sentiment may suggest that what they complain about is not necessarily what bothers them; it is just easier to express.

There is as yet no way of gauging the sympathies of the Roman Catholic clergy except from personal acquaintance and anecdotal evidence. I have sensed a wide range, from the maintenance of habitual forms at one end of the spectrum to tacit agreement with ill-at-ease lay people at the other. Along the spectrum as a whole, my frequent impression is of a search for identity against the background of an official commitment to the universal priesthood of all believers, a personal loneliness in chill presbyteries where in former times there would have been a pair or trio of priests. Whether distraction or solace, there is a desperate problem of keeping up with growing administration demands, including that of church schools (whose rationale is increasingly questioned), most often with the assistance of no more than part-time secretarial help.

In spite of the complexity, it is possible to infer from the evidence (such as it is!) that Catholics are not on the whole deriving from their faith practice an experience which touches their lives deeply and which is typified within, say, the spirit of the 'Rule of St Benedict' mentioned earlier. Furthermore, although this aspect does not bother a significant proportion of those who continue to practise, it seems to be a big factor in the unease of some of those who stay or those who finally cease to attend. Put simplistically, they do not associate their experience of church with a real 'communion of life'. Instead, they see church as a set of formal procedures within a hierarchical organization extending from a high profile pope, through the diocesan bishop, to their local clergy 'representative'. Even bishops themselves can experience this constraint; prior to the 1998 Synod for Asia, the Japanese bishops complained: 'From the way the [preparatory] questions are posed [by Rome] one feels that the holding of the synod is like an occasion for the central office to evaluate the performance of the branch offices.'[9]

It may be accurate to suggest that both clergy and laity are somehow locked into a system which gets in the way of the Good News for them, and yet is hard to question *because it also accords with the traditional ('Henry Ford') idea of an organization*. If so, it would help *if people could unfreeze their fixed ideas about what an organization must be like* – hence my unconventional approach in this chapter.

Additional help would come from any realization that so many of the structures, titles, dress and procedures which most people consider intrinsic to the church were originally borrowed from imperial Rome. The process was reinforced from the fourth century onwards by the increasing reliance of provincial governors of the Empire on bishops and priests to perform secular offices, such as civil magistrates. Also, from the time when the secular Empire disintegrated, the name of Rome has become forever synonymous with organizational order and rationality. This would have dismayed a late Roman bishop (and magistrate) like Augustine of Hippo who was far more concerned about imperial deficiencies such as the brutal obscenities of the gladiatorial games which seemed to be bound up with the repressive civilization of his day.

In other words, a lot of organizational features which we have come to associate with church are incidental elements not necessarily intrinsic to the Good News or the leadership characteristics needed, although in their time they may have served a good purpose. *The alternative does not have to be 'anarchy'.*

What kind of leadership is needed?

What kind of leadership is needed if the picture I have painted does approach reality? *To continue with the existing methods is surely likely to be one of 'managing an orderly decline' in membership, with previous trends continuing'* – as some church organizations openly speak of. No doubt there will be attempts to 'try harder' at this or that practice; perhaps there will be concessions to pressures, especially by encouraging more lay pastoral workers, both women and men, to become involved – but all within the existing framework.

Alternative forms of leadership which would promote a self-organizing church would certainly produce a riskier, messier and less predictable process. Nevertheless, the evidence from other organizational settings is that they would promote vitality and growth of faith, together with a sense of 'ownership', even though there is no knowing whether that would produce a growth of formal membership. The church, in such a period of personal searching as now, is likely to have a large element of the 'virtual' in it. Never mind; the uncertainty and spontaneity would be in tune with the early church and the Gospels. Indeed, today's social and economic environment has actually much in common with the fragmentation and change which surrounded the early communities of Jerusalem, Corinth, Rome and Antioch. Also, in later centuries, new initiatives have invariably come from holy individuals and groups working at the *boundaries* of the system. Furthermore, an increasing number of studies in recent years have been showing how frequently in history there has been a vibrant popular faith, which is relatively unchronicled beside the institutional annals.[10]

If the stark choice *is* between orderly decline and messy, vital and authentic growth, what characteristics of leadership are needed? First, the primary focus must be on a vision of faith and its original charisms, a major emphasis of the Second Vatican Council in the 1960s. However, that has to entail a willingness, indeed an encouragement, to 'let go', to allow the non-professional members of the church to find their own faith, in their own lives and their own work; this *is* Incarnation, not an add-on. Secondly, the focus must be on *facilitation*, not direction and an understanding of the process of facilitation. Typical approaches are the four sections with which I began this chapter. Thirdly, there will need to be a focus on the awareness, values and competences required. It is with this third area that I would like to close the chapter.

3. New awareness, values and competences required

Systemic understanding of our situations

'If only . . .' can be a great give-away phrase in management, just as it is in faith: 'If only . . . I had the resources, then I would meet that target, balance the books and reach a state of equilibrium!'; 'if only I was holy, I would lead a perfect life!', somehow returning to the garden of Eden. How easy it is for us to forget that holiness means 'wholeness', living full and messy lives, not some steady state of other-worldliness. Death is the only equilibrium. The admonition to 'Be perfect . . .' is literally to make *full* use of the gifts we have available, to be *completely* aware. Growth and decay in constant flux are an integral part of the life which we have to manage; that God is to be found in our experience is surely the modern understanding of the Incarnation and is underlined by the Second Vatican Council's message on Revelation.

A hitherto unknown sense of the whole bio-system and eco-system has developed in this century, even though it has much in common with a mediaeval kind of wholeness. So has the inter-relatedness of the economic system of the globe and its various sub-systems and overlaps. Doesn't all this give us a new awareness of the *relationships* between persons and things which is as important as a knowledge of *what* the components are and how they work?

The first requirement therefore is surely the capacity to see with the intuitive eyes of our faith a much more 'systemic' view of creation – as something more continuous and as a more all-embracing *process* than seemed the case in the past. Above all, it is something which is an integral part of our lives; we are all with each other co-creators.

That kind of understanding can allow us to see our own parish, congregation or communities of faith as a systemic process, as related to our wider responsibilities and opportunities, whether to the excluded here at home or to the rest of the planet. That can replace the fragmentation of simply seeing a series of compartmentalized tasks to be tackled and achieved.[11]

The new vision is surely a prerequisite of mature leadership in a world of complexity and is being made more and more possible by explorations of the patterns of complexity in the natural world of micro-biology or physics. It allows us to appreciate that we live and make our choices always in a state of creative tension, in a zone of possibility which lies between the non-existent ideal of perfect order and the real threat of chaos.[12]

Feminine blessings

The second requirement is the recognition of what feminism has taught us about ourselves, that is about men *as well* as women. To date, discussions about women in leadership positions whether in secular management or in the churches have been understandably preoccupied with the issues of justice, equality of opportunity and sexism, both direct and institutional. Sadly, this has distracted attention away from the opportunity which is offered to explore and practise different styles of leading. Those of us who have worked in organizations which have given priority to equal opportunity have also been struck by the different emphasis which a woman leader can bring.

Although one cannot generalize, there is frequently a greater, albeit subtle, emphasis given to *relationships* in preference to the *task*. A difference of this kind can produce a healthier and more effective atmosphere of 'connectedness'; incidentally, the manager in the earlier section 'Self-implementing organization' was a woman. This connectedness is particularly important for the quality of the psychological contract, which assumes much more importance in voluntary settings, especially churches. Even the achievement of women's ordination is no guarantee that there will be recognition of their special gifts, hence a growing hesitation among feminists about ordination as it now stands.[13]

The kind of leadership styles and awareness advocated in this chapter lean far more – to get away from pure gender – to the 'yin' side of our personalities rather than the 'yang'. In my experience of having worked at a senior level in two public sector organizations which gave high priority to equal opportunity, the net effect of preference towards the feminine can be very liberating to the feminine *inside the male personality* too. In other words, mature leadership will also recognize the potential for a more open and creative atmosphere when what the feminine has to offer is seen not just as an obligation of justice but as an opportunity towards a richer, fuller and more complete creation.[14]

Group awareness

This is the third area requiring special awareness. 'Parish teams' are becoming commonplace replacements for parish committees, with the effect of focusing attention on the tasks to be done together and their coordination, rather than discussion and decisions about them. A shared respect for different personality types as well as common team processes are essential. All this needs to be explored systematically, say, by 'away days' together as well as casually all the time, *so long as the group does this voluntarily and openly with each other* and it is *never* imposed, with the usual compact that 'what goes on here stays here'.

The most straightforward range of personality styles is Belbin's eight ('Shaper', 'Finisher', 'Plant', etc.), but to some it may savour too much of the project syndicate or the boardroom for church use. The most complex and thoroughly researched is probably the Myers-Briggs® 16 (ENTP, ISFJ, etc). Personally, although a qualified assessor for the latter, I am tending to find that the Enneagram nine (Two 'Giver', Three 'Performer', etc.) is the most sensitive in a spiritual context; it is certainly the most popular in religious communities.[15] And there are others. Each can be assessed with self-administered questions, but some experienced guidance is helpful, if only to emphasize the margins of error and to reassure during any emotional stirring.

It is a common tendency to get hooked into answering the question '*what* am I?' as if that was absolute. However, as the 'results' are inevitably approximations it matters much more to use the information interrogatively, for instance: '*if* I incline towards "x", how could I learn to use this knowledge in the best way?'. This provides a foundation for moving to the second and more significant stage: 'how does this help me (us) to understand with how our "gifts differing" (Romans, 12:48) are used by each of us to maximum benefit for us all?' It is then that the group starts to understand the power of synergy, the combined benefit being more than the sum of each.

Having an observer in a group meeting (who can be a facilitator or elected from within the group) to give the group feedback on what has happened, by mapping who spoke when and how often (especially after a ball of wool has been passed round to create a 'cat's cradle'), or at which points the energy level was rising and falling and whether each was aware of others' styles and so on, is invaluable for working together. So is an awareness of the stages which groups so frequently pass through of 'forming, storming, norming and only then performing'.[16]

Underlying the work being done, there is an emotional underside which groups are said to pass through (and which has convinced me after taking part in experiments of group dynamics).[17] There is an easy tendency towards a group indulging its dependency instincts by over reliance on some official or informal 'leader', who can just as easily be scapegoated later. Alternative patterns are the tendency to 'flight', say, by evading the business, or to 'fight' by concentrating on some real or imaginary threat from outside. Then, it is said, there can be other fantasies which distract a group from getting to work. Leadership in this context can be ensuring that there is some sensitive facilitation to help a group recognize these tendencies as they occur and so become more effective in the tasks they have to do.[18]

One might paraphrase St Paul on a group basis: 'What a group wills for the best, it doesn't somehow get done, but what it wants to avoid is what actually happens. If the group does what it doesn't really prefer, it isn't the group but some failing inside itself which causes it to fall short' (Romans 7:19). What I christen the group 'genie' can also haunt the large group (like part of an organization) as well as the small group (typically a team of five to eight people). In some situations, one has the impression that there is a kind of institutional defence mechanism which prevents an organization from functioning as it wants – recalling St Paul's heartfelt cry. The most telling case study involved a large teaching hospital where, in spite of themselves, the nursing staff got locked into behaviours towards their patients which were impersonal and uncaring. When the nurses were able to explore this with an industrial psychologist, they started to see what they were doing as a response to the anxieties they shared in the face of all kinds of ambiguities in their roles.[19] Church contexts are full of ambiguities, so that we should always be asking if we can recognize the potential for those Pauline and institutional defence mechanisms which obstruct our true search.

'Right brain' problem solving

This is the fourth requirement. On the fringes of 'new' management, a great deal of effort has been expended in collating and developing more creative methods of solving problems in an organizational setting. These offer a substitute to traditional ways of logical problem solving performed by 'expert' individuals. The most common form is the brainstorming method, which does not censor even the zaniest ideas, because often those spark off hitherto unthought-of connections. It is a management proverb that planning can be done by the 'left brain', but management has to use the 'right brain' to cope with unpredictables – especially human beings.

The benefits are multiplied when problems are worked at through parallel processing, that is, by methods which allow as many people at a time to take an active part, instead of through a single discussion group where only one conversation can take place. This means working in small groups, or better still where everyone simultaneously writes their ideas on post-it notes or index cards which can be clustered, shuffled, explored and prioritized through a common display on a wall or on a table (interactive computer programs can do this for remote conferencing).

Successful examples of 'lateral thinking'[20] use metaphors, symbols or object associations (perhaps after going for a walk, just as Edward Gibbon or Charles Darwin, or St Augustine of Hippo before them, used to do round their favourite gardens) to make connections and insights. For instance, problems can be understood far more profoundly when examined by a group of us each 'wearing' one of six differently coloured thinking hats: white for factual knowledge, red for feelings, black for fault finding, yellow for optimism, green for novelty, blue for the cool overview. This is a further variant of the problem-sharing method of St Ignatius of Loyola, who suggested in the sixteenth century that insight in situations would come only after examination of our *feelings*.

Diagrammatic modelling of ministry responsibilities was a more recent method of the ecumenical consultancy Avec, through whose doors some thousands of ministers passed in the years when it could pay staff. Some important case studies are well documented.[21] The method can be further enriched, whether through pictorial representation, symbolic representation, meditative visualization or role playing. Creative thinking tends to be done intuitively and the intuitive mode is retained when the thinking is recorded in 'mind map' or spider diagrams, for which there are now also computerized versions.[22]

Creative play offers a major contribution, especially in team building, whether through orienteering which helps the extroverts at last (after they have hurried themselves into a jam) to trust the introverts in a group. And there is nothing like abseiling down a cliff face or crewing a sailing boat together to establish trust. It's not so far away from another team of leaders which was once developed by the most empowering leader of all around the Sea of Galilee.

References

Details have been kept to a minimum in order retain a practical approach. In the texts cited, preference has always been given to sources which are most readable or easily obtainable, rather than those, say, where the ideas were originally formulated. I am happy to give more information (Tel./Fax 01252 84 3133 or bk22@tutor.open.ac.uk).

1. Arthur Battram, *Navigating Complexity* (Industrial Society, 1998), pp. 82, 120, who led the seminar referred to, hosted by the Association of Management Education & Development, and based on work done at the Local Government Management Board (LGMB) and published in its Complexity Pack. This is perhaps the most 'user friendly' introduction to the new study of complexity theory in the organizational context using observations of nature, particularly at micro-biological levels. Ralph D. Stacey, *Complexity & Creativity in Organizations* (San Francisco: Berrett-Koehler, 1996) is excellent but dense, with other good leads like Wheatley (1992).

2. 'Open Space' is the brainchild of an American Anglican priest turned consultant, Harrison Owen, drawing on his experience of African village democracy. A number of Owen's books describe the process, notably *Open Space Technology: A User's Guide* (San Francisco: Berrett-Koehler, 2nd edn, 1997). Details of other books, videos, etc., are available from me. There are some similarities to the 'Charette' method used in community development from the 1960s and to later

methods for large groups, such as 'Future Search', for both of which references are available. The COR Conference has been written up by its facilitator, Liz Murphy RSM, *in Signum* 26. 4 (April 1998), obtainable from Tel./ Fax 0151 548 4924.

3. *Self-Organising for Success: Creating a learning culture*, direct from Local Government Publications Management Board, Fax 0171 296 6523.

4. Ricardo Semler, *Maverick!* (Arrow, 1994).

5. Stephen Pattison, *The Faith of the Managers: When Management Becomes Religion* (Cassell, 1997) offers a very telling criticism in his final 'Coda'.

6. A number of translations of the Rule exist. Joan Chittister, *The Rule of St Benedict* (St Pauls, 1992) includes a daily commentary with an up-to-date relevance by this Sister of Erie whose community is described briefly by Annie Murray in (Catholic Women's) Network 53 (December 1997) obtainable from 0181 979 5902.

7. Philip Richter and Leslie Francis, *Gone But Not Forgotten: Church Leaving and Returning* (DLT, 1998).

8. Peter Kaldor *et al.*, *Shaping a Future: Characteristics of Vital Congregations* (Openbook, 1997) and earlier publications of the (Australian) National Church Life Survey. Valuable insights into the British Roman Catholic scene are offered by Desmond Ryan, *The Catholic Parish* (Sheed & Ward, 1996,) and some clues in Annabel Miller, 'The Pain of Renewal' (conference report from University of Surrey) in *The Tablet*, 13 June 1998, p. 793.

9. *The Tablet*, 2 May 1998, p. 571.

10 A supreme example among many would be Eamon Duffy, *The Stripping of the Altars: Traditional Religion in England 1400–1580* (Yale University Press, 1992). And Shakespeare!

11. From the many sources on a systemic view of all kinds, in the leadership context I would instance Peter Senge, *The Fifth Generation Fieldbook* (Nicholas Brealey, 1994) and the landmark but less digestible study by Peter F. Rudge, *Ministry and Management* (Tavistock, 1968).

12. On natural complexity and chaos, see 1 above. Also Fritjof Capra, *The Web of Life* (Flamingo, 1997).

13. Ivana Dolejsová, 'The Gender Agenda' in *The Month* (May 1997) suggests that, in the Czechoslovak Hussite Church, which has been ordaining women for 50 years, actual recognition cannot be taken

for granted. See also Hilary Wakeman, *Women Priest: The First Years* (DLT, 1996); Catherine Wessinger, *Religious Institutions and Women's Leadership* (University of South Carolina Press, 1996); Christie Cozad Neugar, *The Arts of Ministry: Feminist-Womanist Approaches* (Westminster/John Knox Press, 1996), Paula D. Nesbitt, *Feminization of the Clergy in America* (OUP, 1997).

14. Apart from the ground-breaking study on general feminine style by Carol Gilligan, *In a Different Voice* (Harvard University Press, 2nd edns, 1993), in the context of leadership I would cite Sally Helgesen, *The Female Advantage* (Doubleday, 1990). There is not yet enough written about 're-inventing masculinity', but one excellent source is James Nelson, *The Intimate Connection: Male Sexuality, Masculine Spirituality* (SPCK, 1992).

15. For Belbin, see initially Ch. 4 in Charles Handy, *Understanding Voluntary Organisations* (Penguin, 1998); for Myers-Briggs, see initially David Keirsey and Marilyn Bates, *Please Understand Me* (Prometheus/ Oxford Psychologists Press, 5th edn, 1984) 01865 510203; and then Bruce Duncan, *Pray Your Way* (DLT, 1993); Karen Webb, *The Enneagram* (Thorsons, 1996); and then Suzanne Zuercher, *Enneagram Spirituality* (Ave Maria, 1992). *Retreats* annual of the National Retreat Association (0171 357 7736) lists workshops for both Myers-Briggs and the Enneagram.

16. Sequence described by B. W. Tuckman, in *Psychological Bulletin* 1965. The liveliest picture of team dynamics I know is a video by Lynn Lilley, *Teaming Up* (Hawkshead Productions for the Open College), shown November 1990 (BBC2) about team dynamics in an industrial company.

17. Pioneered by the Tavistock Institute of Human Relations, London NW3, and copied elsewhere using the same principles. To be convinced, you have to take part.

18. The processes are well described by Stacey (see 1 above). Many good guides to group working do not delve into the unconscious processes described by Wilfred Bion, based on wartime observations working for the British Army and later at the Tavistock Institute (previous note). Alas, his masterpiece Experiences in Groups (Tavistock, 1961) seems quite obscure at first.

19. Isobel Menzies-Lyth, *Containing Anxiety in Insitutions* (Free Association, 1988), Ch. 2, building on Elliot Jaques and Melanie Klein. Stacey (*Complexity*, Ch. 8) also refers.

20. The term coined and publicized by Edward de Bono who has published many readable paperbacks, like *Six Thinking Hats* (Penguin, 1987).

21. George Lovell (ed.), *Telling Experiences* (Chester House, 1996) has 18 case studies by Avec participants, ministers and religious, women and men. The process is well described in his *Analysis and Design: A Handbook for Church and Community Work* (Burns & Oates, 1994).

22. The process coined by Tony Buzan, *Use your Head* (BBC Publications, rev. edn, 1989); generally see Tony Proctor, *Essence of Management Creativity* (Prentice-Hall, 1995).

8

Mission, ministry and marketing

JULIAN CUMMINS

In one of the few serious considerations of marketing from a religious perspective, the former Archbishop of York, John Habgood, argued that, 'there is only a very limited sense in which it is possible to make a religious faith adaptable to consumer demand without changing its character to the point of destruction'.[1] For those who understand marketing as a process by which products are created and adapted in response to consumer demand, it follows that its application to the mission of the church can only be peripheral.

Marketing people see the situation differently. Philip Kotler, whose massive work *Marketing Management* has reached nine editions and informed a generation of business studies graduates, writes, 'Whether religious organizations should do marketing is not the question. Religious organizations are always doing marketing by attempting to satisfy needs via exchanges with internal and external markets and publics.'[2]

Is the church engaged in marketing? How should it understand what, by any measure, is a powerful discipline in the public as well as private sector? This chapter argues that, as a descriptive science, marketing illuminates the practice of mission, and deepens our capacity to reflect theologically on it. Contemporary changes in mission parallel changes in marketing theory and practice. The two worlds face common challenges of meaning and behaviour and are already closer than is generally recognized. By engaging more openly and consistently with marketing insights and techniques, the church can both understand and proclaim the gospel more effectively.

Prescriptive and descriptive marketing

Marketing is generally understood as a management process by which an organization anticipates and meets customer needs while at the same time meeting its own objectives. For commercial firms, those objectives are normally to maximize long-term profit, or earnings per share. Marketing is not simply about meeting customer needs, but about anticipating and reconciling them with organizational needs in a competitive environment. Firms look to marketing people for strategies and techniques that will enable them to do that better than their competitors. Marketing is thus understood as a prescriptive process. To 'do marketing' is to organise the product, its price, its distribution and promotion to optimize customer and shareholder benefit.

There is a second and parallel meaning to marketing. It describes and seeks to explain what is going on when people try to meet their own needs and those of their customers. To 'do marketing' in this sense is to discuss buyer behaviour, the identification and prediction of consumer needs, and the trade-off that firms make between market share and unit profitability. Descriptive marketing has enabled a number of generalizations to be made about the way people choose between one product and another, the way that distribution chains work and the way that price is used by both consumers and firms.[3] Marketing in this sense is a social science that focuses on exchange. Exchanges are made whenever people trade with each other or communicate values or ideas, and the way in which they do it is the subject of this particular field of social study.

Kotler is right to say that the church is inevitably involved in marketing. It makes exchanges with people whenever a sermon is preached, a eucharist celebrated or a baby baptized. To use marketing language to illuminate its practices should now be as commonplace as to use literary, historical and sociological language to illuminate our reading of scripture. There is no hint of reductionism here. To describe the church in marketing terms is not to claim that it is the only language in which it can be described, simply that it is one among many.

Marketing is also a conscious process of trying to manage exchanges to the organization's benefit. This raises a central question for the church: whose benefit? If the church were simply a human organization, created for human benefit, it could apply marketing techniques without qualification. The church is much more than that. It is understood to be, in the most widely used metaphor, the Body of Christ.[4] It draws its origin from, points to and is centred on the action of God in Jesus Christ. It derives its being from its divine origin. Hans Küng has argued that, 'The real Church is the Church we believe and yet is visible; it is at once visible and invisible. Its visible aspects are therefore of a particular kind, having an equally essential invisible inner dimension. The decisive aspect of what is revealed remains hidden.'[5] That decisive aspect is the continuing action of the Holy Spirit.

To discuss marketing and mission is to discuss the work of the church as a community called into being by Christ and sustained by the Holy Spirit that through word and sacrament actualizes the saving purposes of God for humanity. It is, in the words of the Turnbull report, utterly Trinitarian in its ground, being and hope.[6] A discussion of marketing and mission is grounded in the incarnational reality of its simultaneous existence as a visible organization engaged in exchange and subject to the descriptive analysis of marketing science.

1950s marketing, 1950s mission

Marketing was formalized as a discipline in the immediate post-war period. It was a time of mass consumer markets, of increasing product standardization and of the emergence of mass communi-

cation. Its exponents were the great toiletries and food companies
– Procter & Gamble, Unilever, Heinz. Its abiding symbol is the
side-by-side comparison of the whiteness of shirts washed by Daz
and Persil. Recalling those ads recalls a society forever past.
Clothes were washed exclusively by women with detergents
bought at high-street grocers. Shirts were invariably white, worn
by men for whom a suit was weekend leisure-wear. Fabrics were
natural, washing machines top-loading. When I began my career
in marketing at Procter & Gamble in the late 1970s, these ads
were still used to teach the practice of advertising.

They were associated with a theory of advertising which has
enjoyed a surprising longevity. It is known as the 'logical sequential' or persuasion model, made memorable by the acronym AIDA
(Awareness, Interest, Desire, Action). It describes a process in
which consumers are led from ignorance to awareness of a product,
and thence to interest, which leads to desire and finally to the
action of making a purchase. This description of advertising has
been powerful with both proponents and critics of marketing. It
dates from one of the earliest advertising writers, St Elmo Lewis,
writing in 1898. Proponents have used measures of awareness and
attitude as means of measuring advertising effectiveness, on the
assumption that sales would follow. Critics have used it to demonstrate that advertising is responsible for wasteful consumer expenditure, for creating 'needs' that consumers do not really possess.

But does advertising actually work like that?[7] Most of us cannot
remember when we were not aware of products like Marmite or
Persil. In most consumer goods categories, we do not follow a
logical process. Studies of shopping behaviour have shown that
70% of brand purchasing decisions are made while in the supermarket.[8] Winston Fletcher, a leading advertising agency director,
has pointed out that there are 9,500 products and services in the
UK with spends of over £50,000 a year, sufficiently large to be
monitored by the industry. Few of us, he suggests, buy more than
400 different advertised products or services in a year, leading to
the engaging suggestion that perhaps 96% of advertising is

wasted.[9] Of course, our spending is biased towards products with larger spends. But despite universal awareness, only 35% of us buy Coca Cola in any one year[10] and the more we buy of any single category, the more we are likely to buy several competing brands within that category.[11]

The logical sequential model of advertising has fallen out of favour with practitioners today, particularly in the UK. The change can be seen on our TV screens in the replacement of factual, product-performance advertisements with stories, humour and off-beat teasers. We are no longer persuaded to buy a product in any way that could be considered logical or sequential. Rather, we are engaged in a story in which we have to search for the product, supply our own answers to clues given about it, or relate to people like ourselves whom we find to be users. The process can be seen in the 'Nicole' series of ads for the Renault Clio. The relationship of Nicole, Papa, car and young men is a narrative in which we can choose to engage or not. To the extent that we are influenced, it is as participants in the story.

The 1950s was also the age of Billy Graham rallies. His first rally in England took place the year before commercial television began. It was made possible by air transport, the lifting of wartime limitations on travel and entertainment, and the growth of mass media. In every respect, Billy Graham is of an age with the side-by-side advertising of Daz and Persil. The process of conversion, focused on the moment of decision at the mercy seat, followed the model of awareness, interest, desire and action that contemporaries discerned in advertising. But did it actually work? People who studied the converts at Billy Graham rallies found them to be at the point of conversion, if not converted. Missioners began to wonder whether large-scale appeals to repentance described how people found faith.

Reacting to the Billy Graham approach in the 1990s, Robert Warren writes, 'Whereas in the past the primary symbol of the Church's evangelism was the pulpit, today it is much more likely to be the party.'[12] Out goes the mass rally, the sermon, the call to conversion. In comes the discussion group, the celebration, the telling of personal stories. People come to faith, John Finney discovered, by a long process, often instituted casually through family or friend.[13] Only later do the symbols and meanings of the church's teaching and liturgy become to be understood, to connect with lived experience. Our engagement in the narrative of scripture is understood by many critics to be one of 'reader response'.[14] This transition in approach exactly parallels the change in marketing thinking that took place in the same period.

2000s marketing, 2000s mission

Both mission and marketing today work on the assumption that consumers are not passive recipients of messages beamed at them, ever at the mercy of their persuasiveness. Rather, they engage with messages which make sense to them. They screen out messages they see as irrelevant – a quality of 'selective attention' that every preacher will recognize. They often take note of advertising for a product only after they have begun to use it, perhaps by chance substitution in a supermarket, or by trying it at a neighbour's house. Even then, the message can be 'viscous', unrelated to experience, unless it begins to engage with the physical and emotional use they make of the product. Advertising is thus about involvement. It is a process in which consumers engage with products and services on their own terms and advertising illuminates or fails to illuminate that experience.

This reassessment of the role of advertising has been associated with a more modest view of marketing, of which it forms a part. Far from being an unstoppable, persuasive machine, it is seen to be a hit-and-miss process of involving people in products and their use. The success of new products is estimated to be 30% or less. Advertising has been replaced as the dominant means of communication by sales promotional offers that give often transitory reasons to try out or continue to use a product or service.[15] The confidence managers placed in generic strategic solutions has declined. In their place has arisen a more modest understanding that successful marketing resides in building relationships.[16]

This reassessment has been associated with an increasing emphasis on the qualities that have made Richard Branson's personal interests and characteristics inseparable from the success of his diversified businesses. Branson's approach has a pedigree that reaches back to the beginning of modern business. Jesse Boot founded the stores that bear his name in the 1880s with a string of sensational offers. He would buy up a stock of salmon and sell it at half the normal price, package soap in double the quantity people normally bought it, position assistants in his windows to cut and wrap it, and sell it at a substantial discount. A colleague recalled, 'Always, Mr Boot had something striking, something to make people talk about Boots.'[17]

This process has been described as 'postmodern marketing'. It is not, in fact, either pre-modern or postmodern. It is the way marketing has always been conducted in the great majority of markets. It was obscured for a few decades in a small number of consumer goods markets by the extraordinary impact that television made on a society of small shopkeepers and settled social habits. For a while, marketing seemed to be summed up by the titanic battles of Persil and Daz. It never really was in industrial, professional, retail or service markets, all of which continued to compete and promote with little recognition from marketing academics, though often unconsciously and inefficiently. Marketing can be seen more clearly today as an adaptive, opportunistic process of involving people in using and making sense of products at a sufficient level of mutual benefit for the exchange to continue in the light of the alternatives available.

From the 1970s, the increasingly competitive quality of modern life led organizations of every kind to take marketing more seriously. They began to examine what they did to communicate with their customers, and why. They initially adopted techniques from the consumer goods sector – at the time the only source of marketing expertise. The direct transposition of consumer goods techniques generally failed.[18] Today's pattern is more sophisticated and pluriform. Organizations use marketing insights and techniques to improve what they already do, rooted in their own distinctive relationships. The church is no exception, though it remains reluctant to understand it as marketing.

Evangelicals, liberals and catholics in the mainstream denominations are all taking mission seriously. It may be the result of declining attendances finally posing a threat to congregational viability. It may also be the result of the Decade of Evangelism forcing those of different persuasions to focus on the call to mission that was so central to Jesus' ministry. From the evangelical Alpha course to the more catholic Emmaus course, they have discovered processes of evangelism that are remarkably similar. They are centred on the small group, the discussion, the party. In marketing language, this is network marketing, the technique popularized by Tupperware and Avon Cosmetics. Is it simply a new form of engagement with people? Or does replacing the pulpit with the party change, or at least adapt, the message?

Asking these questions focuses John Habgood's concern about the extent to which religious faith can adapt to consumer demand. Using marketing language to describe the evolution of contemporary mission helps us understand it better, but it does not tell us whether it is right. The practice of mission today raises theological questions which are illuminated rather than obscured by simultaneously thinking about them in marketing terms.

Small groups and their messages

In a major study of small group religion in America, Robert Wuthnow argues, 'it does not overstate the case to suggest that the small group movement is currently playing a major role in adapting American religion to the main currents of secular culture that have surfaced at the end of the twentieth century.'[19] Safe and self-selecting communities, he suggests, provide a form of domesticated spirituality in which God is experienced as a God of love, comfort, order and security. Engagement in the group, at once personal and social, replaces commitment to creeds and liturgies as a badge of membership.

If this is the case – and Wuthnow's argument is based on substantial survey data – it represents exactly the kind of adaptation that Habgood warned against. Those involved in promoting the small-group approach to mission argue otherwise. Robert Warren is careful to say that the 'party' does not mean a revitalization of Christianity. He warns that, 'it is important the Church does not abandon or downgrade the truth content of the Christian message.'[20] Philip Kotler takes a similar view of the application of marketing in the church: 'Since people and environments change, the religious organization must adapt and customise its specific "products" and "packaging", while remaining faithful to its doctrine.'[21] But is it possible to draw a distinction between substance and presentation in this way?

Both party and truth are strong elements in the Alpha course. 'Laughter and fun are a key part of the course, breaking down barriers and enabling everyone to relax together ... Alpha is a place where no question is regarded as too simple or too hostile.'[22] Its leading popularizer, Nicky Gumbel, is nevertheless clear where truth resides: 'It is very important to hold on to the fact that all scripture is inspired by God, even if we cannot immediately resolve all the difficulties ... There are some things that are very clear in the Bible. It tells us how to conduct our day-to-day lives, for example, when we're at work or under pressure.'[23]

The difficulty is that the process of the discussion group makes Gumbel's view of the Bible an input into discussion, not a determinant of it. The Bible no longer 'tells us' in that context: the inspiration resides in the event of discernment. The story of a very different type of Christian gathering brings out the point. Dave Tomlinson, a former New Church leader and now an Anglican priest, runs Holy Joe's, a 'church' which meets in the lounge bar of a South London pub. He describes it as follows: 'People behave as they normally would in a pub; they can drink or smoke, they can participate as much or as little as they wish, and if they really do not like it, they can just move through to the main bar. We have worship evenings, which tend to be quite contemplative, with plenty of candles, symbols and ambient music, and we have Bible study evenings where people eagerly take part in trying to understand and interpret the scriptures.'[24]

How different are Alpha and Holy Joe's in reality? Tomlinson believes the Bible is God's word, so long as we understand the 'word' to be an event mediated by scripture and not the book itself. Though Gumbel would take a more literal view, the process he adopts, and the emphasis placed on the action of the Holy Spirit, in practice makes the 'word' an event of engagement and interpretation. Tomlinson ensures there is an informal chair to keep the discussions on track despite the apparently open structure of his meetings. Gumbel appears more prescriptive, offering time-tables, agendas and notes. In reality, Alpha can only be structured to the point that a group of articulate adults allows its leaders to lead. The medium makes the messages far closer to each other than Tomlinson and Gumbel would allow.

What, then, of the claim that truth is in some sense sacrosanct and unchanging? In the sense that both Kotler and Warren want to claim it, it is unsustainable. The attributes of God understood and approached through the small group are not the attributes understood and approached under a three-decker pulpit. Qualities of justice and mercy are seen in a different light, and with a different weight. This is not to say that either is necessarily invalid. It is to say that Christian truth claims cannot be abstracted from their manner of presentation. Every means of presenting Christ presents a different interpretation, actualizes a different theology. The question is not whether these theologies are different, but whether they are true to the core of the gospel.

Theologians know this question as the challenge of incultur-ation. Here, surprisingly, marketing people can empathize with the question. In 1992, Hoover ran a promotion which offered two free flights to America to purchasers of its products. The offer has been used many times before and since, but Hoover miscalculated its terms. The value of the flights was greater than the cost of its products, so people bought them for that reason. Faced with unexpectedly high demand, Hoover sought to limit its losses through over-rigorous interpretation of the terms of the offer. It suffered a £40 million loss, a serious drop in consumer confidence, and was eventually sold for a fraction of its former value. Hoover had allowed a single offer to fatally undermine its core proposition, its most valuable relationships.

A happier story is offered by the familiar Oxo cube. Oxo was launched in 1847 as a fluid beef concentrate to provide a dietary supplement to invalids. It changed its form (but not its positioning) in 1910 to the familiar cube. During both world wars, it was positioned as a cheap and accessible means of adding flavour to low-quality meat dishes. In the post-war period, its positioning (but not its form) has changed again: now it is a flexible additive to continental dishes, part of an instant-cooking culture. A key element in its continuing success has been a series of long-running advertising campaigns which have identified it with the shift from formal to fragmented eating, from mutton stew to Chinese stir-fry, from nuclear family to eclectic household.[25]

The more one examines what is core and what is peripheral in this story, the less clear it becomes. Is it the cube? There are own-label versions in every supermarket. Is it the purpose to which the product is put? That has clearly changed. Is it the persistent identification of Oxo with changing consumer eating habits? It is hard to separate that from the cube itself. Or is it in fact all of these, which together go to make up that powerful, intangible concept of the brand?

Brand owners are faced with the question of the relationship between presentation and substance every time they run a special offer, make their products available in unfamiliar outlets and engage in temporary discounting. Does adapting a brand to contemporary needs change, and perhaps undermine, its nature? The distinction between the Hoover and Oxo examples is not between tradition and change, but between developing and subverting the essence of the brand. To understand how marketing people make this distinction, we need to look more closely at the idea of the brand.

The idea of the brand

Hugh Davidson, an alumnus of Procter & Gamble, United Biscuits and Playtex, has written, 'Well-known brand-names are a company's most valuable assets. They represent the accumulation of years of favourable consumer experiences and heavy investment in advertising, packaging and quality.'[26] One measure is the difference between a firm's book value (its tangible assets) and its market value (the amount people will pay for it). In the last decade, the proportion of market value accounted for by tangible assets among Wall Street quoted companies has fallen from 60% to 30%. When Nestlé bought Rowntree in 1988, it paid thirty times the earnings for the company. It was not the machinery they were after – it was brand names like Kit Kat, Polo and Smarties. When Virgin diversified into financial services, it was not its record as a fund manager, which was non-existent, or the nature of its financial products, which were little different from others on the market, which attracted investors. It was the strength of the Virgin name that led millions of people to trust it to look after their money.

Brands have a pre-history dating back to markings on Egyptian bricks. In a modern sense, they originated in the eighteenth century in an attempt to mark a product as having a particular origin, a particular guarantee of quality and reliability. The first brand symbol was the red triangle used to this day by Bass. Brands clearly mean much more than confidence in the origin of a product. They accumulate emotional associations, loyalty, familiarity, a series of stories associated with their use and advertising. All these factors enable brands to be priced at a higher level than unbranded commodities. They are reflected in the often passionate response made by consumers to changes in familiar brands. Marketing people have tried to find a single concept that embraces goodwill, image, market strength and reputation. The most widely used concept is that of 'brand equity'.

There is no disagreement among practitioners that the under-lying phenomena exist and that they exist primarily in the minds of consumers. The problem is defining and measuring them as a single concept. Here there is a great divide. On the one hand, there are those who argue that brand equity, though slippery and difficult to measure, is a crucial concept, summing up value that exists in consumers' minds and in the market value of brand-owning companies. They suggest that marketing activity cannot be measured without using it as a reference point.[27] On the other hand, there are those who argue that since brand equity cannot be accurately defined and measured, it cannot exist. A leading advertising practitioner, Paul Feldwick, has argued: 'When we look for an operational definition of brand equity, we are asking the wrong question. Brand equity is necessarily a vague concept, like "personal health and fitness", or "a sound economy". These concepts imply general questions: how well are we doing now? how well can we expect to do in the future? Such questions are not fully answered by any one measure.'[28]

The conclusion we can draw is paradoxical. Marketing people spend their lives developing brands that have evident impact on the value of companies and the decisions of consumers. They can talk about the manifestations of the brand – its packaging, image, emotional values, financial results. They can say that it exists in the mind of consumers. But they cannot say what it actually is. Those who argue that brand equity exists do so on the grounds that something that impacts so greatly in our lives must exist, even though it cannot be readily measured or defined. Those who start from the difficulty of measurement and definition conclude that to talk about brand equity is to talk about its manifestations.

Junior brand managers tend to despair at this point. They are entrusted with the management of a major asset. They know that ill-judged changes to its price, packaging, formulation or advertising can cause havoc to its value. They know also that unless they constantly refresh the brand it will be overtaken by its competitors. They look into the heart of the brand for guidance – and find that they cannot capture the essence of that most valuable asset. Church people who have assumed that marketing is an unstoppable, mechanistic process can, however, take heart. The nature of marketing suddenly seems much closer to mission.

It is particularly close when we ask what the church's brand actually is. John Habgood argued that, whatever marketing may mean for the church, it could not mean brand marketing. But marketing is always brand marketing; it is simply the strength of the brands that differs. Christianity has sometimes presented its denominations as brands: to be a Roman Catholic or a Baptist was to inhabit two wholly different worlds. Closer ecumenical relationships have made it possible to see that the brand is shared between them and other Christian groups. Persil can be found in biological, colour, ultra and other versions, and in a wide variety of pack sizes. It does not cease to be Persil. One benefit to the church of thinking about brands is to extend its understanding of the wide range of versions in which it can be manifested.

Living with an elusive core

Habgood, Warren and Kotler agree about one thing: that to whatever extent the church adopts marketing, it must not change what it is at its core. The difficulty lies in the definition of that core, on which there has never been the kind of agreement between Christians that is capable of simple, unambiguous expression. The creeds have always been understood to point beyond themselves to a reality that words can never contain. The unity of the New Testament has been found in modern scholarship to lie in the unifying experience of the identity of the earthly Jesus and the risen Lord, understood and expressed with great diversity. It is a strand, a centre, but not a single phrase or story or description that we can call 'the gospel proclamation'.[29]

Yet central Christian concepts of salvation, reconciliation and love point to a real but elusive core. In proclaiming salvation, Jesus announced the possibility of a right relationship with God. It was a relationship fully expressed in his perfect knowledge of the Father. To 'know' in the New Testament is not just to understand, but to feel and engage with the heart. It is both to understand, and to be understood, forgiven and accepted by God. In following Christ, his disciples were asked and empowered to take on that relationship, to be Christlike. It is this that comprises salvation, and it is of this that the Kingdom of God consists.

A characteristic of relationships is that they are fluid, dynamic, unpredictable and unknowable. This gives rise to the apophatic tradition in Christian theology which emphasizes that which God is not as the surest means of approaching Him. The conflicts that wracked the early church are witness to the sheer difficulty of capturing a right relationship with God in human language. In understanding God as Trinity, the church is driven ultimately to talk about mystery and manifestation. God is understood as Trinity, as one substance, through being experienced as Father, Son and Holy Spirit.

At the core of Christianity is thus the right relationship with God which Jesus made available to all. To bring all people into that relationship is God's mission, in which the church participates. It is here that critics and proponents of marketing in the church may be less far apart than they think. Richard Chartres, the Bishop of London, is one of the critics. He told a GMTV interviewer: 'If you start thinking in terms of customers and churches being supermarkets, dealing in a commodity called God, then the essence of the Christian faith, which is a personal relationship with the Divine can easily get lost in power play and marketing strategies, so it is a terrible blasphemy to make a commodity of God.'[30]

Chartres is right about the core of Christianity, and about the dangers which beset its expression. But he is wrong in the particularity of his criticism. It is not just in marketing strategies that a right relationship with God can be corrupted, but in choral evensong, episcopal order, church doctrine and every other means by which we seek to express that relationship. All are capable of becoming idols, and lost in power play. Yet without them, we have no means of expression. It is here that contemporary marketing thinking offers a crucial theological insight.

In talking about God we are invariably drawn to talking about His manifestations. We know that when we do so, we are talking about God as mediated through our own experiences. These are formed through the experience of liturgy, of fellowship within the church, of the characteristic doctrines and structures of denominations. The sacred is experienced through the specific and time-bound. Theology teaches us that they all point sacramentally beyond themselves. Yet in practice, they do not always do so. They are permanently in danger of being idolised, of being confused with the reality to which they point, of becoming substitutes for God. Yet without them, it is not possible for us to approach God.

In a related way, marketing people are driven to talk obliquely about what they understand the core of their brand to be. They are driven to use the specific and time-bound, recognizing that it is in danger of being confused with the reality to which it points. Jeremy Bullmore points out that comedians do not come on TV and say 'I'm funny, you should laugh'. Rather, they tell a joke. He writes of brand advertising: 'When we say "That commercial isn't sufficiently branded", we usually mean: "The brand isn't mentioned or shown often enough". We ought to mean: "The clues in that commercial aren't appropriate enough to our brand's desired image." '[31] To understand the liturgies, structures and teachings of the church as clues is very close to understanding them as sacraments.

The question that Christians can ask of any piece of marketing is similar to that proposed by Bullmore. It is grounded in our fundamental profession of faith. We can ask: 'are the clues in this presentation Christlike?' It means taking with absolute seriousness the Trinitarian ground, being and hope of the church. It means eschewing the 'cheap grace' that Bonhoeffer warned against, the comforts of a pietistic or bourgeois Christianity. Any marketing technique that fails to respect personhood formed in the image of God dishonours rather than furthers that which the church is called to be. These challenges need to be addressed to every form of presentation, inherited from history as much as adopted from contemporary marketing.

A useful analogy can thus be drawn between mission and marketing. They show a similar evolution in practice over the last forty years. They share a delicate interplay between substance and presentation. And, most important of all, they both live with an elusive core. That core is at one and the same time their most priceless asset, and that which cannot be measured or defined. Reductionists can argue, as Feldwick does with brand equity and Dawkins with God, that something you cannot measure or define cannot exist. But most people know better. Most people can live with an elusive core. They can experience God as real, actual and personal, and also as unknown, absent and wholly other. The spiritual life is an engagement with that dichotomy.

To draw an analogy between our relationship with God and brand equity is not to draw a facile parallel between God and brand, much less to make God a commodity. All analogies have their limits. Two dissimilarities between mission and marketing need mention. First, a company may choose to discontinue a brand that it owns, but that is not an option open to the church. Human relationships with God cannot be closed down, because from Old Testament times, God has been experienced actively calling people to his service. Secondly, there is an inverse relationship between company and brand and between church and relationship with God. Companies legitimately see brands as assets, to be bought and sold. God's relationship with his people stands in the different mode of gracious gift, made possible by his grace and will. To identify these limits to the analogy strengthens rather than weakens it in the area of the church's life in which it is of value.

As people called by God to his service, we are sent to proclaim the gospel in every age. The church participates in God's mission because 'he has no hands or feet but ours'. From the earliest times, the church has faced the challenge of inculturating and actualizing its faith in different cultures and historical settings. This challenge is not accidental to Christianity, but central to its incarnational and historical character. It is in this aspect of the church's life that the analogy between mission and marketing is of value. It is here that we find that an elusive core and much contemporary practice are common to both marketing and mission.

Building on the links between mission and marketing

This chapter has not set out to provide a marketing strategy for the Church of England, much less for the church as a whole. At best, it is a foreword to such a strategy, clearing away misunderstandings about the nature of marketing that have made it suspect in church circles, and identifying areas of commonality. If the analogy is accepted, secondary questions arise. Does thinking about mission in marketing terms have any practical value? Can marketing people add anything that experienced missioners do not already know? Can they provide concrete help in the particular circumstances facing the church today?

A marketing practitioner might note a number of features about the present practice of mission. There is a wealth of sociological analysis, much of it negative about the prospects for Christianity in the modern world, but some (notably from Robin Gill) concerned to identify the positive opportunities that exist. A growing base of research in the UK and comparable countries (particularly Australia) provides valuable evidence about how and why people belong to the church. There are libraries of books about how to grow individual congregations, much of which parallels businesses self-help material. Several denominations are putting in place structural changes to support a long-held wish to move 'from maintenance to mission'. All this would encourage the view that a great deal of marketing is already underway in the church.[32]

The marketing practitioner might also note that the Church of England is completing a Decade of Evangelism which has not succeeded in arresting decline in either belief or belonging. The research material is curiously erratic. Much of the English data derives from a small and under-funded voluntary body, the Christian Research Association. With rare exceptions (notably the work of Leslie Francis), academic analysis is conducted as unconnected projects. Advertising is conducted by another small and under-funded voluntary body, the Churches Advertising Network (CAN). Training of clergy does not include systematic training in mission either before or after ordination. Intelligent reports produced by central church bodies on everything from church planting to youth work to the challenge of postmodernism are seldom reflected in the concrete plans of church committees at regional and local level.

The practitioner might conclude that the ingredients of a marketing strategy and plan are in place. The problem is that they are not composted, integrated and worked through, theoretically, practically or organizationally. The speed of dissemination of new ideas is impossibly slow. Research and advertising is overly dependent on voluntary finance and personal interest. Structures and training programmes have a long way to go before mission is central to the culture of the church. All this, the practitioner might say, is like so much of British industry two decades ago. And that gives hope – because change in human institutions is possible.

There are five practical ways in which building on the existing links between mission and marketing will be of value to the church.

First, *marketing can help the church understand its unique calling*. The church is not short of well-intentioned but often misleading advice about how to become 'relevant'. Much of that seizes on surface aspects of the church – its music, buildings or administration. Marketing analysis has brought us to recognize that a relationship with God in Christ is our brand equity. Everything else springs from that. In an immensely complex world, the value of a clear focus cannot be underestimated. Far from drawing the church away from its unique calling, marketing analysis draws the church into a deeper understanding of it.

Secondly, *marketing can help the church grapple with meaning and communication*. John Habgood concluded his generally critical review of marketing the church by writing, 'Somehow we need to find ways of rehabilitating those powerful messages which, through the centuries, have carried religious claims and made them meaningful to all sorts of people who are outside the inner worshipping life of the Church.'[33] The issues involved in doing so are a central marketing concern. How do you make whisky relevant to people who think it is something that grandpa drinks? How do you adapt the 'Scotch' heritage without destroying it? To engage in the debate, the church needs to understand that it is involved in exchange, in symbolism, in seeking to involve people within their culture while at the same time trying to hold its side of the exchange.

In 1996, CAN produced an ad with the headline 'Bad Hair Day?!' It was criticized by many as cheapening or misrepresenting what they understood the Christmas message to be. By others, it was lauded as using imagery and language which resonated with young people – which indeed it did. The problem was that there was no relationship between the advertising and the nature and practice of the majority of churches. People in the churches did not see themselves in the advertising and people outside the churches did not think they could find a church that was like the advertising. 'Bad Hair Day?!' could no more be grafted on to the average English congregation than a Volvo ad could be grafted on to a Daewoo.

The way in which people use symbols of meaning is central to influencing beliefs and attitudes. The attractiveness of Nike and Calvin Klein for teenagers is understood by every parent who has been obliged to buy them in preference to lower-priced alternatives. Branded merchandise for teenage boys is about self and group, identity and aspiration. It is a particular example of the way in which people use brands as a means of personal and social self-symbolism to make sense of who they are both in themselves and in relation to others.[34] The symbols and liturgies of the church have historically played a formative role in this respect, but have largely been supplanted. To ascribe this to malign advertisers or 'materialism' is to miss the point. By understanding how teenagers use the symbolism contained in Nike and Calvin Klein, the church can hope to understand how its symbols can re-connect with them.

A third area is that *marketing can help the church understand its own practices*. To talk of outreach as customer acquisition and baptism follow-up as retention strategy is to illuminate at least part of their role. Taken to extremes it can be absurd and replace one jargon with another. It can also obscure the particularity of the church. Churches do not engage in outreach and baptism follow-up just to fill the pews, or even just to encourage a right relationship with God, but as part of a call to serve the community in which they are placed. To deny that they also hope to bring the people they visit to an active, engaged faith is equally absurd. Using marketing language will at least illuminate the grounds on which an activity is undertaken, and the expectations held of it.

In pursuit of what marketing people would understand as customer acquisition, churches deploy a wide range of techniques. They knock on doors, hold special services, run groups for particular age groups, distribute community magazines and much more. Time and resources mean that no church can do all of them. So what should a local church do?[35] A marketing perspective would suggest that they should choose the technique which most accords with the nature and character of that church. Further, that its success should be evaluated over a sufficient period of time to allow for insiders to be bored long before outsiders are even aware of the activity and that it should be applied consistently in every aspect of the church's presentation. This is, in marketing terms, simple stuff. It rarely surfaces at PCC discussions of whether to launch a 'mum's and toddler's service'. By understanding it as marketing, the church can simply do it better.[36]

Marketing practitioners have developed a series of tools that help them understand how people relate to offerings made to them. The Product Life Cycle models patterns of birth, maturity and decline. The Product Portfolio Matrix models the segments into which a market can be divided and the range of products that can be designed for them. Geodemographic analysis helps us understand how purchasing patterns, age and social class interact with location. Tracking studies enable us to plot changes in attitude and behaviour, and to make reasonable predictions about the immediate future. These tools are used in some extent – for example, in Robert Warren's analysis of why large-scale door-drops of evangelistic literature produce low returns.[37] But this type of analysis is largely foreign to the church. It would help us understand the means by which the world offers opportunities to the gospel and the effectiveness of our presentation of it. It is as mistaken to ignore it as it is to ignore the contribution of literary scholars to our understanding of scripture.

Fourthly, *marketing can help the church understand the relationship between attitude and behaviour*. One of the key sociological insights into contemporary religion is the persistence of high levels of 'belief' in the light of declining 'belonging'.[38] The fourth way in which marketing can be applied to mission is concerned with the behavioural reasons why people buy one product rather than another or buy one more often than another. It is about action rather than belief. Most retailers in the UK run loyalty programmes designed to increase frequency of purchase and retain existing customers. There is an extensive literature examining how and why these schemes work, if indeed they do. Why should the church be interested? Because the comparison of counted church attendance and declared attendance has shown that absolute attendance is falling less fast than frequency of attendance.[39]

Church statistics have traditionally been collected on the assumption that being an attender means attending once a week. Without this assumption, it would not make sense to count attendance on a single random Sunday. But why once a week? Why not daily, or indeed seven times daily? Marketing people have often been misled by a similar statistical quirk. Usage of a brand has been based on asking whether a brand had been used in the last month. But why not the last three months? The longer the period, the more people are found to be users. If the church wishes to understand why frequency is declining, and what, if anything, it can do about it, it could learn from this debate. Similar considerations apply to the marketing analysis of reasons why people try out a product and the techniques that can be used to encourage it.

Finally, *marketing can help the church organize mission above the congregational level.* If every marketing person could be a Richard Branson or Jesse Boot there would be little need for systems and processes. Boots has continued to grow because it found means of enabling lesser people to work in like manner. If every church leader could be an Ignatius or Graham there would similarly be little need for systems and processes. The church has slowly begun to recognize this. It has talked about a shift 'from maintenance to mission' for some years, and the Diocese of Wakefield has taken to calling itself a 'missionary diocese'. The effect has been a levelling-off of decline. The church has many people – both clergy and laity – with professional marketing experience. It does not need to appoint a director of marketing so much as to engage the skills of those already in the church. It urgently needs concerted training for clergy and laity in marketing and mission.

This needs to be carried out on a far larger scale and with far greater consistency than the church is used to. Jeremy Bullmore tells the story of a middle-aged colleague who received a substantial share dividend and immediately bought an Aston Martin. Why? he asked. Because he had seen it in an ad – when he was fourteen. Neither marketing nor mission work in the short term alone. For the long term to work, there needs to be a high level of consistency over time and space. To achieve this, the church needs to organize its mission as the multinational organization that it is, the herald of the first and most powerful global brand.

Some Christians will regard these proposals as forsaking the church's focus and dependence on Christ. We are called, it is often said, not to be successful, but faithful. The relationship between the two is more complex than this catchphrase allows. It is a paradoxical characteristic of successful organizations that they succeed by not making success their primary aim.

A study conducted in America of the twenty companies voted 'most visionary' by other firms makes this point.[40] In each case the visionary firms were compared to equally well established firms in their industry. They were extremely profitable, achieving a stock return six times better over a sixty-year period to 1990 than the comparison firms and fifteen times better than the market as a whole. A striking finding was that these firms did not have profit maximization as their primary goal. Relative to the comparison companies, they were far more likely to have non-economic values and ideologies as their primary drivers.

A second finding from the study was that, by facing outwards, the organization itself becomes the creation. It is able to transcend any specific project, any generation of managers, not by inwardness, but by seeking to achieve objectives outside itself. This finding makes sense of the paradox that Jesus founded a church by proclaiming the kingdom of God, that Benedict founded a great monastic order by seeking to recover monastic life. The church cannot engage in mission because a higher level of church attendance is an end in itself. It can engage in mission because focusing on Christ helps it to understand attendance as being useful if people are to enter a personal relationship with him. Plans and programmes follow from that. In a visible sense, a larger and more vibrant church is the creation, the great sacrament of incarnation.

Conclusion

This chapter began with two opposed view on the applicability of marketing in the church. I have sought to show that this opposition is misplaced. Marketing and mission are part of the same history of ideas and practice. Contemporary views of marketing place an emphasis on involvement and relationship which closely parallels thinking in the church. In both cases, there is a vital but elusive core, a need to engage in the adaptation and presentation of messages and symbols, an ever-present danger that the attempt to make the presentation relevant will undermine the core. In both cases, meaning is held in the minds and emotions of people who are themselves not wholly knowable.

The church ceases to be church if it ceases to be focused beyond itself in the saving action of God in Jesus and his forgiving of all our failures. The church is descriptively engaged in marketing because it is incarnate. In trying to make sense of its elusive core, trying to find messages, symbols and means of involvement that make sense to people today, in could make better and more explicit use of marketing insights and techniques. The things that marketing people have learnt about the way people think and behave can and should be used by the church in the mission that Jesus calls it to.

References

1. John Habgood, 'Marketing the Church of Englands', in *Making Sense* (London: SPCK, 1993), p. 173.
2. Norman Shawchuck, Philip Kotler, Bruce Wren and Gustave Rath, *Marketing for Congregations* (Nashville: Abingdon Press, 1992), p. 267.
3. The issue is discussed in 'Empirical Generalisations in Marketing', *Marketing Science*, 14.2 (1995).
4. Paul Minear, *Images of the Church in the New Testament* (London: Lutterworth Press, 1961), identifies this as the 'controlling image' of the church among the 96 images he identifies in the New Testament.

5. Hans Küng, *The Church* (Tunbridge Wells: Burns & Oates, 1968), p. 37.

6. *Working as One Body* (Church House Publishing, 1995), para 1.6.

7. For a useful discussion of this question, see Colin McDonald, *How Advertising Works: A Review of Current Thinking* (Henley-on-Thames: NTC Publications, 1992).

8. Myers Research Corporation for POPAI North America, 1995; UK research has shown similar results.

9. Winston Fletcher, *A Glittering Haze: Strategic Advertising in the 1990s* (Henley-on-Thames: NTC Publications, 1992), p. 38.

10. Fletcher, *Glittering Haze*, p. 49.

11. A key finding in modern marketing research is that the more people buy of a particular category of goods, the wider the variety of brands they will buy within that category. See A.S.C. Ehrenberg and M.D. Uncles, *Dirichlet-Type Markets: A Review* (University of Bradford Management Centre, 1995).

12. Robert Warren, *Signs of Hope: How Goes the Decade of Evangelism* (London: Church House Publishing, 1996), p. 72.

13. John Finney, *Finding Faith Today* (London: Bible Society/Church House Publishing, 1992).

14. For a excellent introduction to this and other approaches see J.L. Houlden (ed.), *The Interpretation of the Bible in the Church* (London: SCM Press, 1995).

15. Julian Cummins, *Sales Promotion: How to Create and Implement Campaigns That Really Work* (London: Kogan Page, 2nd edn, 1998) discusses in the introduction and Chapter 1 why sales promotion has overtaken advertising.

16. For a review of the relative lack of success of traditional strategy see John Kay, *Foundations of Corporate Success* (Oxford: Oxford University Press, 1993). Chapter 21 offers a brilliant 'Brief History of Business Strategy'.

17. Quoted in Christian Petersen and Alan Toop, *Sales Promotion in Postmodern Marketing* (London: Gower, 1994), p. 177.

18. A classic example of this was the launch of the Vector and Orchard bank accounts by Midland in the late 1980s. People were supposed to fall into 'segments' which these bank accounts represented. Unfortunately, the segments did not really exist, and Midland in due course dropped them.

19. Robert Wuthnow, *Sharing the Journey: Support Groups and America's*

New Quest for Community (New York: Free Press, 1994), p. 7.

20. Warren, *Signs of Hope*, p. 70.
21. Shawchuck *et al.*, *Marketing*, p. 60.
22. Alpha News, November 1996.
23. Nicky Gumbel, *Questions of Faith* (Kingsway, 1975), p. 75, 77.
24. Dave Tomlinson, *The Post-Evangelical* (London: SPCK, 1996), p. 13.
25. C. Baker, *Advertising Works 7: Papers from the IPA Advertising Effectiveness Awards 1992* (Henley-on-Thames: NTC Publications, 1993), p. 103.
26. Hugh Davidson, *Offensive Marketing* (Harmondsworth: Penguin, 1987), p. 293.
27. I am grateful on this subject to Tim Ambler of the London Business School for his seminar paper 'What is Brand Equity?' (University of Bradford Management Centre, July 1997) and for subsequent comments on early drafts of this chapter.
28. Paul Feldwick, 'What is Brand Equity Anyway, and How Do You Measure It?', *Journal of the Market Research Society*, 38.2 (April 1996), pp. 85–103.
29. James D. G. Dunn, *Unity and Diversity in the New Testament* (London: SCM Press, 1976).
30. Quoted in the *Church of England Newspaper*, 17 April 1998, p. 1.
31. Jeremy Bullmore, *Behind the Scenes in Advertising* (Henley-on-Thames: NTC Publications, 1991), p. 61.
32. See in particular John Clarke, *Evangelism that Really Works* (London: SPCK, 1995); *Breaking New Ground: Church Planting in the Church of England* (London: Church House Publishing, 1994); William Kay and Leslie Francis, *Drift from the Churches: Attitude toward Christianity during Childhood and Adolescence* (Cardiff: University of Wales Press, 1996); Peter Kaldor *et al.*, *Winds of Change: The Experience of Church in a Changing Australia* (NSW: Anzea Publishers, 1994); *The Search for Faith and the Mission of the Church* (London: Church House Publishing, 1996); Robin Gill, *A Vision for Growth*, (SPCK, 1994); *Transforming Congregations for the Future* (Maryland: The Alban Institute, 1994).
33. Habgood, 'Marketing', p. 183.
34. Ricky Elliot and Kritsadart Wattanasuwan, 'Consumption and the Symbolic Project of the Self', *European Advances in Consumer Research*, 3 (1998, forthcoming).

35. I am grateful to the Revd Andrew Sewell, Assistant Diocesan Missioner in the Diocese of Ripon, for comments on these points and earlier drafts.

36. See Clarke, for an excellent analysis of what makes toddlers' groups effective for mission.

37. Warren, p. 51.

38. Grace Davie, *Religion in Britain since 1945 Signs of Hope* (Oxford: Blackwell, 1994).

39. See the *UK Christian Handbook*, Christian Research Association, 1997, which compares denominational head-counts with declared attendance as measured in the British Social Attitudes Survey.

40. James Collins and Jerry Porras, *Built to Last: Successful Habits of Visionary Companies* (London: Century, 1995).

9

The challenge of change

MALCOLM GRUNDY

To be young at heart is to keep on asking challenging questions. At the core of any religion is the attempt to provide answers to the hard questions of life. The Christian churches live within a recurring tension between the demand for firm answers and the provisional uncertainty which attempts to make sense of experience. They live with the creative ambiguity of a religion based on events in the past and a faith which by its very definition cannot be a certainty but which has hope for the future.[1] The genius of a faith such as this is that it only comes alive when the tradition from which it stems engages in an intelligent way with the real questions of its day.

Vitality within our churches is demonstrated by their willingness to engage with questions both from outside and inside the faith community. In any institution with a venerable past, change is not the most welcome possibility. This poses a dilemma for those who move into positions of responsibility. The thruster, the innovator, the organizer, the specialist, the orator or the applier of pressure suddenly find themselves the focus for differing projections and with the task of holding together a coalition. When are they leading and when are they managing? Are they ever true to themselves or do expectations and pressures conspire to create another public face – sometimes unwilling to be accepted by the person they know they still are? It is because every alert manager or leader can feel the imprint of that bed of nails that I want to raise a number of questions about managing and leading which face all those with responsibility, particularly those within our churches.

I want to begin by outlining some changes which have already taken place within the churches. I call these discontinuities because they have made carrying on as before an impossibility. They are discontinuities because they have broken a sequence of adaptation and accommodation which are the characteristics of any maturing organization. The breaks which they have brought about are all the more significant because they have been the result of different patterns of behaviour by those within the church, which are caused by changes in other parts of their lives. Once I have set out these discontinuities I want to go on and explore some of the unavoidable questions which these changes present.

Four discontinuities

There are four great discontinuities that have disrupted the equilibrium of life in our churches and have frustrated the expectations of their most loyal members:

- we have fewer clergy than we expected or hoped for;
- there are far higher costs than ever before, which have to be borne by members of congregations;
- people do not go to church every Sunday;
- there is a gradual lowering of denominational allegiance.

I want to expand on these discontinuities because I believe that unless they are acknowledged by those accepting responsibility, church leaders will live in a world of increasing unreality and will understand neither the religious demands of their country nor the pressures of life weighing on their adherents.

Fewer clergy

Projections for every denomination show that the number of those entering the ordained ministry is considerably less than those reaching the age of retirement. The immediate consequence of this is that many more congregations will not get a minister of their own. The stress of this on already overworked clergy is enormous. They find themselves with ever bigger units or groupings of churches without the necessary recognition and support to allow a leadership style to change. The expectation is that they will 'manage' several parishes in just the same way as they would if they had only one church with one congregation. Attempts at rural, multi-church groupings have not given us an inspiring model for the future. Inner-city congregations have perhaps been the most vulnerable to cuts and groupings. Some denominations have withdrawn altogether. The challenging questions of how to work collaboratively and about the nature of oversight and authority are ones which have to be explored in such a situation.

Higher costs

No longer can the endowments and benefactions of the past pay for our present churches. Some denominations have always had to 'pay their own way' but many others have lived on investments and property inherited from landowners or in buildings financed by industrialists. No longer will the local family firm build the church, the coal owner provide free fuel or the squire pay to repair the roof. Those who go to church have to pay in full for the maintenance of the minister and the building. Those who are relatively wealthy in the wider church have to support the poor. Most do it willingly once they have understood that the denominational Share is not a tax to be avoided wherever possible.

With higher financial commitment comes the appropriate desire for a greater say in church life. Bishops and priests have to be accountable. While the sick among the clergy will be cared for it is a questionable expense to carry passengers. Congregations have to pay for the maintenance of their own ministries. There is a fundamental question here in leading and managing about the corporate nature of a denomination. Do we really want to 'bear one another's burdens', or is the need to survive and maintain the local building leading to a greater parochial defensiveness?

Occasional attendance

People do not go to church as often as they used to. The pressures of families at great distance, the need to take children to sport at school on Sunday mornings, the need to work on Sundays and to play together as a family mean that fortnightly or even monthly attendance is becoming a characteristic even of the committed. The consequence of this for planning church activities and rotas is horrific. It also diminishes the corporate sense of a congregation. On the other hand churches have now developed a feature of the 'big service' with some frequency. The less committed will come in hundreds to Christingle, Mother's Day and four or five other occasions in a year. But as soon as they sense they are becoming regular attenders, get approached about planned giving or to join a rota, they back off. Believing without belonging is with us in a big way. There are enormous questions for managing and leading here. We are, in the main, operating structures which are too large for our membership to sustain. We have too many activities and we are bad at closing things down. We assume that churchgoing implies joining a community of believers but are we making the wrong assumptions about what the active level of that commitment should be?

Lower denominational allegiance

When I run congregational consultations I frequently ask how long members have been in that particular church. Very many people will say that they have belonged to more than one denomination in their life. Our mobile populations demonstrate that when a family or an individual move they do not necessarily search out a church of their own denomination. They make new friends and get taken along to their church. Or, they shop around until they find one which is friendly and has the feel and approximate size of their old congregation. Once there they begin to ask about denomination and, within limits, make every attempt to accommodate themselves to it. This may be just as pragmatic as I describe or it may be more about a person's journey of faith and the kind of church they want to attend while they have small children or when they are at some other stage in their life. Whatever the reasons it has already become clear that denominational allegiance is lessening. In spite of some church leadership, or because of the obstacles and barriers which church teaching often presents, there is a great sense that the laity are redefining what they mean by belonging to a church. Leading and managing within the denominations will have to take serious account of what lay people are saying and doing as they determine the ground-rules for their allegiance.

A new series of challenges

The consequences of such a new situation, brought about by breaks in traditional practice, are serious for each denomination and for us all as at least supporters of congregational life. They bring what I want to regard as challenges to all those who want to see that organized Christian religion continues. Such challenges are not a criticism of the work which has gone into developing life in local congregations over the centuries. We are where we are, with the strength we have, because generations of faithful clergy and devout lay people have made tremendous contributions. Their work enables us to approach the new challenges with a confidence borne both of a tradition bearing sacrificial work and also of a spirituality which affirms the presence of an incarnate God who is active in the pressures and changes of this created world. The focus for my exploration of the implications in these 'discontinuities which present challenges' has to be in one particular area. It is in a discussion about the styles of management and the nature of leadership which will enable Christian congregations to face a future which they may come to see as full of tantalizing promise.

Any change makes us ask something about what is going on. It would be foolish to leap to conclusions about what needs to be done for the future without a brief analysis of the consequences of such discontinuities. Through a series of questions I want to explore in a little more detail what is contained within a discontinuity. This might give some pointers for our own understanding and a few inklings of what kind of action we might need to take for the future. The first challenge is the unavoidable question about internal tension which already faces every congregation.

How do we live with difference?

It is just because such great discontinuities characterize the life of almost every congregation that the need for dialogue and an understanding of different points of view becomes so important. Managing and leading are about providing a vision. This has to be one which is understandable and presented in ways which can be open enough to allow others to take initiatives of their own. The development and sharing of a vision needs to begin with an understanding and a clear analysis of things as they are now. The first 'cold shower' in coming to terms with the present is to be able to recognize what changes have already taken place. Organizations and structures live in a permanent time lag and leaders have to spend enormous amounts of time and energy getting their members to recognize and accept the inevitable. It is in the debate which has to take place within a church, as change presses hard that differing theologies and beliefs emerge. In open discussion, which requires the handling and releasing of conflict, hidden differences and hurts come to the surface.

Life in a church or within a local congregation is like life in a village, or some would say on board a ship. In an unspoken way the residents have learned to live together and to ignore what they do not want to see. They have also developed ways of living with the irreconcilable. They can tolerate tremendous amounts of deviant behaviour. They have learned to celebrate and to mourn together. In a negative way, they may have developed a corporate memory which will not let old grievances die and which will continue a feud when the original reasons for a division have been forgotten.

Congregations are not made up of like-minded people. They contain groupings of those who want different things from church-going and from their minister. There are always the newcomers and the 'old guard'. There are the modernizers and the conservers. Nowadays there are very likely to be the charismatics and the traditionalists. Within a congregation, as well as a denomination, there may be those who accept and those who oppose the ordination of women. Nowadays there are certainly those who have strongly differing attitudes to homosexuality and gay relationships. Concerning the restoration of buildings, there are now those who oppose the use of money from the National Lottery Charities Board and those who see this as the only route to the sums of cash needed to restore a building.

Unless churches are to move even more towards the clubiness of the like-minded a primary task of managing and leading will be to recognise the pressures, conflicts and social changes which have brought about different attitudes to Christian living and to church order. Managing involves the holding together of differing groups in a congregation. Leading asks for the reformulation of a renewed vision around which most of those in the differing groups can agree and be drawn together. Maturity is shown in a community by how its members can tolerate difference. It can also be shown in a willingness to let those who want to, leave with good grace and not with an almighty row – or with a sense of failure among those who remain.

How do we understand consent and authority?

To those who like to work in co-operative and even collaborative ways it is always sobering to be reminded that hierarchy is a word originating within the mediaeval church. Hierarchy brings with it mental pictures of a pyramidal structure and figures exercising authority and power. It contrasts with more modern concepts of democracy and participation. Words do change in their meaning and ideas are altered through time. Authority and power have an explosive emotional content for each of us when we remember that we have ourselves been both victim and oppressor. Paul Avis has achieved a major study of authority and leadership and we might begin with one of his instructive quotations, 'Thus Leonardo Boff defines domination as authority without consent, while Stephen Sykes claims that authority without consent is tyranny'.[2]

Authority can be used and experienced as compulsion or force. There are situations where power and coercion can be used. There are rules to be obeyed and punitive sanctions to be enforced when they are not. In the churches, although many leaders might be tempted to stray in this direction, the voluntary nature of the organization and the very limited sanctions which a church can exercise make compulsion or force an unlikely option. The legalism of a denomination may feel like a cruel authority when, for example, rules about divorce and remarriage or the sanctions against single sex partnerships are used as a barrier to the sacraments or full participation in a church.

Authority can be experienced as oppressive when officeholders take advantage of their reputation or position. In the churches, as in many ancient institutions, some authority is given through the achievements and distinction of those who have gone before. There is a genuine respect for those who are ordained through the valued place clergy have won in society. Similarly, bishops have a kind of deference paid to them just through the office they hold. Often the people holding the office have done nothing of themselves to earn the regard for their position. They have the responsibility to exercise that office with restraint, conscious of the enormous 'door opening' opportunities which such privilege affords. The abuse of such an office by taking into it ideas of personal power will accentuate the risk of the erosion of privileges for those who come after. Within the churches leaders who try to manage through the use of sanction and self-taken authority rather than by consent will not be held in high regard even if, for a time, they may be seen as getting their own way.

Authority can be acknowledged through competence and expertise. Staff in the various departments I have belonged to have sometimes been anxious that they will not be accepted by a parish either because they are lay or because they are women. I have always said that they gain their respect – and sometimes authority – through the professional way in which they do their jobs, not through who someone else says they are or are not. Increasingly it is this kind of authority within the churches, as elsewhere, which will gain respect – whether it be skill-based or through a presence in spirituality and teaching. In the most collaborative and egalitarian regimes there has to be a focus for an idea. Often the role of inspirer and interpreter is needed, as is that of someone to articulate hopes or frustrations Such authority rises and falls according to need, acceptance and physical staying-power. It is also transitory, fitting the need of the moment. We have all seen with, some sadness, the inspirer of a previous age repeating a message which no longer has any resonance – past its 'sell-by date'.

Power in these contexts can be experienced in almost a sliding scale where authority diminishes the more it is taken. The attempt to exercise authority without consent can be an uphill task indeed and is very close to oppression or bullying. It has to be used on the occasions when boundaries have been overstepped or when laws or freedoms have been abused. It is 'Canute-like' in essence if what is being enforced relates to an inappropriate way of doing things and uses a set of sanctions no longer acceptable to those within the wider group. The impersonal exercise of inherited or delegated power has to be taken with extreme care. Without the human compassion needed to explain and support actions it can be experienced as severe and oppressive. Power won through competence and expertise is hardly experienced as power at all. It comes to a conscious level only in its abuse.

The use of these words in an exploration of managing and leading are fundamental. Unless we are prepared to ask the searching questions about how power and authority are experienced in times of transition and change we shall not be able to go beyond a superficial exploration. There are forces here which are just as much at work in the collaborative or participative organization as they are in one which is unashamedly hierarchical. In the experience of this I am sure that I carry with me friends in the Free Churches and not only the disaffected in Anglicanism or within the Roman Catholic Church. Perhaps more importantly, none of the ways in which these forces are experienced in the churches is exclusive to that province. This is a debate about the potential within any human being to abuse whatever power they may become aware that they have. Christians have the same task as that set for all humankind to resolve. What is there in our understanding of ourselves and in how we organize our corporate tasks which can save us from the corruptions which authority and power can offer?

How do we hear questions from outside?

A church that is only concerned with its own internal matters may grow and flourish for a while but if it does not 'connect' with the questions posed by those outside it will rapidly become out of touch. It will act as an Ark for those who are disillusioned and who need to feel that they are not of the world. It will grow in its own distinctiveness, it will have characteristics of exclusiveness, but it will nurture only its own. In writing such a description I am not only describing churches which are clearly sectarian in their self-understanding. I am anxious about trends of these kinds in the mainstream consciousness of our denominational life. The pressing question in this section is what are the responsibilities placed by a wider society on those who are managing and leading the churches today?

Such questions from outside are brought into the churches by their members, especially their new ones. It is easy to speak of believers holding a range of religious views and to accept or deny this as a necessary part of modern life. It becomes real when congregation members are asked to expand somewhat on their basic beliefs. Rarely do these stem from the faithful teaching of one denomination, and sometimes not even from one faith. More and more believers appear to be putting together for themselves a 'spiritual survival kit'. This will have different things in it according to need and to temperament. It is absolutely clear that Christians are now able to cull from a wide range of reading, worship and religious experience the articles of faith which will nurture them. From my own present experience I can endorse this from my reading the potted biographies of those who come to me when I am a senior selector of candidates for the ordained ministry. Equally I come to understand, when I speak to churchgoing visitors in some of our Yorkshire Dales villages, that they only go to church with any regularity when they are on holiday! Questions or experiences from the outside make church members and their leaders reach for what is real to them. Can managing and leading tomorrows churches cope with this pluralism of belief, or will there be a tempting desire to impose an orthodoxy stemming from the past?

There is now not only the pluralism which gives the searcher a wide range of opportunities for belief, there is also the pluralism with which we can come to understand how organizations work. Another significant question for this section is about how churches can understand themselves in relation to the many studies which now exist of other organizations. Conversely, how can churches contribute to a dialogue about organizational analysis from their own pictures of themselves? The exploration of such questions is clearly an area in which MODEM has a primary interest.

Richard Higginson has drawn from the ideas of many organizational thinkers in writing about the 'culture' which a company may have.[3] He has attempted to explain that the characteristics of an organization might well be set by the 'genes' which give it life. Quite entertainingly, he describes the type of 'second wave' company where order and stability are prominent where title and rank go with preferment and where tradition informs future goals. He compares this with the 'genes' of a culture which make a company more interested in networking than hierarchy, keener on flexibility than structures and looks for risk and growth rather than security. Both views represent the sometimes creative sometimes oppressive tension with which all managers wrestle.

Within our churches there is pressure to understand ourselves according to a variety of interpretations which better fit other organizations and companies. We feel condemned if we do not display the 'enlightened' characteristics of some of them. These are not appropriate feelings. They could lead us down the illusory path of following what is right for someone else but not for us. But we do need to know how others have seen themselves and what they think about us. There are other ways and our questioning has to lead us towards an understanding of them.

For the present generation an interesting and relevant area for us to listen to the world and to question ourselves about is in the area of devolution. How can an essentially conservative organization like a denomination plan for changes within its structure? The United Reformed Church, the Methodist Church and the Church of England have each undertaken national restructuring in recent years. Each has experienced the tension of wanting to follow recommendations which enable flexibility and decentralization either from a personal hierarchy or from a hidebound committee system. Each has experienced a pulling back, blamed by some on conservative bureaucracy. Would it help to see that what has happened is more probably a product of the genes? It is institutional inertia which has frustrated the ability to shake off the encumbrances of the past and prevented us embracing the new shape church already being formed by many of our members. Higginson's pen pictures of organizational behaviour from outside do help us to understand ourselves.

The reciprocal part of this question concerns how churches can dialogue with other organizations and contribute something to an understanding about how they might operate in the future. There are a number of levels to this. One might be the degree of professionalism with which we attempt to understand ourselves. Only by operating in that way can we have any credibility elsewhere. An appropriate professionalism goes alongside a certain necessary self-confidence about our beliefs and values which can withstand the rigours of scrutiny. Another is in valuing the integrity of ways in which we can conduct some levels of debate. The contribution of the churches to major questions of morality in Britain give credit to this. Again, there is a considerable wealth of experience which can be shared in demonstrating to others how commitment can be gained – and held – in a primarily voluntary organization.

The way in which values and beliefs can develop through time is of interest to any organization. Most corporations have had to respond to external pressures as well as to 'market forces'. There is little doubt that churches can contribute widely to the new ways in which employment can be understood – from the imaginative experiments in its community projects to its acceptance of different ways of employing its ordained ministers. If only we can see and display it we are in the vanguard of experiment in maximizing the commitment and potential of our personnel.

How do we lead and manage inside the churches?

A leader in any organization will need to focus energy on the primary task. If that task is blurred, or unknown, the leader will either embody a new task or enable a debate which will work at redefinition. A leader is also a voice which articulates the deep aspirations of a community, speaking for others in ways they dream they could speak for themselves – if only they knew what they thought and could find the words.

But leaders also have to manage. More than anything else, leading is about managing the shared values of an organization. In this role leaders exercise more oversight than control in the way goals are achieved and tasks performed. Within the churches this kind of oversight is called 'episcope'. It is particularly bishops but also moderators and chairmen and senior staff members who exercise this kind of oversight. Confusion in the public mind, as well as in the minds of church leaders, occurs when they see themselves as a kind of chief executive. They cannot 'do something about' awkward clergy, they cannot 'tell congregations what to do'. They can manage by consent to legitimize the actions of others and steer a process whereby a coalition of players try to move forward without tripping one another up.

This leadership style requires me to foray into the changing understandings of leadership in episcopally-led churches. The permanent nature and position of those in senior appointments and their lack even of peer accountability means that it is necessary in episcopally-led churches for control and executive function to be elsewhere. The very parochial nature of our churches, which are really congregations with a wider sense of belief and loyalty, means that authority has to be dispersed. It is the parish or local congregation which really sets the shape of a denomination. This is even more so in our partner north German and Scandinavian Lutheran churches than it is in England. Our church order stems from the same kind of root which is closely linked to civil and state authority. We have each had to work hard at a theology and a pragmatism which gives this unusual situation its aura of virtue. Bishop Stephen Sykes has written widely and helpfully on these subjects.[4]

With the development of synodical government in the Church of England from 1970 onwards, control for many functions has found a new home. It is not always easy to see what is the difference between the authority which a bishop has as president of the Synod and that which is held in the apostolic role as guardian and teacher of the faith. Synodical government has made bishops more accessible to clergy and laity with all the extra demands on their time which that implies. It has also widened the possibilities for devolution of power and for shared responsibility in decision-making. Executive responsibility now lies with the chairs of specialist committees, with diocesan secretaries and with chairs of boards of finance. One of the good things about synodical government is that it has established an appropriate 'separation of powers'. When synods work well they manage the task of enabling a church to move towards its short- and medium-term objectives. Synods set budgets and exercise a form of financial control. Bishops can embody the hopes of their people and articulate them to the parishes and to the wider public. Most importantly, they exercise pastoral and doctrinal oversight of that collective part of the local church.

The form of government now known as 'Bishop in Synod' allows different constituencies within a church to debate together. It works well when a broad spectrum of opinion can be represented and when all involved can accept the decisions of the majority. It has a less attractive underbelly where ecclesiastical party politics have been able to flourish and where members can get themselves elected, not because they command a certain authority among their constituency, but because they hold a strong view on one or more issues.[5] There are significant organizational lessons and yet more questions here. Each of our denominations, in their different ways, is trying to demonstrate a new balance between the participation which encourages open debate and the necessary trust which needs to be placed in individuals to allow them to get on with the job.

How do we manage and lead for the next phase?

My great question for this final section is about the kind of leading and managing needed to take organizations like the churches on to the next phase of their life. One clever author has said that, 'Management is doing things right; leadership is doing the right things. Management is efficiency in climbing the ladder of success; leadership determines whether the ladder is leaning against the right wall.'[6]

Leading and managing for the future will involve a tremendous amount of relearning. New walls have been built against which we must lean our ladders. There will still be authority structures, churches will still have hierarchies, but they will not be the places where control is exercised. More than ever before, the members of an organization have the ability to determine its future. In churches, without the willing commitment of members and their generous giving, there can be no future. The consequence of this for leaders and managers is a significant shift in the balance of authority. From now on leaders will need us more than we will need them.

Management ideas and organizational structures will need to be re-drawn in order to empower a larger number of the members. This will be a response to the need for all the committed to be able to share in the debate about developing a sense of purpose. Clergy and congregations need to feel that they have risen above the weekly grind of fund-raising and property maintenance and that they share in an over-arching vision. Inspired by this kind of leadership, people feel more confident to become active themselves in the wider church. They will feel that they can be more creative in the control of their own congregations because there is a mutuality of trust between the main players in the organization. Ecumenical dialogue about managing and leading will not produce an amalgam of Reformed and Catholic understandings of church order. Such essential dialogue will produce a new way of understanding leading and managing, still within the present denominations, but which speaks much more about enabling and working together than about authority and control. It will embody in its debate and in the actions of its leaders, the concept of ministering – a key word in this book's title.

Leadership and lifestyle

The consequent new piece of learning needed for leaders and managers is to show more openly in their lifestyles that they believe in the vision because they live it themselves. In writing about the characteristics of successful companies Peters and Waterman say that, 'Organisational values and purpose are defined more by what executives do than by what they say.'[7] In our Western world there is a tremendous gap between the message and way of life of our churches and their leaders and the life of Jesus, their founder and inspirer. This is not to say that poverty and no possessions are the only route to salvation. Jesus spoke to and ate with the rich and powerful. It was the unencumbered nature of his attitude to life and the re-focusing of issues through his moral teaching which gave authority and made an impression. A new approach to leadership is about a lifestyle which speaks of an inner integrity. It makes us say of a person when we are in their presence, 'I felt ten feet taller and ten years younger', or, 'When I was with them I felt they only had time for me and my concerns.' There are great figures of this kind and they do inspire. On occasions, Christian figures who catch the public eye have this effect on a wider public. For most of us that kind of feeling comes from the special people who are around us. Sometimes we bear that responsibility for others. There is no doubt that a major piece of learning for leadership in the church is to give more attention to the message given through the life we live.

Innovation and dissent

Churches are not good at innovation. The learning needed for a next generation of leaders and managers will be about how to bring in innovation to their denominations. Congregations, dioceses and districts will need to be confronted with the need for innovative new solutions to pressing problems arising from, among other places, my four original discontinuities. No doubt there are many other disruptive factors alongside them.[8] The learning needed is about how to confront constituencies with the need for change. Leaders will need to use their charismatic function to articulate pressing questions. They will need to re-learn how to use leading and managing skills to enable the kinds of discussion to take place which will enable community solutions to be found. Synods and Councils can only go part of the way in this. They belong to a 'local government', committee-based understanding of public debate. The new learning, to produce the next wave of activity and structures, will have drawn more from community action and community development models and experience than from models with use formally elected 'representatives'. Authenticity for the next generation of leaders and managers will be demonstrated by their ability to listen, articulate and reinterpret as much as from the use of their inherited positions. Senior leaders and managers will then want to walk alongside those community-oriented inno-vators, those in parishes and congregations who will choose to take the local responsibility for managing whatever change is both agreed and possible.

Innovators are essentially dissenters. Here is a paradox: how can leaders in the mainstream of an organization, trying to take a majority with them, also be dissenters? It is much easier than might be imagined. Leading and managing, for the more alert, contain within themselves the discomforting itch of unease with things as they are. The best leaders and managers want to change things.

Leaders who can live with the difference inevitable in com-munity dissent will find themselves holding together groups who may well promote radically opposed solutions to a problem. Some will have cultivated a life which is only really content when it is on the fringe offering alternative solutions. Churches have a commitment to foster responsible dissent. In a phrase commonly used by churches in the former Eastern Germany, they hold a 'critical solidarity' with their wider societies. That critical solidarity may well have already become much more a characteristic of life within our churches. The great new piece of learning in managing and leading for the future is to create and sustain a body of Christian belief which can support its followers as they wrestle with difference and as they try to live responsibly within their present societies, jobs, families, communities and churches. It also has to foster – and perpetually renew – a body of belief which is never happy with things as they are. A vibrant community of believers will welcome discontinuities and use them in order to be able to promote a lively debate about how to live with difference while choosing to support and sustain one another.

A framework for the new learning

It is perhaps too easy to say that the only certainty in life is its uncertainty. Many will testify to the truth of that experience. In this series of questions about managing and leading we have put ourselves at the heart of a debate about how to move forward in our own lives, in our churches and as communities. But people who only ask questions can become tedious and irritating. My questions have a different function. A debate which is willing to explore key issues rather than defend polarized positions or leap to premature conclusions is full of promise. It is enabling a conversation to take place between those who can listen to one another. A leader who can hold to this task is allowing a culture to be influenced by open, collaborative, debate.

Any community which is prepared to work together at a redefinition of its aims and goals is one which will also come close to examining and understanding, perhaps for the first time, its fundamental values and its basic beliefs. These are times when it is right to feel both fragile and vulnerable and also to know the need for some securities as we go on. What can be offered through management and leadership which contain within themselves imagination, innovation and inspiration is a secure framework for sharing, debate and redefinition. Within the security of a trusted framework, all those who want to can participate in a debate about a developing faith and a changing church. They will feel that they are welcome. They will sense that there is a place for them here in this open community of Christian dialogue, just as there is a place for all of us both at the foot of the cross and at the table with our risen Lord.

References

1. See John Habgood, *Faith and Uncertainty* (London: Darton, Longman & Todd 1997), Introduction.
2. Paul Avis, *Authority, Leadership and Conflict in the Church* (Mowbray, 1992).
3. Richard Higginson, *Transforming Leadership* (SPCK, 1996), pp. 21ff.
4. Among many studies see: Stephen Sykes, *The Integrity of Anglicanism and Authority in the Anglican Communion* (Mowbray, 1978).
5. For a fuller exposition of this see: Wesley Carr, *The Priestlike Task* (SPCK, 1985), Ch. 9, 'The Bishop and the Synod'.
6. S. Corey, *The Seven Habits of Highly Effective People* (New York: Simon & Schuster, 1990), p. 101.
7. Peters & Waterman, *In Search of Excellence* (New York: Harper & Row, 1986), p. 97.
8. Such ideas were first set out by Peter Drucker in *The Age of Discontinuity* (Pan Paperbacks, 1968). See also, Peter Rudge, *Order and Disorder* (Australia: CORAT, 1990).

10

Leading in urban priority area parishes

ANTHONY HAWLEY

Introduction

The purpose of this chapter is to give some consideration to managing and leading in urban priority area parishes (UPAs). *Faith in the City* (the Report of the Archbishop of Canterbury's Commission on Urban Priority Areas, published in 1985), set out its definition of UPAs at the conclusion of its first chapter.

> We have described the UPAs in secular terms as places of absolute poverty, of 'the relative poverty which is integral to an unequal society; and of increasing poverty by comparison with national norms and the favoured minority of middle Britain: this has to be termed polarisation. We have further described the UPAs in terms of their three essential characteristics of economic decline, physical decay and social disintegration.'

Although it can be claimed that much has happened in many UPAs in the last thirteen years, there can be no doubt that the picture of a divided Britain has not yet been painted out. The effects of a different political administration remain to be seen. Is there such a thing as UPA culture? And if there is, what does it consist of, and why is it important for church and society? These questions will be considered by means of a brief analysis. Then follows a look at the role and task of the priest or minister in UPAs and of the congregation, as they interrelate. In conclusion, some questions of management and leadership in UPAs will be raised for the church to consider.

Why this emphasis on UPAs? The very existence of such areas within society mean that they must be considered part of the responsibility of the church as a whole. The parochial system of the Church of England ensures that every part of England falls within a parish and is therefore under the care of a designated minister. Other Christian denominations prioritize their work and mission depending on their policy and resources: both the Roman Catholic Church and the Salvation Army have historically placed great emphasis on the importance of a presence and a witness both in inner-city areas and on inner-city issues and much of this work remains a priority. The Methodist 'Mission alongside the Poor' is a further example of an attempt to target resources towards areas of poverty. St Paul makes much reference to Jesus' followers as the Body of Christ in his letter to the church at Corinth, a trading city with evidently many of the urban difficulties of today. Indeed, in Paul's day, it was given a bad name similar to some of our own inner-city areas. But Paul's message to the Christians in Corinth was one of solidarity with one another: each and every one had a vital part to play in their witness in that troubled city. Not surprisingly, the church as the Body of Christ is one of the best known models. Used in the context of today's church and society with our urban priority areas, it emphasizes that each part affects the whole. We simply cannot close our minds, our hearts or our corporate wallets to urban priority areas and expect the life of the nation to continue as before. The disturbances in Brixton and Toxteth in 1981 brought that message home. For the church it is a constant impetus to examine what it is trying to do and how it is doing it, in such areas.

Moreover, these UPAs are not small in number. With regard

to the Church of England, the survey undertaken by the writers of *Faith in the City* showed the heaviest concentration in the dioceses of Birmingham and Manchester (over 40 per cent of their parishes), London and Southwark with over one third and Liverpool with about a quarter. Out of the twelve dioceses analysed, with significant urban populations, there were calculated to be 718 UPA parishes out of a total of 3048, a figure of 23.5 per cent. Further, the tables produced in *Faith in the City* regarding the distribution of the Parochial Stipendiary Clergy (p. 380), show a total deployment in 1984 of 879 clergy in UPA parishes against diocesan totals of 3,182. Over the intervening years, these figures will have changed, but the total will remain high enough to underline the point that the number of UPA parishes alone justifies consideration being given to the ways in which they are managed and led. The UPAs represent a substantial part of the church's concern and responsibility.

UPAs cannot expect to be exempt from scrutiny in today's 'performance-related' world. We live in an age where results matter. Schools produce details of exam grades achieved; train companies of how many trains ran on time and how many complaints were made; hospitals tell us the length of their waiting lists, and so on. 'Charters' of different kinds offer a benchmark by which people can measure the effectiveness of performance. It is the new form of accountability. There are no exemptions, certainly not on grounds of location. Inner-city schools receive the same rigorous treatment from OFSTED inspection teams as schools in well-heeled suburbs. Hospitals in cramped conditions with antiquated buildings will be measured against the same criteria as those just built and resourced with modern, state-of-the-art equipment. There may be a justifiable case to be made for more help and resources, but it is the results which count. The way the church is managed and led in UPAs should also be the subject of critical scrutiny.

A further reason for the need to raise these important issues of managing and leading in UPAs is that, as has been hinted at above, that there are considerable cultural differences between the inner-city and outer estate areas and other parts of Britain. Discussion of these differences may lead us to consider whether there may be different or more appropriate management methods or styles of leadership. The second section of this chapter will deal in detail with analysis of some of the characteristics of a UPA 'culture.'

Finally, if it is agreed that special consideration needs to be given to UPAs, then it follows that there are implications for training, particularly for those in the full-time stipendiary ministry of the church. How best to deploy their resources of people is a burning issue for all Christian denominations in Britain today. Most current figures indicate that the number of those offering themselves for full-time ministry is diminishing (whether the recent upturn in the Church of England will be sustained remains to be seen). At the same time, the average age of those coming forward is rising. Much time is currently being spent across the country by senior management planning groups trying to work out how best to preserve what is best in their existing ways of working while taking into account the predicted reduced figures in the future. Issues of managing and leading in the future are clearly crucial in this debate, not least over what management and leadership skills may be required in those who will have responsibilities for more of the work than their predecessors.

UPA culture: why should the church take note?

Before attempting to define what is particular about UPA culture, it must be admitted that there is no one simple definition, any more than there is one UPA that demonstrates all aspects. Rather there are pointers, characteristics, which may be agreed as more likely to be found in UPAs than in other areas. The popular method chosen, known as the SWOT analysis, highlights the strengths, weaknesses, opportunities and threats perceived as being illustrative of UPAs. It has some limitations. Strengths in some UPAs will not be found in others, nor will some of the opportunities ranging from tight Victorian terraces in a multi-ethnic inner-city to the almost exclusively white outer estates of the 1960s, such as Killingworth on Tyneside or Kirkby on Merseyside. No brief analysis can bring out every aspect of the rich culture that lies within such a range of peoples and places. Nevertheless, it is possible to make some general observations which may help us ask some serious questions.

Strengths

So what are some of the strengths of 'UPA culture'? Many people possess the often unnoticed qualities of perseverance and resilience, born out of a life of having to 'make do', of making the best with slender resources. They have cut their coat according to their cloth. This can hide an untapped potential of ability and energy, only released when a real opportunity arises (such as 'second chance learning'). The sheer hard work involved in simply 'living' can inhibit any real growth. But given the chance there is a readiness to rise to the challenge. This is most noticeable amongst women, who still largely keep to the tradition of being responsible for all domestic matters. Indeed, the importance of the role of women in UPAs cannot be overstated. Women provide the glue which holds the whole fabric of UPA life together. They know one another through such contact as meeting at the school-gate and in the shops. Men may go out to pubs and men's clubs, but (apart from a few) their range of contacts is much more restricted. If leaders are people who can command a following, then an exercise to identify local leadership in a UPA will most often produce the names of women. Many are already active in women's health issues, advice and counselling and in schools and colleges, performing an invaluable task in all these places, often with only basic levels of education. Thus, to add the skills of managing to their gifts of leadership, they need training.

In many UPAs there is a warmth of welcome not so easily

found among those who can retreat behind the gates of a large property in the suburbs or the country. Life is more precarious, but far more relaxed and uninhibited. Spontaneity and, in some places, entrepreneurism flourish.

Weaknesses

Many studies have highlighted weakness in UPA culture: deprivation of choice, lack of self-esteem and confidence, little strategic or long-term planning, people often weighed down by ill health, often exacerbated by the plight of high unemployment, the single greatest cause of the malaise in so many UPAs. Women, in spite of the strengths listed above, are seriously under-represented in local politics and local trades union movements. A 'dependency upbringing', which in the past taught reliance on others to do the simplest tasks, has produced a generation of 'damaged' people lacking in confidence and skills. Many lack what others in our modern society regard as basic, such as their own transport and telephone. Communication is thus slowed down, and everything takes longer to achieve. It is not surprising that life at this pace in the modern world leads to short-termism, and reliance on what is often termed the 'money in weekly'.

Stories abound of the long memories that exist in deep-rooted parishes in the countryside and of reasons given by villages to preserve their independence when ecclesiastical amalgamations are suggested. ('We couldn't possibly unite with them – they were on the other side in the Civil War' or, even better, 'They didn't warn us when the Danes were coming.') This short-term planning, in turn contributes to a 'chaos' theory that everything will turn out all right in the end as long as we can overcome the crisis of the present. Some are left without hope, having little energy or enthusiasm to engage with local life. Many UPAs have been described as communities of the left behind, where those who have had the ability and wherewithal to get up and go have done just that. The result is that there is a shortage of skills. Those with professional qualifications have mostly moved out: they may retain their family links, but they live, work and educate their children elsewhere.

Opportunities

But some of what are identified as weaknesses can be seen in a positive light as opportunities, and both individuals and groups have proved this to be the case. The untapped potential of many who left school at fifteen is one example: it is not an easy road for someone in their late thirties to return to college to study for GCSEs and A levels. It is even harder to sustain a course of study and proceed to university. Yet many have achieved this against the odds. The determination of one such mother from a Merseyside outer estate enabled her to gain a PhD and she now holds a teaching post in John Moores Liverpool University. Interestingly, her PhD thesis was a study of poverty. The source material was all around her. As more people from UPAs proceed to further and higher education, a belief is strengthened that 'the experts can be challenged'. But the training is vital, within content and method. Several Anglican dioceses have produced lay training programmes where much thought and concern has gone into the preparation and formation of people from UPAs. One model which has emerged in Britain in recent years is broad-based organizing (BBO), imported from the USA in the late '80s and early '90s. Based on the ideas and practice of Saul Alinsky, its main membership both in Britain and the US is drawn from church congregations. It sees itself as having a faith-based collaborative approach with an emphasis on family values. Its method is to involve individuals who are identified as local leaders on a personal one-to-one basis. Their task is to mobilize a following in their church or organization and, in collaboration with others from similar groups, listen to local issues, prioritize and decide which are winnable and then set to work to achieve them by applying analysis, pressure and the use of allies. A national, central co-ordinating foundation arranges training for these individuals, which local organizations buy into. As well as the organising method, this stress on training is one of the hallmarks of BBO. It is thorough, thought-provoking and practical, and involves little input. For UPA parishes and groups it can provide a good opportunity for confidence building and training in organizing and leading. In spite of being based on the importance of the initial personal contact, it is intensely collaborative and decision making is essentially collective.

It is one of the few organizations that seems able to unite people of different backgrounds, races and creeds to address common local issues. In the US where BBO has been in practice for three decades, some issues now are tackled in a state wide basis; for example the establishing of a minimum wage in California was the result of this method of working. In Britain it offers the further opportunity of drawing in the hopes and aspirations of often marginalized ethnic communities, as well as utilizing their skills and talents. There are lessons to be learnt from those who are at present involved in managing and leading in UPAs: much experience, expertise and thinking about the issues deserves to be debated and shared.

Threats

Will the church be able to commit itself to a vision of training and confidence building for those in UPAs? It will not be easy. As *Faith in the City* observed, for the Church of England at least:

It is clear that the Church of England has traditionally been mainly middle class in character: it never attained the kind of pervasive influence, transcending the boundaries of class, that was achieved by Catholicism in Ireland or nonconformity in Wales. Equally, as it moved into the twentieth century, it carried with it a clerical paternalistic legacy of a male-dominated Church in which the clergy held the power (1985:31).

Whatever the opportunities that collaboration may present, there is always the temptation for clergy in particular to take short cuts and maintain a culture of dependency. There is the threat that other issues may press more urgently upon the church, such as revising its internal structures, or considerations of finance and these could have the effect of sidelining issues of the UPAs. Much of what is of real value in UPAs can also be of value to the wider church. In some areas, positive attempts to offer this have been made, notably in the Dioceses of Liverpool, London and Manchester.

Collaboration, which was listed above as an opportunity, can also be a threat. There is evidence that many leaders in the church pay lip service to the notion of working together, but do not practice what they preach. Often much action is justified on grounds of expediency ('there wasn't time to consult'). All human organizations contain those who desire and enjoy power. The church is no exception. The road to power is scarred.

The priest in a UPA: role, tasks and some questions

There are particular issues to be addressed when we consider managing and leading in UPAs. In the Church of England, the calling of priests is set out in the Ordinal, where there is a reference to leading the people in prayer and worship. Although there is no mention of managing, it is clear that many of the other duties of the vocation such as baptizing, preparing the baptized for confirmation, teaching, ministering to the sick and dying and the role of being messengers, watchmen and stewards, all require both personal and parish management even on a modern scale. The keeping of a diary and arranging meetings are in themselves management tasks, whether people call them that or not. The fact that many UPA people may not keep diaries or be familiar with meetings and how they work, does not obscure the fact that clergy in those areas need to be as well organized as their colleagues elsewhere, and possibly even more so.

Whatever the parish is like, there are particular tasks which the priest will have to do in order to manage his or her day. In this section I shall be looking at the tasks of planning, decision-making, organizing, leading, communicating and evaluating. Each of these will be considered along the factors of UPA culture which I discussed earlier. From this exercise will emerge questions both for clergy themselves and, indirectly, for the wider church and for society. The word 'priest' is chosen because of the earlier reference to the ordinal: it could as well be substituted with 'minister' or any equivalent recognized title.

The priest as planner

It is no longer possible to be entirely reactive to life in a parish, even if it ever were so. There is a need to plan, not just for next week or even next month, but to take a more strategic view of the future: where do we want to be in our church in three, five or seven years' time? To reach that goal, an analysis of the present must first be made and then the steps by which progress will be made towards the destination. What are the strategic objectives of the parish? People may assume that others know what the goals are but unless the question has been asked, there can be no guarantee that everyone understands and is pointing in the same direction. To achieve this, further planning is required, to get people together for the task of setting goals.

None of this, of course, is restricted to any one kind of parish. What are important here are the questions this throws up for working in UPAs. An obvious obstacle occurs immediately. If it is true that one of the characteristics of 'UPA culture' is short-termism, then one may have to be creative in thinking how best to talk about strategic objectives when the minds of many people are geared to thinking of results in the short term. Where to look for allies in this? Where there is a future vision to be shared in a UPA setting what skills might be needed in communicating this? And when can these be taught? What practical help is the wider church offering to those who are asking these questions?

The priest as decision-maker

Inadequate planning may result in wrong decisions being made. The process of making decisions is really a particular part of planning and requires that specific questions be answered:

- do I have all the information I need to make this decision?
- how much of this decision-making process can I share with others?
- where does my authority in this decision begin and end?

For the priest in a UPA situation, two further questions might emerge:

- do I need help in unleashing the potential of people?
- how can I do this when people appear to lack confidence and want to leave the decisions to me?

The phrase 'unleashing the potential of people' is to be preferred to the currently more popular one of 'empowerment'. Empowerment suggests that those being 'given power' are somehow in a deficit position, waiting to receive what is to be handed to them by others. But the potential is already there. All that is needed is for that to be released. It is easier said than done. As we have said above, there is often both a reluctance to do this and an ignorance of how to do it. The first may involve changing an attitude of mind, the second the acquisition of skills. The latter may particularly be necessary when attempts are made to address the confidence issue. Building up people's confidence is not something that can be done overnight, and requires skill and patience, knowledge and determination.

The priest as organizer

Although not exclusively confined to the priest in a UPA parish, it does seem to be more commonly the case that a number of responsibilities fall to someone in that situation, such as dealings with professions, financial matters or practical work on buildings. Small, non-professional and elderly congregations often do not contain sufficient human resources to meet these regular demands. Sometimes these demands are emergencies, cutting across what may be planned work and the priest must be sufficiently flexible and well organized to cope with the disruption. The task becomes one of organizing the time available and then co-ordinating all the resources effectively and efficiently. In a UPA parish, there is the long-term challenge of enabling people to have the skill and confidence to deal with many of these responsibilities, whether they are emergency or routine work. The short-term question is often: how do I get people away from a 'chaos' theory, that everything will be all right in the end and encourage some organisation, without losing the energy and spontaneity which they bring?

The priest as leader

All clergy would agree that there is a need to exercise leadership. The question is what principles of leadership are adhered to. There are several understandings. It is the definition of the Drucker Foundation that:

> The only definition of a leader is someone who has followers. Some people are thinkers. Some people are prophets. Both roles are important and badly needed. But without followers, there can be no leaders. An effective leader is not someone who is loved or admired. He or she is someone whose followers do the right things. Popularity is not leadership. Results are. Leaders are highly visible. They therefore set examples.

Leadership is not rank, privileges, titles or money. It is responsibility.

This echoes Drucker's earlier distinction that 'managers are people who do things right', and 'leaders are people who do the right things'. Or is it more to do with what Peters and Austin call preaching the vision:

Attention, symbols, drama. The nuts and bolts of leadership. More is called for than technique. You have to know where you're going, to be able to state it clearly and concisely – and you have to care about it passionately. That all adds up to vision. (1985: 284)

Or as Charles Handy neatly puts it:

A leader is someone who is able to develop and communicate a vision which gives meaning to the work of others. (1993: 117).

In his book on leadership (King 1987), King lists seven essential principles for leaders:

- leadership is to be shared;
- leadership is for equipping others;
- leadership is varied;
- leadership is flexible;
- leadership is to be both settled and mobile;
- leaders are to be servants;
- leaders include both men and women.

All the foregoing can apply equally to UPA and non-UPA parishes. The difference is in the execution. Sensitivity to the pervading culture will determine the manner in which principles are applied. Important too for the priest is the availability of someone with whom this can be discussed.

The priest as Communicator

Although all clergy see themselves as very much in the business of communication, many do not communicate either enough or effectively. They often give up too soon. With the increasing sophistication of communications technology, many of the church's traditional methods of teaching and preaching sit uneasily with the desire for 'soundbites' and slick instant answers. Media presentation is a skill that is expected of all who take part and there is a demand that all information be reduced to a simple message. This demand spills over in other areas with the result that clergy are expected to perform in a similar way. For the 'natural' communicator this transition can be made with good effect, but many find this hard. In every situation clergy will ask the question whether what they have communicated has been heard and understood. In UPAs a further question is whether there are ways of communicating which are particularly suited to UPAs? Is it possible to generalize and speak about communicating with tabloid readers being different from those who are broadsheet readers? Most dioceses have communications officers, part of whose job is to deal with the media: some also offer assistance with questions such as these.

The priest as evaluator

Most clergy subscribe to the value of reflection. The best way of learning and benefiting from this is done if there is a structure to the process. Because much of the task of the priest in the pastoral role is responding to people's needs, there is a danger of allowing all work to be done without adequate planning and preparation. If objectives have been set, in those areas where they can be set, then, with proper evaluation, progress and achievement can be measured. Help is at hand in many places for those clergy who want it. But many do not avail themselves of this opportunity, despite the acknowledgement of the need to reflect on what they are doing. Questions arise for those in UPA settings. How do I involve others in a UPA to plan for results with me and monitor our objectives? Who might these other people be?

How do I decide who is best to do this work in a culture where these may be alien concepts? How can this process of reflection – action – reflection be applied as much to building up people as to the maintenance of buildings?

UPA congregations: managing and leading – shared or delegated?

At a recent conference for rural/area deans, members were asked to dream dreams about how they would like to see the future. The overwhelming response was that of an ideal where clergy worked collaboratively, both with fellow clergy and with lay people. Again, in a survey of a small number of deaneries in the Liverpool Diocese in 1995, the results were that 'all were agreed on the main area of focus, which they . . . identified as sharing of resources, sharing and working together, and co-operating in a mission-orientated deanery.' The intention is the same, echoing Robert Warren. 'Churches whose lives are most healthy and alive are almost invariably churches which have worked out how to encourage and support clear and creative leadership and active participation in discerning and implementing the vision owned by all. Clear leadership and good collaborative styles are great when properly harnessed together.' (Warren 1995: 179)

What, then, might be the tasks and difficulties encountered, particularly by congregations in the area of leading and managing in UPAs?

Confidence building in fragile communities

A common feature of the local church in UPAs is its fragility. Numbers are often small, money and resources are stretched and the population transitory. Individuals of today with strength and tenacity are often gone tomorrow. The challenge for the manager and leader in such situations is to locate the strength and build on it. The question is often how to do this. Have the managers and leaders been given the training by their church which they will need for this task? And if they have, will their church follow this training with the offer of resources?

In some UPAs, particularly those on outer estates, there is a strength in the community, a strength made up of strong family ties and with a history of having had to pull together through thick and thin. This mutual support, which is the glue that holds such communities together, often has a reverse side, a mistrust of outsiders or bitter local infighting. Such xenophobia, while creating a strong parochial defence, does nothing to build positive relationships with the outside world. It breeds a lack of confidence which is recognized as a major stumbling block to progress. What part can the church play in this, recognizing the value and strength of family ties, yet wanting to enlarge the vision and opportunity? It is not a challenge only to the church. Schools, colleges, employment agencies can all work together. One practice that has been identified as helping this progress is the linking with outside organizations: many schools now have links with businesses and places of higher education locally. Churches have tended to forge links further afield, but the value of this cross-fertilization at its best is that it can play a useful role in eroding a limited local vision and in a small way, crossing a national divide.

Visions and decisions

Whilst a vision may be initiated by an individual and articulated by a few, for it to succeed it must be shared by many. True leaders will enable others to share. Over thirty years ago Cardinal Suenens wrote:

> The fundamental role of the leader is to make collegiality possible. The role of the one in charge is not that of making a

'personal' decision after taking the advice of others into account. For in that case it would still be 'his' decision. His role is rather to make it possible, in so far as depends upon him, for there to be a common decision which commits each member to the decision ... A true leader, ultimately responsible for the pastoral work in a locale, will find his place when he has succeeded in helping the others to find theirs.

This is particularly true in UPAs as we have observed earlier. *Faith in the City* commented on the Liverpool Diocese's UPA report which noted that 'no church can be a truly local church so long as leadership and decision making is in the hands of people who do not live there', by saying, 'we would go further than this: not only must local leadership and decision making be shifted towards those who live in the area, but it must be shifted more to those who belong to the predominant social class or group.'

There is a skill in being concise, getting over what is important, so that there is a clarity of expression with which others can associate. Again, for churches there is a challenge here in assisting their managers and leaders in doing just that. In some places, churches encourage and enable local ministry teams. One of the issues they will wrestle with is how to cope with long-term strategies and decreasing numbers of short stay clergy.

Train – communicate – reflect

Beyond the sharing of the vision and decisions is the step of training together. Robin Greenwood, amongst others, has written on the church's need to be a 'learning organization', acknowledging Peter Senge's work at the MIT Sloan School of Management, where he emphasizes that the new work of the leader is to build learning organisations. We have already underlined the importance of communication: if this is working well, it will be a two-way process, building up the confidence and effectiveness of both priest and congregation. To complete the process, there is the value of shared reflection. For those who through the training become local leaders in the life of a church community there is a continued need to keep up communication with the whole body. Both those who through membership of local ministry teams are ordained as local ministers and those who exercise lay leadership, will be in a new situation in the church. The danger of divisions within the body can be eased by good communication and common reflection. For UPA congregations this whole exercise of training, communication and reflection is vital for a truly learning and collaborative approach. Sustained commitment to the principle is required from those who manage and lead, for it to succeed. Those who resource and manage the church at other levels also need to be aware that there are no quick fixes. Continuity and a sticking with it count for a lot, particularly in UPAs.

So what is needed?

There is a temptation to go beyond the title of this book and dare to suggest solutions, instead of posing questions for reflection, which may in turn lead to appropriate answers. The underlying question of this chapter is: How best to change hearts and minds in a 'dependency culture'? We have looked at aspects of the so-called UPA culture and examined the role and tasks of clergy and congregations as they, at least in representative form, manage and lead in these areas. At the end of the day it has to be recognized that the church is composed mainly of volunteers and that both clergy and lay people are to a huge degree independent. People may be open to persuasion but not coercion. As Robert Warren has recently observed, 'power to command has been relinquished' (1995: 11). This is a fact that has to be acknowledged and any strategy of managing and leading which assumes that this is even partly true will need to be re-examined. The subsidiary questions and challenges are to do with formulating and sharing a vision of UPA ministry and then identifying and channelling the energy which is found there. The following seven points for consideration

are in no way exhaustive, but may encourage both those who plan
and lead in UPAs and also those who have a wider responsibility.

Vocations

A good starting-point is the encouragement of vocations to the
ordained ministry, in all its forms in the Church of England,
stipendiary, non-stipendiary and as ordained local ministers. A
balance is desirable in the wider ministry of the church and whilst
pastoral planning can only properly take into account those who
are deployable, that is, the stipendiary clergy, the possibilities of
a vocation to local or non-stipendiary ministry should be open to
all. Opportunities for training for all forms of ministry are now
so flexible that imaginative ways of learning and building up the
required 'course modules' are available to help students at every
level. The experience of those who have found their vocations in
a UPA parish may provide a valuable resource for helping to
promote vocations in such areas. In most dioceses there are clergy
who will have useful insights and suggestions in this field.

Selection and training institutions

There are still a number of clergy whose entire ordained ministry
has been spent without any contact with a UPA parish. Though
such contact has been recognized as a valuable experience by the
Church of England's Advisory Board for Ministry and by those
responsible for providing training, it is still nevertheless the case
that many students do not have a short placement in UPA ministry. This is to be regretted, as not only is the opportunity for
understanding and learning missed, there is also the possible loss
of a real call to serve. Experience shows that even where a vocation
may subsequently lead people in a different direction, many never
forget their brief experience in a UPA parish, and value what they
learnt there. One diocese has recently set up a fund, part of

whose object is to provide financial help to ordinands to gain such experience.

Although the placements can only be 'tasters', they are much more than tokens. They can play a major part in fostering a sympathy and understanding of UPA ministry and provide an encouragement to serve. Most theological colleges now include the placement experience as an intrinsic part of training, but it is important that this is extended to the increasing number of individuals whose training is provided by non-residential courses. It is also important for ordinands from UPA parishes themselves to take this opportunity and not consider that they 'know it all': as ordinands on placement they will find themselves in a very different role.

Promoting acceptability of UPA ministry

UPA parishes cover both inner-city areas and outer estates. Some of these areas still have a stigma attached to them which acts as a barrier to acceptability, even amongst Christians. For many they remain unknown parts, little visited by those with no particular reason for going there. The Centre for Environmental Studies, in a report published in 1984, described outer estates of Britain as 'forgotten areas of deprivation'. Even though their fortunes, at least for some, may have improved in the past fifteen years, they are often still forgotten.

Part of the task of the church at diocesan level must be to encourage UPA parishes to feel as much a part of the diocese as middle-class parishes. James O'Halloran sees this as an issue of injustice:

I am often baffled by references to what is called the middle class church. I realise, of course, that this may be a convenient sociological rather than a theological description. But looked at theologically, there is no such church. There is only the church of the poor (the materially poor and those who identify with them), a community of the faithful, all equal through baptism. So we should not lightly use the expression middle class church. Surely classism is as abhorrent to the Christian as racism or sexism, and the feminist movement has made us all aware of the importance of being sensitive in the language we use. (1996: 143)

The image of the church as the body of Christ is another reminder of the church's call to be at unity in itself giving an equal value to each of its members. Then there is the intrinsic value of just being there, like Ezekiel's presence with the exiles by the river of Chebar: 'I sat where they sat' (3:15). Important, too, in this process is a clear understanding of and sympathy for UPAs by the diocesan communications officer.

Resourcing UPA ministry

Important for the confidence, morale and effectiveness of those who are engaged in UPA ministry are the resources that are available. Continuing Ministerial Education (CME) opportunities are vital in this area: one diocese has designated a member of the CME team to work with those in UPA ministry, to support, challenge and advise in theology and in practice. At the very least it avoids clergy having to reinvent the wheel and at best it can stimulate and encourage new creative ideas. But there has to be a diocesan 'bias' to this work. There needs to be the ability to provide practical help at short notice, for example in vicarage security. Clergy will often need help in working with local people in long-term planning in how to identify and work with 'allies' in the community. Peter Brierley has written helpfully about this resourcing of the individuals and many organizations and people are available to provide such assistance on a practical level.

Collaborative working

Linked closely with the above is the need for collaborative working. In talking of today's full-time ministry David Sheppard has often said, 'There is no place for gifted loners.' One answer being worked on and achieved in UPA and non-UPA parishes alike is the formation of local ministry teams. A flexible definition of such teams is helpful: important is the evidence of real collaborative ministry. In the UPA situation it is increasingly clear that those called to minister there should not be asked to 'walk alone'. Again CME and diocesan training schemes will be available to assist and encourage, together with those responsible for pastoral planning and deployment.

Partnership working

Collaboration of another kind is joining up with other denominations and secular agencies in an area. Many if not most UPAs are targets for special attention: government or European funding, and grant charitable trusts and voluntary groups are often all actively seeking to meet particular needs. The church, with its unique place in the community, is in a position to be actively involved. The involvement with such allies is often time consuming and if to do with government or European initiatives, complicated as well, with much paperwork and strict deadlines to be met. But the church can often share its resources with others, and play a real part, ecumenically if appropriate, in addressing the needs of an area. In other fields, for example in youth work or community action, membership of a youth forum, or of an organization such as Broad Based Organizing (referred to above) can result in church members (and not just the clergy) being involved in partnership with local allies. Training or information sessions are offered which can be of value to church members. Particularly in youth work there are significant opportunities for churches in UPA parishes which have an interest, to be involved in imaginative developments. One youth centre on Merseyside, managed by the local churches, is currently running a scheme in collaboration with four local secondary schools in which the most difficult pupils attend the youth centre instead of school and receive specialist professional youthwork. This is paid for by the schools but managed by the centre; it's hard work, but has proved so successful that a further four schools have asked to join the scheme.

Spiritual support

This is an additional vital strand of the support network to be offered to clergy and especially those in UPAs. Practical administrative suggestions, encouragement to form collaborative ways of working and maintenance of morale and confidence, all need to be undergirded by strong inner resources. Patterns of individual daily prayer and public worship are for many the bedrock of their daily ministry on which the strength to keep going, the ability to take hard decisions and face difficult situations is based. Also there needs to be built in opportunities for prayerful reflection where individuals can share their spiritual journey, whatever name is given to this process. Church leaders and those responsible both for the training of assistant staff and for offering CME and spiritual support will be the people looked to in this category to ensure that such inner resources are being replenished.

What are the implications for the institution in all this? Can a church which has such a middle class dominance really accept what an acceptance of the process of UPA parishes could imply? Fifteen years ago under the chapter heading of 'Can the Church Bear Good News to the Poor?' David Sheppard wrote:

'The poor have a deep instinct that Jesus is on their side, but they are not so sure about the church. It is seen to be kindly, especially in serving the elderly and children. But to the poor it seems to be primarily for the settled and successful and unwilling to stand for justice on behalf of the poor if its own security might be threatened.' (1983:200)

So will the church change and will those responsible in the church for leadership and management help those who are working in UPAs, on changing hearts and minds in a dependency culture and at the same time change themselves in heart and mind to address what the urban priority areas may be saying? These are challenging questions for the future.

Bibliography

Archbishop's Commission on Urban Priority Areas *Faith in the City* (London: Church House Publishing).

Brierley, P. *Priorities, Planning and Paperwork* (London: MARC Europe, 1992); *Outer Estates in Britain* (London: Centre for Environmental Studies, 1984).

Handy, C. *Understanding Organisations* (London: Penguin, 4th edn.).

King, P. *Leadership Explosion* (London: Hodder & Stoughton, 1987).

Morgan, G. *Imagin-i-zation* (California: Sage, 1997).

O'Halloran, J. *Small Christian Communities* (Dublin: Columba Press, 1995).

Peters, T. and Austin, N. A. *Passion For Excellence* (Glasgow: Fontana/Collins, 1985).

Sheppard, D. *Bias to the Poor* (London: Hodder & Stoughton, 1983).

Warren, R. *Being Human, Being Church* (London: Marshall Pickering, 1995).

11

Organizational culture in congregations

CHRISTOPHER BURKETT

Introduction

A leadership that deals with meanings: appreciating the power of organizational culture in congregations.

The commonly observed decline in organized religion in post-war Europe illuminates some aspects of religious practice but obscures others. One such often unnoticed element is the ubiquity of religious congregations. In all the discussion of decline, the remarkable fact is that religious belonging, as represented by being a member of a congregation, has held up better than many types of belonging in other voluntary organizations.[1] In a social climate in which institutions of all kinds are viewed with suspicion and individual preference without associated social ties is lauded, the relative strength and persistence of congregations is remarkable. A systematic appreciation of what belonging to a congregation achieves in the lives of its members can greatly enhance effective leadership. Indeed, analysis of meaning creating mechanisms might provide fruitful ways into understanding similar processes in other organizations.

Hidden meanings

Very ordinary, everyday expressions and behaviours hide deeply felt and significant interpretations of life. Consider the following comments gathered by a churchwarden in a small, rural, Anglican parish church, prompted by a dispute about the relative merits of two altar frontal cloths – one, an ancient and rather tatty one; the other, a newly worked one meant to replace it.

- This shouldn't be a big issue. I didn't realize it was until some time after I had put lots of free hours into [working on] the new altar frontal.
- This shouldn't be a big issue. The Ns [the former squire's family] presented it [the old cloth] many years ago and it should be respected, not binned. They lost two young sons in World War One.
- The diocesan adviser on fabrics says the item [the old cloth] has no great artistic merit and is probably beyond normal repair.
- It [the old cloth] is of great historical value and all that is worn is the bit at the front where the vicar's hands and wrists have rubbed whilst preparing communion.
- Vicar, may we have the new altar frontal at the dedication of the kneelers, as requested by others?
- Yes [do use the newer frontal], provided this is not the thin end of the wedge. The old frontal should be out soon, and in any case definitely for Armistice Sunday.
- Fred N [the last surviving and indirect heir of the squire, who lives many miles away] has said, 'What a nice new altar frontal you have.'

This is the kind of dispute about apparently trivial things that can be the bane of those who exercise leadership. In this particular case, even the brief comments recorded here suggest that rather more than the aesthetic appeal of two tablecloths is at stake. If alongside these views some of the facts about how the village has changed and what that might be doing to the local church are added, the depth of concerns being expressed begins to surface. This is a village whose population has all but doubled in one generation due to building developments, whilst in the same period the resident vicar has been lost, the local school closed and employment opportunities in the immediate locality have declined sharply. In the light of these changes it starts to be apparent that feelings about the altar cloths are suggestive of all kinds of crucial issues, such as belonging, continuity, local rootedness, social divisions, authority, boundary maintenance and congregational purpose. A cultural, or more properly sub-cultural, analysis that can lay bare these things so that local leadership can work with them is what I want to explore.

The social significance of congregations

What is a Christian congregation? Most obviously, of course, a congregation is a gathering of people whose aim is the worship of God. That religious aim brings with it a range of social characteristics that will apply in varying degrees. A congregation creates a sense of identity in that people know themselves to belong together and recognize each other as part of a particularly entity, albeit in varying degrees. That identity serves a social function, that is, it contributes to the working of social relationships. From the perspective of the worshipper that function is usually seen very positively because it provides reinforcement of values and a strong sense of belonging. When that function is damaged, for whatever reason, it becomes easier for a person to leave the congregation. Each congregation offers strong reinforcement, albeit in very different ways, to its members own individual senses of identity. The congregation's activities strengthen and enhance its members' senses of self and self-worth.

With identity comes the creation of boundary – that is, the congregation's life establishes a particular position in relationship to other social groupings. This boundary depends not only on membership, doctrine and practice, but also on how participants feel and the categories they use to describe themselves. Visitors often perceive these boundaries as hard to cross, and sometimes they are described in terms of being in foreign territory. It is all too easy for a leadership that is enthusiastic about growth and keen to encourage a congregation to be 'outward looking' to underestimate the importance of boundary. Boundaries in this sociological sense will always be there and are essential to the commitment that comes from particularity; the question is how best to understand them and work with their consequences. Like other organizations, a congregation has to function with a constant tension between boundary maintenance and boundary transcendence. Being alert to the dilemmas inherent in this tension is a particular leadership skill.

In sociological terms, each congregation acts as a 'cultural frame' – that is, a social setting that generates its own distinctive 'subculture'. In other words, there are recognizable distinctive qualities inherent in what goes on in any congregation. Often these qualities are simply assumed by those involved, but the newcomer has to learn them and be 'socialized' into them. It is, therefore, to be expected that newcomers will feel that they are in some sense in foreign territory. Induction processes, although unlikely to be labelled as such, are just as necessary in congregations as in other institutions.

All these social functions are very contextually specific. As every leader knows, what 'works' in one place will not necessarily 'work' in another despite similarities of church governance, theology, congregation size, and the like. It is important to note here that although 'social context' is a very important aspect of what makes for a worshipping congregation, that is not to say that factors drawn from that context wholly determine what a congregation might achieve. For example, some approaches to church growth[2] have insisted that 'social homogeneity' within a congregation is essential to its positive development, that is, that a prerequisite to growth is a membership of people from relatively similar social backgrounds. That degrees of such social homogeneity do figure in the make-up of congregations is evident, but the relationship to a congregation's sub-culture is more complex than simple determination. This should be reassuring to church members, since, as Peter Cotterell observes[3], although social homogeneity facilitates a stressless community it is also a very poor reflection of the Kingdom of God that embraces all. The symbolic nature of congregational structures and behaviours allows a range of interpretations, meanings and experiences to co-exist.

The five dimensions of congregational existence

These social elements, with supporting theological ideas, figure with varying significance and in varying relationship to one another, through five identifiable aspects or dimensions of congregational existence.

The social context

This refers to the setting in which the congregation is found and to which, in one way or another, it responds. This means the directly surrounding locality in terms of the social, political, cultural and economic forces that are operating there, but is not only limited to the immediate environment. National and global issues may also impinge in some way.

Programmes

This dimension refers to those things that a congregation *does*, and can be defined as those organizational structures, plans and activities through which a congregation expresses its mission and ministry both to its own members and those outside the membership[4].

These are the things a congregation plans and executes across time – its liturgical seasons, its social calendar, its planned education and fellowship programmes, – indeed, all those activities which a congregation undertakes. This is the aspect of a congregation's existence that is normally the most obvious.

Processes

If programme is about what a congregation does, then process is about *how* it does what it does. This is the flow and dynamic of the congregation – how leadership is exercised, how problems are solved, the way conflict is managed and what communication strategies are used. Frequently, formal and informal processes will not coincide. Denominational standing orders or canon law may well lay down how something is to be done, but, on the ground, people are aware that much more informal things have to be dealt with as well if the thing planned is going to be achieved. Analysis of process must include not only formal committees and the like, but also those informal parts that 'just happen'. Often that 'just happening' has a regularity about it that should not be ignored.

Theological imperatives

The style of analysis presented here is given largely in sociological terms since the contribution of such a perspective is often given insufficient attention in Christian organizations. That does not mean, however, that theological understandings can be ignored. In every church congregation Christianity's essential teachings are expressed, and no one feels they are free to do just as they like. Issues of orthodoxy, continuing tradition, denominational understandings, and the way behaviour is judged to fit with theology figure large. By definition every Christian congregation regards God as the principal framing category of all that it does and is. Here it is quite proper for theology to exercise an ideological role.

Organizational culture

This I see as the overarching dimension that determines how the others work. By a congregational culture (or more properly, sub-culture) I mean that persistent 'story' of itself that its members use in describing themselves. It includes a whole repertoire of elements that create a sense of 'we' that persists over time and through changes, creating a sense of belonging and distinctiveness. Symbols, stories, values, patterns and style are all aspects of this dimension.

Methods like mission audits have increased the awareness of the first four dimensions, but systematic attention to this last one remains under-developed. This cultural dimension will therefore be the one on which the rest of this chapter will focus.

Analysing sub-culture: looking for stories

Much of the cultural frame is constructed symbolically. This idea is based on an approach to culture that sees it as a huge communication network in which meanings travel along elaborate and interconnected pathways. In these networks each meaning depends on another meaning, rather like each strand in a spider's web leaning on other strands. Symbols are the things that carry the meanings along the pathways of the web – that is, they are the bearers of messages and meanings. Just how symbols achieve this is dependent on the 'rules' of the culture or sub-culture concerned and the circumstances at any particular time. The meanings are created or constructed by the people involved. To take an everyday example: a smile may be a symbol of happiness, scepticism, welcome, humour, love, ridicule or revenge, among other things, depending on the culture (or sub-culture) in which it is employed and the 'rules' that are taken to apply. Within the small-scale cultural frame of a congregation, objects, behaviours and activities come to mean particular things. For example, a pulpit

Bible, as well as being understood to represent the seriousness with which the congregation views the word of God, may also represent the family who gave it in particularly tragic circumstances. If that in turn is taken to represent the caring attitude of the congregation itself that supported the family through terrible times, attempts to have it replaced are likely to be fiercely resisted. The pulpit Bible has become a bearer of meanings which have great emotional power about them. Symbolic construction is all about the meaning people give to things and how we 'think' ourselves into belonging. Appreciating this process is crucial to sympathetic leadership. Through a growth in such local knowledge and careful reflection on it, leaders come to understand the significance of things and behaviours that casual visitors do not even notice.

Fundamental to symbolic construction is the outlook a congregation's members have developed by their allegiance to the story or stories they tell of themselves. Narrative creates and maintains the sub-cultural system. Simply put, I believe congregations are defined primarily by the stories people use of themselves, or the stories of which they feel themselves to be a part. It is this story or stories that will ultimately determine what the congregation can achieve, not institutionally assumed or set goals. Needless to say, that congregational story must be related somehow to the story of God in Christ. Effective leadership, therefore, has to recognize the power of congregational narrative, find ways of positively engaging with it, and constant strive to relate it, positively or even negatively, to God.

This is a challenge to the usual ways of describing congregations that dwell on categories like denomination, churchmanship, doctrinal persuasion, ritualistic expression, socio-economic class, organization, or the wider residential communities from which members are drawn. A perspective that looks first to (sub-)cultural analysis suggests that such descriptions do not offer an adequate appreciation of the complex entity 'congregation' and that an alternative description is needed that gives full weight to the particular culture of a particular congregation. For example, an Anglican congregation may contain a number of people who would describe themselves as nonconformist by upbringing; it may express its worship solely through modern texts, yet a number of its members will describe themselves as 'Prayer Book Anglicans'; it may describe itself as a Parish Communion church, yet a substantial number of its worshippers will not be frequent at receiving communion; it may order its life in terms of the geographical parish, but a good number of its members may not be resident in that parish; it may have a preponderance of members who have been through further education and therefore order its style of worship accordingly, yet it will have some who have had only the most basic of educational opportunity. Wherever the lines are drawn there always remains a significant number of people for whom the defining criteria are 'wrong'. But a congregation is not a casual assembly of individuals, rather there is, to use an expression drawn from James Hopewell's seminal study,[5] a 'we' of a congregation that persists through changes, doctrinal differences, worship alterations, socio-economic boundaries, and the like. This 'we' can be identified and analysed through the symbols and stories a congregation uses to describe reality.

This 'we' is tenacious and not easily destroyed. It is established from resources drawn from the widest arena of human experiences not just from those labelled 'Christian' and it is expressed primarily narratively. Don Cupitt[6] has argued that story draws us into a social world; the conviction of this chapter is that it has a similar power in establishing belonging and identity in regular religious gatherings. Leadership that utilizes this perspective examines the congregations it serves in terms of 'internal or inner history', in Niebuhr's expression, for as he put it,

> The constant reference is to subjective events, that is to events in the lives of subjects ... such historic recall ... refers to communal events, remembered by a community and in a community. Subjectivity here is not equivalent to isolation, non-

verifiability and ineffability; our history can be communicated, and persons can refresh as well as criticize each other's memories of what has happened to them in the common life; on the basis of a common past they can think together about the common future.[7]

A semiotic understanding

Broadly, the analysis advocated here is a semiotic one. Semiotics sees the world of human activity as an interconnected array of 'signs' or 'symbols';[8] hence the word 'semiotic' itself, from the Greek *semeion* or 'sign'. To the semiotic theorist, culture is a vast communication network in which almost every element may function as a bearer of signification. The use of the system of signs is seen as being governed by still other signs functioning in a way that denotes the relationship between signs. Most of this usage is tacitly assumed rather than explicitly acknowledged. A culture consists of signs functioning silently in a way that allows its members to speak and act understandably in a huge number of ways. A semiotic approach allows the practitioner insight into the symbolic construction going on in a congregation. This is a way to interpret the cultural frame that is a congregation so that its own sets of codes and rules for using them are made apparent. The task is to present a hermeneutic of those congregational cultures that can offer analytical insight into why they are as they are and what they might realistically achieve in the future. As the anthropologist Clifford Geertz puts it, this type of analysis has to do with 'sorting out the structures of significance . . . and determining their social ground and import'.[9]

The leadership skill I am emphasizing is an interpretative one that goes in search of meaning.[10] Behaviour, organization, structure and artifacts that appear on the surface similarly can have a huge range of interpretative meanings when they function as symbols. Indeed, it is this multivocality of symbols that lies at the heart of a congregation's existence and the particular culture that is its own. Symbols allow a huge variety of interpretations, meanings and experiences to co-exist under the umbrella of an identifiable and delineated pattern of behaviour. As Anthony Cohen says, 'People can find common currency in behaviour whilst still tailoring it subjectively (and interpretively) to their own needs.'[11] The meanings differ but the symbols are shared. The imprecision of story and symbol allows individuality and communality to live together. The members of the congregation have both something in common and something that distinguishes them from others, although those things may not be apparent at first sight. Semiotic analysis can lay those things bare.

Three vital concepts

The style of analysis being advocated here is essentially hermeneutical, and treats congregations as systems that are structured narratively and seeks to analyse the exegesis of life and faith they represent. The approach being advocated is one that strives to 'read' a congregation as if it were a text. This is the method advocated by Lewis Mudge. He writes,

> To see the situational shape of faith, we must bracket out, or deconstruct, the established institutional and conceptual forms in order to see what is there prestructurally. That can perhaps be done through a form of 'hermeneutic phenomenology' that sees the social world as 'text-like' and thus can study different lived 'readings' of that text.[12]

This perspective utilizes concepts drawn from narrative theology, social anthropology and organizational studies, and it is worthwhile examining those concepts at some length to establish the nuances crucial to congregational analysis.

Organizational culture

In organizational studies it is commonplace to use the concept of organizational culture as a key analytical tool, particularly in dealing with change, for example, Handy,[13] Daft[14] and many others. Schein[15] defines organizational culture in this way:

> . . . the pattern of basic assumptions that a given group has invented, discovered, or developed in learning to cope with its problems of external adaption and internal integration, and that have worked well enough to be considered valid, and, therefore, to be taught to new members as the correct way to perceive, think and feel in relation to those problems.[16]

Framed in this way, the concept can be directly applied to the analysis of local churches. Indeed, many Christians would consider the assumption by an individual of a particular set of key values, guiding beliefs and understandings, as an essential part of becoming a faithful believer. This is, however, to use the concept at a 'macro' level where the culture that is referred to is that of the denomination, or the universal body of true believers, or the ongoing tradition of faith in broad terms. Here the concept is used in a local and particular sense where the sub-culture analysed is that of a single congregation, although there will necessarily and properly be many correlations with the wider understanding.

The wider use of the concept assumes that the local group is a subsidiary of a larger grouping, but when it comes to the analysis of a local church it is of vital importance that the nature of that church as perceived by its membership is taken with the utmost seriousness. Only by such a focus can the operation of symbolic meanings be uncovered. This is genuinely 'local knowledge,' to use Geertz's expression.[17] For example, when talking of their belonging people will speak of being part of 'St Peter's', 'Little Middling Church', 'Commonbank Chapel', 'the study group', 'where our family has always gone', not 'the Church of England', 'the Diocese of Wansbury', 'Anglicanism' or 'Christianity'. Fundamentally, experience-near concepts[18] are the ones most readily used. Geertz defines these as concepts that an informant or subject,

> might naturally and effortlessly use to define what he or his fellows see, feel, think, imagine and so on, and which he would readily understand when similarly applied by others . . . [These are those terms which] . . . in each place, people actually represented themselves to themselves and to one another.[19]

These are the representations of the life of faith into which newcomers are actually integrated. This is the culture, the shared history, that the group 'owns' and it is profoundly localized in its extent. The characteristics of organizational culture are most apparent, and have most force, at this level. A key leadership task is formally and systematically to become aware of these meanings, however they are expressed.

Symbolic construction

As Hopewell suggests,[20] congregational culture is not an accidental accumulation of meaningful elements but a coherent system. This symbolically constructed system does not necessarily rest primarily on any geographical, theological or ecclesiological definitions, although all of these may play a part at a secondary level. The reality of a congregation lies in its members' perception of the liveliness and worth of its culture. It is those who belong (sometimes interpreted in a very wide way) who make of it a 'resource and repository of meaning and a referent of their identity,' as Cohen puts it,

> . . . whether or not its structural boundaries remain intact, the reality of community lies in its members' perception of the vitality of its culture. People construct community symbolically,

making it a resource and repository of meaning, and a referent of their identity.[21]

Cohen was writing of the concept 'community', and it is my contention that a congregation is a type of community and that his analysis of symbolic construction can be directly applied. Cohen makes the point that such an analysis is not concerned with the morphological, structural and objective definitions that are frequently applied to social institutions.[22] This is an approach that attempts to penetrate a structure in such a way that it becomes possible to look 'outwards', as it were, from its core, rather than 'inwards' from some external vantage point. It asks what a thing appears to mean to those involved, and consequently requires data that would allow such meanings to be discerned. This requires a high level of reflective skill on the part of leaders. It also requires a certain scepticism about structural similarities, for as Cohen puts it,

> Homogeneity may be merely superficial, a similarity only of surface, a veneer which masks real and significant differences at a deeper level.[23]

Indeed, the concept of symbolic construction puts a large question mark against ideas of structural determinism, for, as Cohen further writes,

> The greater the pressure on communities to modify their structural forms to comply more with those elsewhere, the more are they inclined to reassert their boundaries symbolically by imbuing these modified forms with meaning and significance which belies their appearance ... as the structural bases of boundary become blurred, so the symbolic bases are strengthened.[25]

I am arguing that a congregation is largely such a symbolic construction. Through it people 'think' themselves into belonging and create symbolically established boundaries of difference. Meaning must, therefore, be a fundamental category in this style of analysis, rather than form. As described above, people may participate in broadly similar behavioural forms and yet recognize differences not apparent on the surface and invest those forms with an enormous range of meanings which can be mutually exclusive. Understanding the boundary creating significance of these meanings enables responsive leadership.

Our mental images of the world are more than miniature projected pictures of what our optical nerves receive. They are interpreted and categorized significations. Applying this semiotic understanding of knowing to the particular network of signs or symbols that is a congregation allows the leader new and vital insight into the task of management. This is a way to establish, in Geertz's terms,[25] a 'thick description' of congregational culture and how that culture has 'read' its environment.

Such an analysis will uncover more than the aspects of a congregation that are embedded in doctrinal formulations and the requirements of formal organizational membership. It will look beyond behaviour to the meanings that are uniquely framed within the congregation's life as a coherent system. This will allow access to that elusive area of activity and understanding that is usually only described through the skills, feelings and intuitions of the experienced 'reflective practitioner,'[26] for as Bosch puts it:

> People do not only need truth (theory, theoria) and justice (praxis), they also need beauty (poiesis), the rich resources of symbol, piety, worship, love, awe, and mystery.[27]

These symbolic ways of viewing reality, worked out in the local context, defy easy regulation and classification, but they demand recognition since they are fundamental to a congregation's effective ministry and mission.[28]

Congregation as narrative

Ordained ministers often bemoan the reluctance of many worshippers to engage in study groups, or the difficulty even longstanding, devout members have in expressing themselves in theological concepts. The analysis offered here, however, suggests that formal conceptual standards are not the only ones that require appreciation if the complex interactions of a congregation are to be better understood. Because a particular kind of thinking comes hard does not necessarily mean that there is no deeply significant thinking taking place. The style of thinking that is paramount in a congregation is a storytelling and anecdotal one. It is not linear and self-consciously reflective, nor is it correlative or of a 'theory to practice' nature, but it is nonetheless thinking. The significance of this style of thinking in its own right must be acknowledged if a congregation's culture is to be understood. It is a foolish leader indeed who simply ignores these things. Or to put it more positively, the large amount of time any local church minister spends in listening to anecdotes, gossip, personal histories, and the like, is a core part of the reflective skills of leadership. The popular and widespread social suspicion that equates storytelling with falsehood and is over-dependent on 'the plain facts' in a mechanistic sense[29] must be challenged by a more multi-layered estimation of persons as social actors and interpreters.

Following Hauerwas, I believe that stories and their consequent metaphors provide the lenses through which people describe the world. In Hauerwas's words, stories show,

> How we should 'look on' ourselves, others and the world, in ways that rules taken in themselves do not. Stories and metaphors do this by providing the narrative accounts that give our lives coherence.[30]

Stories are, therefore, of primary importance in the creation of a sense of a person's own identity and the skilled leader gives them their full weight in order that his or her leadership is received as empathetic and motivational . As Stephen Crites maintains,[31] what kind of story a person believes to have been enacted in the events of that person's own life is determinative of identity. Similarly, stories disclose new possibilities since they allow imaginative projection into the future in a way that conceptual analysis based on what already is, cannot.[32] This ability of story to allow life to be construed in a certain way is immensely creative and enables (for good and ill) the images and fantasies hidden within us to surface.[33] Story is another facet of boundary creation and maintenance. Cupitt puts it this way:

> As animals mark out their territories with urine and other scents, so we cover the world with language; and as dogs live in a world of smells so we live in a world of words. By symbolically 'marking' and structuring experience, and above all by telling stories, we have slowly turned a barren wilderness of white noise into a habitable world.[34]

In a sense, story is the Christian *theoria*, expressed not in metaphysical ideas but in the practicalities of a wisdom that is lived.[35] So it is proper for a Christian missiologist like Newbigin to describe the person of a Christian as one who 'will seek faithfully both to tell the story and – as part of a Christian congregation – so conduct her life as to embody the truth of the story.'[36] This is more than the application of disembodied conceptual truths. The narrative is the interpretation and it extends beyond the confines of what can be expressed as formal dogma. Indeed, the stories that are embedded in the symbols of a congregation may well find their origin outside the accepted canon of Christian belief and practice. One of the frustrations of leadership within churches as perceived by the theologically articulate is the relative weakness of Christian symbols in the determination of meaning in a congregation as against meanings framed with other symbols. On the basis that it is essential that leadership works with what is actually present, rather than institutional expectations of what should be present, leaders need to ask themselves again and again what stories actually predominate here? What I am arguing for is a clear recognition as a vital skill that reflective talent in ministerial leadership that has often gone unregarded.

What kind of evidence?

The narrative that this perspective seeks to analyse is made explicit not only in what people say but also in the rituals and artifacts that are shared in a variety of ways. A situational analysis that is framed in the widest terms is required, which can bring to light meanings that generally go unnoticed. What is aimed at is what Mudge and Poling term 'a humble – watchful and listening – hermeneutic',[37] that expectantly approaches the signs or symbols that each community generates 'in its setting'. I understand this to be part of that style of leadership that is reflective in its determination of policy and understanding. Methods appropriate to that style are those that are based on a willingness to listen patiently and assess as well as dynamically intervene. They will include participant observation that looks for behaviour patterns, types of meetings, methods of organization, styles of response, and the like, both in formal and informal meetings and services. Those methods will require the noting of anecdotes, stories and sayings that are frequently repeated either in the congregations or about the congregations. Alongside these elements, an examination of artifacts and the physical organization of church buildings will also yield clues. From this kind of data patterns will begin to emerge – things will recur at various levels and over time, correlations will be apparent, consistencies and inconsistencies will appear, and the meanings that are attributed to things will become evident. It might be objected that the good leader does this in an unsystematic way all the time, but that is my point – adding some systematic cultural analysis greatly increases the usefulness of what is otherwise a very hit-and-miss affair.

Simply put, my contention is that it is a key management skill to discern what narratives are being expressed in the life of a congregation. Once acknowledged and recognized, such discernment empowers leadership through an increased awareness of the particularities of belonging, identity and meanings being expressed in the life of a local church. This in turn becomes both motivating of collaborative effort and increases the possibility of positive change. A similar analysis is also likely to be useful in many other institutions.

Conclusion

A cultural perspective challenges straightforward theory-to-practice kind of thinking. The tendency is to assume that if people knew verbal formulations and conceptual truths they would automatically experience the truth. Similarly, it is sometimes assumed that policy documents, procedural manuals and the like will inevitably achieve a uniformity of behaviour or performance. Teaching right doctrine, or instituting the right organizational plans, is seen as an inevitable precursor of positive progress. What this perspective suggests is that although doctrine and organization are of course very important, they are weakened in their effectiveness if symbolic, meaning-creating, aspects are ignored. People experience religion much more easily than they explain it. Congregations have symbolic accounts of themselves that are recognizable and into which people can be assimilated. Through a language of belonging that is meaningful in relationship to their own experience and historical situations people identify themselves as the 'we' of a congregation. This is to put meaning and belonging as the absolute fundamentals of congregational existence, and that is a theological issue, after all the words 'Kirche', 'Kirk', and 'Church' are all based on the Greek *Kyriakoi*, which simply means those who 'belong' to the Lord.[38]

People do not believe what makes no sense to them and as I have argued they use stories and symbols as the bridge between reality experienced and their personal and group 'making sense' of that reality. People create a symbolic construction of their intimate allegiances that itself becomes a motivating symbol. For example, the congregation of a church threatened numerous times with closure by denominational authorities might develop a strong sense of identity around 'seeing-off' those authorities. Out of that, faith might come to be seen primarily as something of great tenacity and loyalty. And this in turn might motivate the people towards development and growth 'against all the odds'.

Although individuals understand faith differently, symbols and stories allow those differences not only to co-exist but to be subsumed, to some degree, in a corporate story. Within that story the absolute demands of faith exist alongside an easier and more accommodating perspective. Theology and theologies exist in tension but together. This means it is not the case that only congregations whose membership shares the same social outlook and backgrounds can function effectively. There is, of course, a danger in this in that a cosy sense of belonging can lead to a kind of cultural parochialism that totally obscures the demands and challenges of the Kingdom of God. Awareness of that danger is another reason for pursuing this kind of analysis.

Since particular congregations function as sub-cultures in their own right it is not possible to simply assume that reality categories that apply in one instance will automatically apply in another. Congregations are, in McFadyen's expression, 'proximate contexts of communication',[39] and this is both a strength and a weakness. It is a strength in that it can allow a high level of personhood and commitment to develop. It is a weakness in that the very firmness and meaningfulness of close interaction can establish yet another boundary that would-be members have to negotiate. Hopewell says that critical to the cultural analysis of a congregation

> ... is the discovery of significant motifs, or themes, that through their conscious and unconscious repetition by church members sanction the world view, ethos and praxis of the parish.[40]

Inevitably these motifs can produce not only security but a certain cosiness and complacency. A key leadership task is to signal when that is happening. On the positive side, security of identity provides an environment where new meanings can be experimented with without threat. To create room for this to happen is another key leadership task.

Because symbols do decay and lose their power, it is all too possible for a congregation to be left with little more than 'empty shells of fragmentary memories'.[41] Coupled with this, there is nowadays a loss of symbolic sensitivity in a world of increasing literalism.[42] Empty symbols and literalized symbols can no longer bear the story-making enterprise that is so vital. Writing of organizational culture in the business world, Edgar Schein said,

> One of the crucial functions of leadership is to provide guidance at precisely those times when habitual ways of doing things no longer work, or when a dramatic change in the environment requires new responses.[43]

It is the role of a local church leader to offer just such constructive criticisms and alternatives in the culture of the congregations he or she serves. Discovering what narrative is operating and working with it sensitively and carefully becomes a key task that allows a way into the deepest understandings of the people in a congregation. Acknowledging that stories and symbols are local and particular, and therefore not easily transportable, eases many of the frustrations of managing and leading. This is 'local knowledge' that has to be learnt. My conviction is that the effort involved in this style of analysis is often rewarded by an insightful appreciation of what a congregation achieves in the lives of people. Such insight adds a vital perspective to leadership.

References

1. Grace Davie, *Religion in Britain since 1945: Believing without Belonging* (Oxford: Blackwell, 1994).
2. For example, consider Eddie Gibbs, *I Believe in Church Growth* (London: Hodder & Stoughton, 1990).
3. Peter Cotterell, *Mission and Meaninglessness: The Good News in a World of Suffering and Disorder* (London: SPCK, 1990), p. 148.
4. Jackson W. Carrol, Carl S. Dudley & William McKinney (eds.), *Handbook for Congregational Studies* (Nashville: Abingdon Press, 1986), p. 11.
5. James F. Hopewell, *Congregation* (London: SCM Press, 1988).
6. Don Cupitt, *What is a Story?* (London: SCM Press, 1991).
7. Richard H. Niebuhr, 'The Story of our Life', in Stanley Hauerwas and L. Gregory Jones (eds.), *Why Narrative? Readings in Narrative Theology* (Grand Rapids: Eerdmans, 1989 [1941]).
8. Robert J. Schreiter, *Constructing Local Theologies* (London: SCM Press, 1985).
9. Quoted by Schreiter, *Constructing Local Theologies*, p. 56).
10. See Schreiter, *Constructing Local Theologies*.
11. Anthony P. Cohen, *The Symbolic Construction of Community* (London: Routledge, 1985), p. 17.
12. Lewis Mudge and James Poling, *Formation and Reflection: The Promise of Practical Theology* (Philadelphia: Fortress Press, 1987), p. 107.
13. Charles B. Handy, *Understanding Voluntary Organisations* (Harmondsworth: Penguin, 1988).
14. Richard L. Daft, *Organization Theory and Design* (St Paul: West Publishing, 3rd edn., 1989).
15. Edgar H. Schein, 'Coming to a New Awareness of Organisational Culture', *Sloan Management Review* (Winter 1984), pp. 3–16.
16. Schein, 'Coming to a New Awareness', p. 3.
17. Clifford Geertz, *Local Knowledge: Further Essays in Interpretive Anthropology* (New York: Basic Books, 1983).
18. Geertz, *Local Knowledge*, p. 58.
19. Geertz, *Local Knowledge*, p. 58.
20. Hopewell, *Congregation*.
21. Cohen, *Symbolic Construction*, p. 118.
22. Cohen, *Symbolic Construction*, p. 20.

23. Cohen, *Symbolic Construction*, p. 44.
24. Cohen, *Symbolic Construction*, p. 44.
25. Geertz, *Local Knowledge*.
26. Donald A. Shön, *Educating the Reflective Practitioner* (New York: Josey-Bass, 1987).
27. David Bosch, *Transforming Mission: Paradigm Shifts in Theology of Mission* (New York: Orbis, 1991), p. 431.
28. Mudge and Poling, *Formation*, p. 107.
29. See John M. Hull, *What Prevents Christian Adults from Learning?* (London: SCM Press, 1985).
30. Stanley Hauerwas, *Vision and Virtue* (Notre Dame, Indiana: Fides, 1974), p. 71.
31. Quoted by Michael Goldberg, *Theology and Narrative: A Critical Introduction* (Philadelphia: Trinity Press, 2nd edn.. 1991), p. 12.
32. David Tracy, *Blessed Rage for Order* (New York: Seabury Press, 1975), p. 207.
33. Mudge and Poling, p. 40.
34. Cupitt, *What Is a Story?* p. 90.
35. Groome in Mudge and Poling, *Formation*, p. 72.
36. Lesslie Newbigin, *The Gospel in a Pluralist Society* (London: SPCK 1989), p. 82.
37. Mudge and Polling, *Formation*, p. 159.
38. Robert P. Roth, *The Theater of God: Story in Christian Doctrine* (Philadelphia: Fortress Press, 1985).
39. Alistair I. McFadyen. *The Call to Personhood: A Christian Theory of the Individual in Social Relationships* (Cambridge: CUP, 1990), p. 261.
40. Hopewell, *Congregation*, p. 30.
41. F. W. Dillistone, *The Power of Symbols* (London: SCM Press, 1986), p. 213.
42. Thomas Fawcett, *The Symbolic Language of Religion* (London: SCM Press, 1970), p. 264.
43. Schein, 'Coming to a New Awareness', p. 9.

12

Who sees the vision?

ELIZABETH WELCH

Introduction

I would like to explore the role of leadership and management in those churches that have traditionally looked to decision-making as a function of the whole people of God acting together, rather than as focused in particular individuals. After a brief look at the historic origins of the Free Churches as these have affected questions of leadership, I will examine one significant issue in front of the church in this country today – the decline in their membership – in order to look further at questions of leadership and management.

Historical background to leadership

Historically, the Free Churches in England and Wales have had an ambivalent attitude towards leadership. The Reformation in England took a different route to that of the Reformation in much of continental Europe. The Church of England maintained the episcopal structure of the church, a structure that was perceived by non-conformists in the mid to late seventeenth century as being overly hierarchical. The dissenters from this period stood for certain aspects of church life such as the freedom to order their worship for themselves.

The Christian traditions in England that broke away from the

Church of England were rooted in the sense of the need to break away from what was perceived as the hierarchical structure of that church and to form bodies that were non-hierarchical. This often led to a tension between the struggle against non-hierarchical leadership and the need for strong-willed prophetic individuals in order to carry this struggle forward. This leadership by strong-willed individuals was also held in tension by the desire to have maximum participation in decision-making by the whole people of God in each place. I would like to explore the consequences of these issues, in order to open up questions of leading and managing in relation to prophecy and participation.

The United Reformed Church has its roots in the dissenting tradition of church life in England. In this tradition, 1662 and the Act of Uniformity, requiring conformity to the *Book of Common Prayer*, were held to be major setbacks for Christian life in this country and are still referred to in this way in some parts of the Free Churches. There are United Reformed Churches that point with pride to their origins in time of persecution as '1662 churches'. This sense of pride stands in contrast to a sermon heard a few years ago from an Anglican vicar, where he referred to 1662 marking the great leap forward for the English church and being a valued landmark in the history of the church.

Historical origins of contemporary thinking on leadership

This tradition of dissent has several emphases to it, which have historically affected ideas of leadership and still play a role in the life of the church today. I want to look at four of these strands in order to reflect on the influence that they have had for the Free Churches today in thinking about leadership, authority and management. These emphases are:

- a resistance to a hierarchical understanding of authority;
- a focus on the authority of each congregation;
- a sense of independency of one congregation from another;

- a valuing of the participation of the whole people of God in decision-making.

One emphasis in the history of dissent had to do with a resistance to a hierarchical understanding of authority. This had a particular focus against the personal authority of bishops, or indeed anyone outside the local congregation who might seek to wield authority. Bishops were seen as those who imposed views of the life of the church on the local people, rather than leaving the local folk to make up their own minds or be obedient to their own consciences. However, this did not prevent individual dissenting charismatic leaders exercising sway over people across the country.

The other side of this anti-hierarchical emphasis was an emphasis on the authority of the local congregation in having rights over its own faith and life. Congregationalists, Baptists and Quakers all in varying ways stood for the power of the people of God in each place, gathered together under the guidance of the Holy Spirit, to make decisions for themselves. The only external authority was Holy Scripture.

This emphasis on congregationalism led to a sense of independency in each place, where each congregation was self-sufficient and had no need of other congregations in order fully to be the Body of Christ. The unity of the church consisted in the people of God in each place being faithful to the gospel and was seen as needing no visible bonds in order to be held together in unity with those in other places.

A further emphasis was on the sense of the participation of the whole people of God in decision-making. 'Church meeting' – the gathering of the local believers together to discern the mind of Christ for that community – was at the heart of the church's life. In church meeting, all could speak and as church meeting voted, so the community lived. However, if there was a strong individual in the church meeting, that individual could sway the whole. On the other hand, if there was an individual who voiced strong ideas outside the church meeting, there was the safeguard for the church that these ideas should only be put into action if church meeting agreed. These four emphases led to a particular understanding of leadership within the life of the Free Churches, an understanding that nevertheless had some ambivalence about it.

Leadership couldn't be imposed from outside, because this was seen as too authoritarian and cut against the freedom of each individual to make up his or her own mind on matters of conscience. Yet congregations were dependent on strong-willed individuals, coming from either within or without the local congregation, to sustain a tradition of dissent.

The congregation had supreme authority, which gave strength to the gathered people of God in each place. Yet wider insights from outside were limited and the possibility of sharing resources across a regional area depended on the goodwill of any one congregation. Special appeals could be made from one congregation to another in times of need, but there was not a strong sense of mutual accountability to one another.

Independency encouraged rugged individualism. This had the strength of developing good quality local leadership in each place. However, without a strong local leader, congregations faltered. There were also questions as to the way in which leadership could be shared, either within the congregation or across congregations.

Participation of each individual in decision-making gave a sense of ownership to each decision that was made. When this worked well, the life of the congregation as a whole was well developed. However, it could be a slow way of working in which the impetus of enthusiastic personal leadership became dissipated. There were also occasions when it led to tensions between strong local leaders and congregations who disagreed with the directions being proposed. In some instances, these cases of disagreement led to splits within the congregation and a further separate congregation being established.

The origins of the dissenting traditions within this country lay in an era in which religious and civil authority was held closely together. This had a consequential effect on the lives of both non-conformists and Roman Catholics, whose civic freedoms were limited because of non-adherence to the established church. The establishment of 'dissenting academies' for the training of non-conformist ministers, a result of restrictions on non-conformist attendance at universities, is one example of this limitation of civil freedom. The limitations put upon non-conformists served to strengthen the sense of independency and the sense of a non-hierarchical approach.

Challenges for non-conformity

The dilemma for the dissenting traditions of the church in this country became clear at the beginning of this century. The early decades of the century saw a radical decline in Free Church churchgoing, a decline only paralleled more recently in the Church of England and the Roman Catholic Church. A primary cause of this decline was that there was no longer a need to dissent. The victories of freedom in worship and in civic life that had been struggled for over the past couple of centuries had now been won. The laws of the land had been changed and Free Church people were accepted in most walks of life.

In some parts of the Free Churches this has led on the one hand to an uncertainty about identity and on the other hand to a vigorous holding on to structures that reflected the hard-won battles of certain periods in history. In some cases, the churches that have had a strong local grassroots orientation have developed regional and national structures. However, the sense of participation of the whole people of God in the decision-making life of the church, at whatever level, has been retained, rather than an emphasis on personal leadership being developed.

The United Reformed Church came into being in 1972 when Congregationalists and Presbyterians decided to unite. Not all Congregationalists came into the new church. The tradition of independency meant that individual congregations were free to decide not to join if they believed that this was right for them.

In 1982, a further union occurred with the Churches of Christ. These unions were part of a desire to find a new way forward for the church and yet have also led to a searching for a new sense of identity to undergird the new church.

In the United Reformed Church, as in the Methodist Church, the desire to hold personal authority in check has led to the development of strong national structures. In the Methodist Church, a strong connectional structure has developed, emphasizing a sense of mutual belonging through the councils of the church, rather than through a personally exercised leadership. This structure has its focus in the annual meetings of the national conference, while having at the same time a strong grassroots emphasis with the structures of local circuits in each area, grouped together in 36 districts across the country as a whole.

In the United Reformed Church, the national structure has certain similarities, with some differences in terms of where authority lies and in the size of area bodies. There is a national General Assembly, which meets each year, twelve provinces, between them covering the country as a whole and, within these provinces, a total of seventy-two district councils. Certain authority is given to each of these bodies, but there is still a focus in the authority of the church meeting in each place as the meeting that decides about the life of each congregation.

These national structures have continued to emphasize the participation by the whole people of God in decision-making. This participation has been widened from the conception of each congregation making decisions for itself, to the sense of the councils of the church contributing to the decision-making process for the church as a whole. In the United Reformed Church, this still leads to some interesting debates as to where the weight of authority lies. One of these occurred recently when a district council held that because it had discussed a certain issue and taken a vote prior to the meeting of General Assembly, this was the decision that should be sustained, rather than that of General Assembly, which happened to have gone in the opposite direction.

The traditional emphases on being non-hierarchical and participatory have become formalized in national structures that, in conciliar terms, could be seen to have developed their own hierarchical emphasis. From the perspective of the life of the local congregation, the General Assembly can seem a far removed body with little direct relevance to the grassroots life of the local church. Even the district council (often the size of a county area) can feel like 'those out there who are other than us and yet make decisions for us'.

Applying for a small grant becomes a tortuous matter, needing to be discussed by the local congregation in its elders' and church meetings, the district council executive, the district council and finally, finding approval in the meeting of the provincial finance committee.

It is interesting to note that the important principle of the participation of the whole people of God in decisions that affect people's lives and the consequent ownership of those decisions by each person in each place can become eroded when it becomes too formalized. Two difficulties emerge. First, decisions can only be made slowly. This leads to a sense of a lack of dynamism in the life of the church. Secondly, a lack of distinction between different kinds of issues can emerge. If everything needs to be discussed by everyone, the colour of the walls in a meeting room becomes as important as the mission and outreach of the church.

Authority – corporate or personal?

This sense of a 'conciliar hierarchy' has to a certain extent replaced the sense of the 'personal hierarchy' against which our ancestors in the dissenting tradition struggled. And yet there is still the sense of the people in each place giving weight to their own authority for their own lives. This can lead to a lack of clarity about authority. In some parts of the United Reformed Church it is as if people no longer understand what it is possible for them to do, or not to do, because they do not have a sufficiently coherent idea of the church and its structures to know what's theirs to do and what needs permission!

The emphasis on the participation of the whole people of God in corporate decision-making, whether the body be the local church meeting or the national General Assembly, leads to an interesting discussion about the relationship between management and leadership. This discussion has a particular focus on the balance between corporate and individual aspects of management and leadership.

At one level, the United Reformed Church could be said to be a well-managed body. The finances nationally are in good shape (at the time of writing); there are resources available to undertake new initiatives; the structures are clearly laid out – it might take a while to make a decision, but it is clear who should be involved in decision-making along the way; many different people participate in the various decisions that need to be made about the life of the church – through the committees or the councils of the church.

And yet this church, along with the other mainstream churches in this country, is in a time of decline. There are not enough ministers to serve all the congregations; a certain number of church buildings are in need of radical repairs; membership of the churches is both declining and ageing.

There is an interesting question in the life of the church about whose responsibility it is to turn the organization around. At the heart of the matter is the sense that the future lies in God's hands; that the church has only survived for so long through the work of the Holy Spirit and through the lives of those people who have faithfully followed in the footsteps of Jesus Christ. Should we, therefore, leave the future up to God, and carry on as we are? And yet we believe that God works within the created world and through the lives of men and women. If the church is the Body of Christ, then the body will survive and not just slowly decline into oblivion.

But does the church have a responsibility to help the work of the Holy Spirit? And is the exercise of this responsibility found in management? Does God lead the church directly through the action of the Holy Spirit, or are individual people or the councils of the church necessary that this leadership may happen?

Managing decline or developing growth?

One of the West Midlands' district councils of the United Reformed Church has recently begun a programme at its meetings, entitled 'The future of the church – managing decline or developing growth?' (At the district council meetings, there are lay representatives of each of the United Reformed Churches in that district, as well as the ministers of each church.) One of the questions to emerge is that of 'who takes the lead in raising these issues?' Is it up to each local congregation to look at its own decline? What kind of role does the district have in relation to the congregations to stimulate thinking about decline?

The district, through the pastoral committee, has the responsibility of allocating ministry to churches, in terms of saying whether a congregation can have a minister of its own, or whether congregations need to share ministers with each other. One of the discussions that has emerged is about whether ministry should be allocated to points of growth, rather than to churches in decline.

The district council had already tried to look at developing a mission strategy for the district three or four years previously. A day consultation had been held, and yet the subject had not been pursued further until the proposal for the present programme.

When looking at why the first course of action had not been pursued and yet the second course had, it was clear that it was to do with change of personnel. The people concerned were not part of the structures of the district council, but interested individuals within the life of the district council. In the first instance, the minister who had put forward the proposals for a mission strategy had retired and moved out of the area. In the second instance, the programme was spearheaded by a particular individual engaged in inner-city ministry, who wanted to raise questions for the district as a whole.

In both management and leadership terms, it seemed that the district council was only able to act in pursuing new directions when particular individuals took up the cause and were prepared to give time to pursuing it. The district council gave much time, through its officers and committees, to running the ongoing life of the district. Agendas were always very full. There was rarely enough time for lengthy discussion on any one particular area of concern. When it came to raising a major issue before the churches as a whole, such as the area of decline, it was dependent on particular people other than the officers raising this issue. Then there also needed to be a radical change to the agenda of each meeting to enable discussion to take place.

This example raises the issue as to whether those in the structures of the church can, in themselves, do any more than manage the work immediately in front of them. In a church which believes in the participation of the whole people of God in decision-making, the matters that come on to an agenda of a meeting can be very extensive. If there is a sense that each matter has equal weight, then it becomes hard to give priority and time on the agenda, to any one matter over another.

The question that was put in the programme heading 'managing decline or developing growth?' carried an implication that management was concerned with the better use of diminishing resources, rather than with turning the picture round in order to stimulate the future of the church.

This raises an interesting question about the contrast between management and leadership. Management is seen as that which is to do with maintaining the status quo, and leadership to do with moving an organization on, in sometimes radical new directions. It seemed that, in this example, in terms of the structures of the district council, this was the case. It was only when particular individuals emerged to give leadership that new directions materialized.

The district, through its pastoral committee, had already been wrestling with questions of diminishing resources and how to make best use of these resources. Whenever a minister moved on from a church, examination was given both to the needs of the church and the needs of the district as a whole in terms of ministry. Questions of the finance needed to fund ministry were shared across the churches of the district, in order that lack of finance would not be a bar to having a minister.

There was a certain tension experienced with regard to the district council having a role in management. Certain local churches felt that it was inappropriate for people outside their particular church to have a role in determining future possibilities for the life of that church. Other people within the district council felt that the district should play a stronger part in managing the available resources. There was a question as to whether talking in terms of management was felt to be a right use of the church's time and thinking – is not the role of the church to be depending on prayer and the direct work of the Holy Spirit?

It was clear that management was being engaged in, in terms of using the diminishing resources effectively. There was an acknowledgement that congregations could not just be sufficient for themselves, but needed to share resources and mutual support with one another. Yet this management role of the district council had not in itself led to the underlying questions facing the church being addressed. The decline of the church was being responded to, but in a way that endeavoured to maintain the status quo, rather than to look for more radical options for the future of the church. Here we are looking at the particular area of decline in the life of the church, in order to reflect further on the areas of leadership and management and participation.

If management is about facilitating the best use of available resources in order to further the aims of the organization, the United Reformed Church has endeavoured, within the terms of its ethos and self-understanding, to develop good management. It has held together the concept of the participation of the whole people of God in the decision-making life of the church with the development of an organization that went wider than individual congregations or local groupings of churches. It has endeavoured to ensure that each congregation has at least some share of a minister and that there is the finance available to fund the ministers in post. New ways of grouping and sharing ministry are being raised. Patterns for the development of local leadership are being looked at. The development of a partnered self-appraisal scheme for each minister has just been agreed nationally. A new pattern of in-service training is being developed, with some discussion as to whether it might be possible for it to become compulsory for each minister.

However, there have been two drawbacks to this management approach, when it comes to responding to fundamental change. First, the structure of the church has been unable to respond to the diminishing size of the church. The regional and national organization of the life of the church has reflected a time when the membership has been double the present figures. While there has been some pruning with regard to national and regional committee structures, the basic four-tier system (local congregation, district council, province and general assembly) has remained in place. This has led to a structure which feels top-heavy and in which the people at the grassroots feel at a distance from the centre. It is also an interesting development for a church which had its origins in a non-hierarchical approach to the organization of the church.

Secondly, the church's ability to respond to major shifts in pattern of church-going has been limited. While the objective of managing existing resources in a declining church has been a priority and has been responded to creatively in many places, the tackling of a more fundamental and underlying issue with regard to the future of the church has not been as easy. This is perhaps not surprising when those who hold office within an organization have as their objective sustaining the life of the organization, rather than seeking new directions which mean engaging in radical change.

Responding to decline – management or leadership?

The question then becomes, 'Does a response to the decline of the church require management or leadership?' At one level, the need for management is obvious. Declining resources need to be shared and in order to share these across several congregations and across the church nationally a strategy needs to be drawn up and implemented. There are many creative initiatives, not least those which led to a wider sense of ecumenical sharing, both in looking at the problem of decline and looking at the resources of people and buildings and finance that are available to the churches across the board, in order to see whether these can be better shared. Declining resources require new ways of looking at patterns of ministry, at training for changing models of ministry, at lay participation. However, if managing decline was all an organization was concerned with, it would seem possible to manage an organization very successfully to the point of its ultimate demise.

There is a larger issue at stake here. This issue is about the overall vision for an organization and its future. The answer to the question 'responding to decline – management or leadership?' is then found not in management alone, but also in leadership. Without the leadership that sees the vision and that carries people with that vision, the important work of management can become diminished and more concerned with the organization as it is, especially in a time of crisis, rather than the organization as it might be.

There are two components of leadership. The first is about having a vision and giving direction. The second is about being able to take people along. In order for leadership to be effective, both these components need to be in place. There is a dilemma experienced by those in a particular part of the dissenting Free Church tradition in relation to leadership, as referred to earlier in this article. The emphasis on participation by the whole people of God in the life of the church at every level has a limiting effect on the exercise of personal leadership. Having a vision and giving direction do not always fit easily in to the work of committees and councils.

The history of the Free Churches has nevertheless been dependent on particular individuals exercising considerable leadership, often independent of any structure or organization. Yet the organization of the Free Churches today seems to give more weight to the importance of the participation of the whole people of God in the life of the church than the need for particular charismatic individuals to exercise leadership, whether these individuals be officers of the church or prophetic voices within the church.

In the United Reformed Church, the safeguards against the misuse of personal power have built in a system which mitigates against the exercise of personal authority. The Moderator of General Assembly, the nationally elected figurehead of the church, is elected on a one-off basis for one year at a time, and combines this office with his or her normal other responsibilities. In the district councils, the presidents serve for one or two years only, in a very part-time capacity. The people in the structures of the church who have the most potential for exercising leadership are the twelve provincial moderators. These are full-time appointments, in the first instance for seven years, and then renewable for a further five years. In a time of retrenchment, leading to uncertainty about the future of the church, a greater sense of caution about the exercise of personal initiatives arises. The voice of prophetic individuals is muted when there is a high level of anxiety about the organization and its current directions.

If authority is held within councils and committees, there is a question as to who takes the lead in developing the vision. Councils and committees need motivated individuals to enable them to work. The role of any one council or committee is often seen as being to tackle particular pieces of work, rather than to have a view of the organization as a whole. This more limited view mitigates against setting overall directions. Councils and committees are dependent on the people who are appointed to them. There is an interesting balance to be struck between those who have been going to a particular meeting for many years and whose insights are conditioned by the issues that have developed in that one meeting, and those who come in new and take time to find their way into the issues and concerns on the agenda. The discussion that can ensue between people at the different ends of the spectrum can slow down the development of a new vision for the organization. Effective leadership, which takes an organization forward, needs a person and a voice as well as a sense of corporate accountability.

Leadership and participation

It is interesting to note that the hard-won freedoms of a participatory democracy, for which the Free Churches have historically been influential in campaigning, are seen to be of diminishing significance in England today. In Scotland and Wales, local participation in public life has found a new direction with the two recent referenda about some measure of self-government. In England, voting at local elections is at an all time low, membership of political parties and trade unions is on the wane and there has been a sense of devaluing of those who hold political power. The sense of the importance of participating in public life is diminishing.

This sense of the diminishment of the desire for participation in public life is paralleled in the Free Churches with the diminishment of the desire for participation in the councils of the church. In the United Reformed Church attendance at church meetings is going down. There is uncertainty amongst some about the value of the wider councils of the church.

Yet the importance of the participation of people in decisions that affect their lives has been a strong part of Free Church thinking and remains so today. The need to gain the assent of the whole people of God for the direction the church takes can increase the commitment of the whole people to that direction. This needs discernment as to the areas of life and faith that genuinely affect the whole people of God in contrast to particular issues that can be delegated to individuals and committees to work on. The development of policy-making and strategy is an area in which particular individuals have a key role. Yet the effectiveness of the policy depends on the ownership by the whole people. Personal leadership in the church needs to be rooted within that sense of the participation of the whole people if it is to be effective. But leadership needs to be personal if it is to be leadership.

This effective personal leadership is based on openness, trust and mutual accountability. Openness means willingness for the leader to share thinking and reflecting with those who will be affected by any new direction. Trust means a leader having the confidence of those he or she is called to lead. This trust is both about open appointing procedures for those who hold office and about ongoing support for the leader once in post. Trust is also about the ability to discern those who exercise prophetic roles and listen to their voices.

Mutual accountability means developing the kind of structures whereby both individuals and the people of God as a whole exercise responsibility for one another in a mutually creative and beneficial way. Decisions need to be owned. Even in the church, there is a financial bottom-line. With limited resources, those that are available need to be used constructively in a way that is supported by those who provide the resources.

Effective leadership is about giving life to an organization. In the life of the church, a body committed to the fullness of life, the question 'is this individual or committee or council or meeting life-giving?' is an interesting one to reflect on. For the church to move from decline to growth, the question of new life, the life of Christ, is central.

This new life is the gift of the Holy Spirit, and is found in prayer and worship. The Holy Spirit comes to give freedom to the people of God. Yet, the first actions of the early church after Pentecost were those of mutual accountability for those in need and for the mission of the church. Leadership is a gift of the Holy

Spirit which is prayed for in the life of the church. The exercise of leadership involves particular people. The results of effective leadership involve good management.

Conclusion

I have endeavoured to look at questions of leadership and participation in the Free Churches in order to discern directions for the church today. I have looked at the historical understanding of leadership and participation in the Free Churches and the way that understanding has developed today, in order to argue for a renewed sense of personal leadership. The context of the exercise of this personal leadership in the midst of the life of the whole people of God is one of the insights of the Free Churches offered to the ecumenical movement.

In a time of change in the life of the church, the exercise of effective leadership is an important ecumenical issue. For the church to face the challenges of the late twentieth century, it is important to share insights, experiences and resources from the different Christian traditions, in order that together the churches may be strengthened for the tasks that lie ahead in the new millennium.

13

Organizational transformation

BRUCE REED

This chapter is the result of a number of transformations which I have encountered in my work in conferences and activities which concentrated on learning by experience methodologies. These transformations are summed up in the behaviour coming from a change in understanding the meaning and use of various concepts. Among them can be listed: the shift from 'individual' to 'person', seeing how system and culture interact continuously, knowing when to ignore boundaries; discarding competition as the condition for growth and survival and replacing it with co-operation, and understanding about working in role leading to the ability to distinguish between power and authority.

Since 1963, when I was first introduced to the 'Tavistock Method' of group relations, developed originally by Ken Rice, Harold Bridger, Eric Trist and Pierre Turquet at the Tavistock Institute of Human Relations, I have been trying to find concepts which made sense of my experience in organizational settings.

These theoretical concepts became the key for describing 'the unconscious structuring and conscious organization of working groups'.[1] Those of us who work in the study of organizations are too easily aware of the way concepts lose their freshness and shape and become meaningless jargon. As I worked my way progressively as member, staff and director through these learning by experience modes, it was essential to recall that they were ideas-in-the-mind, and their only valid use was their capacity to encapsulate the meaning and the feeling of actual experience. In this process, I was able to experience a number of transformations only through constant wrestling with the dynamic differences between concepts which just enabled me to avoid the fate decreed by the Zen master quoted by Gregory Bateson, 'To become accustomed to anything is a terrible thing.'[2]

The pressure to sustain the air of 'strangeness' about these ideas came from the work of myself and my colleagues as consultants to managers in business, government, church and voluntary bodies. For example, we needed concepts to use in organizational role analysis with managers, a method of one-to-one consultation with a consultant away from their place of work. The task for managers was to become more aware of the constructs by which they were habitually construing their working environment and their role in it, by studying their own description of their actual working experience. However if my own use of constructs became second-hand to me by losing touch with my own felt experience, they would then be at best third-hand for the client and add no value at all to the manager's understanding of his experience.

I have selected a number of these points of learning, but I recognize that by presenting them here they are only likely to be perceived by the reader as '...the trial and error process through which the individual adapts to his environment, finding a new response or pattern of responses to a given situation or stimulus'. This is 'Learning I' of Gregory Bateson's levels of learning theory. Most of what I need to say indicates my own experience of Level II: 'a corrective change in the set of alternatives from which a choice is made, or a change of how the sequence of experience is punctuated', though on rare occasions I experienced what he described as 'Learning III', which is '. . . a change in the process of Learning II, a corrective change in the system of sets of alternatives from which choice is made'. I hope that what follows will throw light on the denseness of these definitions and might put readers in touch with their own parallel experiences.

The following interacting theoretical concepts, by their similarities and differences, encapsulate a variety of my organizational experiences.

Person / Individual

Common social definitions of human beings are individual and person. Other ideas which cluster around these two also include psyche, mind, ego, soul and spirit. What concerns us here is the experience of someone who thinks of himself/herself as person (or individual) and how that someone is experienced by others as a person (or individual).

To experience oneself as a person makes one aware of a sense of participation in a 'wider field of the experience of others, a feeling of empathy, indwelling, participation, resonance. To experience oneself as an individual makes one aware of one's own unique needs and interests, to be aware of one's identity and private emotions like love, joy, satisfaction, fear, greed, anger.'

John Heron, however, would consider that the theoretical person or personhood is an emergent state of being and that the individual is one psychological mode of the emergent person. He defines person as '. . . the psyche in manifestation as an aware, developed being in whom all its modes are brought intentionally into play. A person in this sense is clearly an achievement.'[3] He proposes a '. . . basic polarity between an individuating function and a participatory one: the former makes for experience of individual distinctiveness, the latter for experience of unitive interaction with a whole field of being. These two poles do not exclude each other; instead the two functions interact along a continuum in which one is more dominant at one end and the other at the other end.'

He extends his theoretical model very widely to embrace the world in its various stages of social, historical and political development. My focus, alternatively, is on our current ordinary experience of life and organizational life in particular. I am in a constant process of 'reading' myself in my reactions to others, and I do this using the concepts of person and individual because they describe quite different sets of experiences, which in turn have a dramatic effect on my own and others' behaviour in organizations. For example, someone who is invited to become a manager may only see himself or herself as individual and may not even want the post because it will involve inter-personal (*sic*) skills, the quality of being a person.

As an individual I am unique and self-contained. I may agree with others but they don't belong to me or I to them. The characteristic is to look inwards, to claim being self-made where my inner world is barricaded against intrusions from the context, a resentment against becoming dependent. For individuals, therefore, institutions are frequently experienced as stifling, procrustean and deterministic. Under conditions of chaos and where people are bewildered, the individual can emerge as a free spirit, the self-motivated expert. Without realizing it or wanting it, such a one can become an unconscious focus for others, at least for a while.

A person is someone who is a nodal point of a network of relations with others. To the degree that I am a person, I can represent others and recognize my influence on them and upon their behaviour and development and in turn recognize their contribution to my own. I exemplify John Donne's concept of person, ' No man is an Island entire of itself . . . Every man is a piece of the Continent, a part of the main.'[4]

Erving Goffman points out two modes of feeling about one's relations with others which to some degree illustrate the distinction between being a person and being an individual.[5] The individual tries to avoid being 'committed' by circumstances. An immature boy and girl whose ill-considered actions have led to an unplanned pregnancy in Erving Goffman's terms, are committed to parenthood: a situation from which there is no way out. But a couple who cannot make a child and cannot become a father or mother may imagine themselves as if they were parents. In Goffman's terms they are attached to parenthood, even though they remain childless. Their attachment is a quality of being persons, compared with individual commitment. Goffman also identifies a third mode of relation calling it 'embracement', which is a positive condition brought about by a person harmonizing attachment with commitment to signify the wholeness of the person.

Both as person and as individual I can develop a sense of 'identity', but the word identity may be conceived differently, the person implying that identity relates to belonging, while the individual's identity relates to being.

What is important for managers is that they are in touch with their experience and thus able to sense the nature of their relations with others. The manager is likely to feel able to relate to those who are experienced as persons, while individuals may prove awkward. However such independent behaviour is what the manager needs at that time. In my experience individuals avoid being managers because it becomes boring and repetitious but embrace the possibility of running special projects where they work alone in the institution.

The same human being can change their way of thinking about themselves from being a member of a group, a corporate community, a church congregation, a football club; or being simply one of a crowd, a statistical unit, being 'one of us', or not being one of anybody. This distinction between person and individual has much wider implications as we turn to consider other theoretical concepts.

Open systems thinking/sustaining systems thinking

Systems thinking is about the construction of mental models in trying to make sense of a bewildering complexity of the patterning of activities, relations and feelings which are characteristic of daily living. To some of those patterns in which figure persons like father, mother, partner, children, a boundary can be drawn and we construct the idea of a family. The continuance of the family metaphor depends on how the people behave, their going out and their coming back, and the renewal of food and other life necessities. Likewise we construct metaphors of business, of churches, of government.

The constant question is to decide how to define where the boundary can be thought of, so as to construct the metaphor. So for example the Milan School of Family Therapy, in working with one child, would draw the boundary around not only the 'immediate family' of parents and siblings but include grandparents, uncles, aunts and cousins who are part of the pattern of relations, considering that the family system is a whole with a total existence, not a collection of human beings.[6] This boundary can readily lead to the realization of community as a system description, where the boundary will be drawn in the minds of people in very different ways.

Systems, if they are to be sustained, need renewal of energy to counter the entropy, the running down as predicted by the Second Law of Thermodynamics. To achieve this the system needs to be conceived defining a circular process or feedback mechanism by which the energy is constantly made available to the system. On this construction two different systems are conceptualized, depending upon how the boundary is located.

First, where there is a purpose in producing an artefact or service then a boundary will be drawn between the productive activities and between the specific people, systems or institutions which receive the outputs of these activities. The boundary measures the internal work done in transforming inputs (the people, energy, technology, materials) from the environment into outputs (product or service) into that environment. The boundary also indicates the outcomes, dependent upon how the specific people, system or institutions receive those outputs. Where the feedback is positive, then the outcomes will provide the energy in the form of inputs to enable the system to survive or grow. Where the feedback is negative, the information can be regenerative by causing the managers of the system to adapt their transformation process and outputs. The boundary marks out two phases of an ongoing cyclic process on which the future of the system is contingent. Open system thinking includes, therefore, both the formal system and its context as one whole, a system/context continuum.

Secondly, where the emphasis is about 'being' as distinct from 'doing', there will be no need to draw a boundary at all. From the point of view of the observer the picture is one of many different parts. The interaction between parts can be noted, but since all the parts are involved inevitably in a kind of dance, any sense of purpose is imposed by the observer and cannot be attributed to the parts themselves. This is the predicament, for example, of those seeking a 'cause' of global warming. The energy is too diffuse and cannot be comprehended except to say it is a function of the whole.

These two constructs of system have been named differently by social scientists and organizational analysts. Peter Checkland develops the idea of hard systems methodology and soft systems methodology.[7] I suggest that the former could be called 'open system', to indicate that the system is open to continual interaction with its environment; the second could be called the 'sustaining system' (Maturana and Varela would term it autopoietic[8]), a self-generating system. The open system model applies readily to business and other institutions like government, schools, prisons or hospitals. The second model applies to such examples as tribes, cultures and societies. Problems occur when different people have different ideas as to how the boundaries are drawn. They can then think of themselves as working in a business based on open systems thinking, but having an experience of being in a sustaining systems model. This becomes further complicated where the managers responsible for the performance of the business – open systems model – appear to ignore the feelings and beliefs reflecting sustaining systems thinking.

Open systems thinking is contingent upon somebody defining the purpose and understanding how to plan the resources, technologies and processes by which the model can be defined by the drawing of boundaries. Open systems thinking is about understanding 'reality'. The task remains for the initiators to communicate to the other persons involved what that purpose is, so that they can carry out those plans and achieve the required targets. If we think of a business as an example, a change in economic or technological conditions in the context requires the management to be prepared to redefine products and services which are necessary for the achievement of the purpose of the system. The success of the business is dependent upon the hierarchy of meaning so that the purposes of different people can be linked together constructively. To do this could be how an engineer can carry out his work for the purpose of the company, while at the same time being conscious that the purpose he has for his family requires that he earns a sufficient income. At a more corporate level, failure to recognize the hierarchy of meaning can be seen in members of the trade unions going on strike to challenge the manager's decision which adversely affects the workers' purposes.

A simple way to imagine sustaining systems thinking is to delete all the boundaries which have been imagined in a world of open systems thinking models. Sustaining systems thinking is about being, whose meaning derives from the nature of the relations in the mind of the observer, between each of the parts and between all the parts and the whole.

It is an 'holistic' approach, when each part is seen to exist in its own right – what Arthur Koestler called a 'holon', which 'exhibits the polarity of part and whole in the hierarchic order of life'. A metaphor for systemic thinking is the holographic plate into which three-dimensional pictures have been imprinted. The unusual feature is that a fragment of the plate will show the same picture as the whole plate: the whole is in the part – there is no division between part and whole. There is no division between inside and outside as metaphorically shown in the Möbius strip where a ribbon of paper is twisted once and then glued at the ends to form one continuous surface which includes the erstwhile both sides.

If only we can understand it, any part of life can lead to the understanding of the whole. Sustaining systems thinking opens a new understanding of parts and whole. As Gregory Bateson puts it 'the resolution of contraries reveals a world in which personal identity merges into all the processes of relationship in some vast ecology or aesthetics of cosmic interaction. That any identity can survive seems almost miraculous, but is saved from being swept away on oceanic feeling by the ability to focus in on the minutiae of life. Every detail of the universe is seen as proposing a view of the whole. These are the people for whom Blake wrote the famous advice in 'Auguries of Innocence',

> To see the World in a Grain of Sand,
> And a Heaven in a Wild Flower,
> Hold Infinity in the palm of your hand,
> And Eternity in an hour.[9]

In the study of systems thinking in learning-by-experience conferences, boundaries are offered by staff in the programme, but sustaining system interpretations are made which ignore them by considering the staff boundaries as a form of scaffolding – containing space rather than content. The interpretations generally focus on the participants' boundaries-in-the-mind which are expressed behaviourally as resistance to learning because of participants' reluctance to face reality. It is from such conferences that the conceptual tools providing the framework of this paper have been discovered, explored and tested over the years, with the support of colleagues and participants.

The social consequence of sustaining systems thinking is cultural awareness. The total material, mental and spiritual 'artefacts' constitute the social pattern of relations called 'culture' by sociologists, it is rich in metaphorical language. As social institutions, the business and service agencies necessarily reflect and are affected by the environment they work in. Sustainability both of the culture of the institution and of the environment, depends on how the institution is able to learn from and relate to the political, economic, technological and social conditions which are being experienced. The change from soviet socialism to Western capitalism has sorely tested Eastern European governments, public institutions and private enterprises in handling these systemic complexities.

In furthering their goals, executives are prone to pay attention only to those elements in the environment which they consider important for their purposes. As they make products and provide services, however, institutions are open to the cultural context and develop their own sub-cultures, which overlay the external social culture. It is managers' pre-judgement about culture that can blind them to factors which could transform the company in the future, if only they could see that. For example, the current culture in this country expresses the importance of human values and spirituality. A management intensely concentrating on profit and market share may treat these as peripheral and as business constraints. Instead of trying to respond to them organizationally, allowing them to influence their policies and to contribute to their sustainability, management have drawn their boundaries in the wrong place.

Boundary / manager

Bateson's definition of 'information as a difference that makes a difference'[10] applies directly to boundary, when it is used as information in systems thinking. Von Bertalanaffy's use of 'membrane' as the boundary between an organism and its fluid context makes clear in his work on systems that boundaries are permeable, not barriers.[11] The task of any purposive system is to decide where to 'place' boundaries that denote the difference between the inside and the outside. This signifies that activities are started up and planned to achieve a purpose. A further management task is to decide the means and conditions and clarify the intentions by which boundaries are crossed. Management's rationale is based

on boundary defining and monitoring: Janus-like, managers themselves work on the institutional boundary, seeing both inside and
outside. I would suggest that these two tasks constitute the world
of management in being accountable for the performance. Management *is* the boundary. So wherever there is management, there is
a boundary; and where there is no boundary, there is no management.

This line of thought can be confusing because of the popular
use of boundary. For many it means, 'thus far and no further'.
To cross it is to break the rules. Not only does this change boundary into 'barrier' with a high wall, but it also implies that managers are sentries and oppressive. Managers are taken to be there
to make things happen or to stop things happening, and consequently it leads to the expectation that unless managers instruct
people to do things, they don't do them. Hence the grotesque term
'man management' which has appeared as part of organizational
training jargon, an expression guaranteed to raise the spectre of
compulsion and dictatorship and which has in the past provided
powerful ammunition for assault by trade unions.

Some countries have grown up with this attitude as part of
their history. For example, I understand the Swedish language
uses the word 'border' to include the idea of boundary. So when
one of its largest companies wanted to stress the urgency for its
staff to penetrate society in order to seize market opportunities,
it instructed them to 'ignore borders' – as if they could do so and
still remain part of the company! In Denmark, the democratic
spirit has meant that the term 'manager' has been dropped from
organization-speak, and 'leader' has to cover both ideas where
boundary is secondary to relations. There are other examples of
usage outside the UK which show the importance of understanding boundary as a concept organizationally.

Boundary as a concept in-the-mind is not static, but dynamic;
its value is always changing, every day. The vigilance of managers
is needed to define and re-define it continuously, like a line drawn

in the sand below the high-tide watermark which needs to be redrawn twice a day.

The philosophy of 'bigger is better' relates to the importance of boundary. I suggest such a notion can be more a sign of weakness than of success. Some growth is monstrous, like a cancer, the larger it becomes the more lethal it gets. The problem of growth is to manage the boundary, so that those responsible for expanding the system accept their accountability for the sustainability of its total context in carrying out its own purposes economically, socially and ecologically. This will most certainly question the values underlying these purposes. One consequence is to recognize the rights of all the stakeholders: employees, customers, suppliers, contractors and local communities whose existence is critical, alongside shareholders and investors.[12]

Globalization of business interests opens new horizons for those responsible for companies whose units are scattered across different culture and countries. In the interests of market growth, suppliers, customers and competitors may agree to co-operate and set up informal interactive marketing and managerial structures and activities The result is the formation of networks across several companies, where boundaries are disregarded as restricting and bureaucratizing. Charles Hampden-Turner and Fons Tropenaards have characterized this by contrasting the business methods of the Western countries with the 'tiger' economies of the Far East. The authors distinguish what they call the finite game from the infinite game.[13] The finite win–lose game is based on competitive action to win market share, whereas the infinite win–win game is based on co-operation whose success leads to overall market growth. They advocate the extension of the infinite game in the West as the more effective way to stimulate economic success. Our reading of these two different approaches is that the finite game is based on defined systems with boundaries and roles, whereas the infinite game is based on trans-company personal networks. However the recent collapse of the Far East 'tiger' economies shows the limitations of this game. The failure of these companies to manage their basic systems of boundaries and roles successfully shows that the infinite game cannot operate without the finite game. Boundaries are necessary for open systems thinking.

Person / role

Social scientists have employed the role concept in different ways – in anthropology, psychology, socio-dynamics, and so on, each with their own emphasis of meaning. We have developed the concept from our work in systems from a socio-psychological standpoint, so that it becomes a tool for those who think and work in purposive system thinking terms. Here, role is differentiated from person, position, job description and task, although it involves them all.

The purpose of role is to enable persons to engage in organizational work to achieve the aim of their particular system. Persons may be given a position, tasks, job and the use of resources but I suggest they cannot be 'given' a role. What they are given is a system to work in and the aim or purpose of that system. From such information a person then tries to discover how best they can engage with the organization and its task, how to work with the culture and to establish working relations with colleagues. This can be understood as the person looking for his or her role in the system. There are two aspects to this – the inward discipline (psychological role) and the outward behaviour (sociological role). A person grows the 'role' in their minds as the means by which they determine their behaviour in the system. Newly appointed managers need to search for the role, then incorporate the discipline, so that they can take the role. We speak of a person-in-role as a holistic notion when the person integrates him/herself into the whole which includes the system, its purpose, the context and the people.

From the outside, others in the same organizational system have expectations of how the person will or should behave. They have in their mind the sociological role of that person, but this is only one of many criteria which will affect how the person-in-role chooses to behave in their psychological role. Where people do not perceive the purpose of a system but only the behaviour of the person, despite his or her own perception that he is exercising authority, they will experience him as using power to further his own interests, which could lead to his rejection by them. It becomes the task of a person in a leadership position to make clear to others the aim of their specific systems so that they can transform leadership charisma into being experienced by others as working with authority.

Because situations are always changing, role is dynamic and the person-in-role needs always to be alert to differences requiring flexibility and skill, for example, the skill to use apparently adverse conditions to one's advantage. Like competent sailors coping with headwinds, unreliable currents, and strong seas which threaten to drive them off course, yet who still arrive at their destination. This compares with the person-in-role working in conditions of stress and not being seduced by the insistent expectations of others. Role is also an art where the values and culture of the system are assimilated and then reflected by the person-in-role as they express their emotional concern for the best interest of the system. Role as an idea-in-the-mind fits with other mental concepts like organization and boundaries.

The energy for being in role is generated from within the person, in relation to external opportunities, so that they can appreciate the variations which facilitate the transformation of their system which are needed to work to the requirements of their vision. This approach breaks through the constraints of bureaucracy. Where institutions are plagued by rules and procedures, it indicates that the persons concerned have the need to be controlled by the outward power of rules, rather than by the inward authority which is possible by role.

Transformation of the role may result when people discover that the role they have taken is dysfunctional with the needs of the system. For example, a software design company was managed, jointly by three different functional managers who met and worked as a team, called the Senior Management Team (SMT). This team model was supported by higher management, but despite their efforts they were not being successful, they were too bogged down in details. On investigation, it was obvious they were each representing their own function , for example, the project manager identified with his responsibilities, but not with the work of other functions. It was pointed out that they were working from their respective sub-system functional boundaries rather than from the company system boundary. But the fact was that they were accountable as a team for the success of the design company. In other words they were the general management of the enterprise. They had access to the role of general manager but they were restricting themselves to the role of function manager. They grasped this point and changed the 'SMT' into the 'GMT' (General Management Team) that same day. Their corporate work improved and they never looked back. It was striking that the term SMT was not used again by them and that in a very short time the company personnel converted readily to their new title.

This instance could be replicated in many management teams even when it is chaired by one executive to whom the other managers report. Meetings often consist of functional managers reporting on their own work, so it is no wonder that they complain they never deal with strategic issues. It is clear that in these cases the senior executive had not invited or expected them to join him on his outer boundary from where they could see the company as a whole. They behaved more like a group of individual managers than a team with a common goal.

In national life, the widespread loss of confidence in institutions indicates the effect on role of the blurring of system boundaries. These national institutions are being experienced by citizens and consumers increasingly as bureaucracies, an endless sequence of petty processes. People have lost their awareness of the institution as a whole system. Instead of institutions serving society as major stakeholders, they are seen as being exploited by their executives for their own interests. With no sense of the service which is conferred by meaningful institutions, boundaries are turned into bureaucratic barriers.

Consequently, this state of affairs changes the balance between role and person. In the political trend towards proportional representation, the concept of representation through role is being replaced with the move towards the delegation of person. Politically, the status of Members of Parliament is reduced to speaking on behalf of like-minded voters. Those voters who failed to elect their chosen candidate do not consider they are represented in Parliament. Under the present constitution the role available to an MP is to represent all the constituents, irrespective of their political allegiance. The system in which they function is the entire constituency. With this conviction they can operate as person-in-role, instead of as someone delegated through a pressure group around which there are no formal boundaries: hence the in-fighting within parties between people who wear the same rosette. Technically speaking, a party may seem to be a system but behaviourally it acts like a clique concerned for its power. We will probably have to regard these new facts of life as normative for the future, whether we accept the consequent changes as progress or as regression.

Ecclesiastically this same problem applies to the selection of bishops of the Church of England as the 'established' church. On their ordination, bishops are asked to take authority for the 'cure of souls' of all the population in their diocese, whatever the spiritual state of the people themselves. In the recent confusion over a new appointment, an Anglican priest proposed that church congregations in a diocese should elect their bishops as is done in other episcopal provinces outside England. If this were implemented in England it would radically alter the role of a bishop because it changes the boundaries of the diocese from including all the people to only the faithful within the diocesan area.

Authority and power

A problem in organizational life is the confusion between power and authority. Transformation requires energy and if transformation is to be effective and not regress to the status quo, it requires the exercise of authority. Our view is that within people and structure there is latent energy. When this energy is being activated by someone who makes personal use of inanimate objects and relations with others to achieve something for their own purposes, whether these are good or not, they are using power. On the other hand, when the energy is mobilized by a person-in-role for the benefit of the system in which they work, then they are exercising authority.

Managers use power when members of staff do what they are told or what they are expected to do because of their relationship with the managers: because they are liked, because they inspire confidence or fear. In doing the job, they may be more aware of pleasing 'the boss' than finding satisfaction in the work and its completion. Under these conditions staff will be concerned to get on well with the manager, not because it is best for the business, but because it makes life easier. Discussion of mistakes, problems and weaknesses is strictly limited because it could lead to pain, arguments and anger, which then leads to breakdown in the relationship they want to preserve.

A manager exercises authority when members of staff know how their work contributes to achieving the aim of the system and what they are expected to do because of their relation to the task. The manager's obligation is to brief staff so that they can grasp the significance of what is to be done, know the extent and limits of the resources available to them and that they are reassured and confident that they have the requisite skills. That is, staff can take ownership of their own work within the system and consequently have a sense of freedom in carrying it out. Their relationship with the manager is one of openness about admitting problems and mistakes, because unless the staff know the real situation the job will go wrong.

People whose own purposes are in accordance with an implicit system but not aware of their own function in it may be taking a role without realizing it. The parable in St Matthew's Gospel, chapter 25, shows that in the way they were ministering to the poor and needy, certain people, according to Jesus, were functioning in role in the system of the Kingdom of God. Whatever their conscious intentions, Jesus praised them for what they did. I suggest that here they were using authority, which was honoured by Jesus when in the parable he offered them seats in the Kingdom in glory alongside himself.

Role transforms power into authority. This introduces another function which conditions this transformation, that of authorization. A person's actions can be 'authorized' by others only if they are considered as working within prescribed limits, limits (boundaries) which enable the actions to be understood as carrying out the aims of the authorizing body by accepting accountability for their actions. Hence others also functioning within these limits experience freedom if they can take the role to exercise their own authority.

Therefore, within a system, a person-in-role can exercise authority, whereas a person in a network of relations without boundaries can only use power. If one party takes up a role in one system and at the same time another party takes up a role in a different system, and the two parties do not share the same boundaries or systems, they will perceive each other as not being authorized. Hence only power relations can operate between them. This explains some of the ceaseless wrangling over some border disputes. The Northern Ireland peace process hangs upon all the stakeholders acknowledging the same boundaries as defined by the Mitchell agreement.

A similar predicament is expressed in *The Ring of the Niebelung* by Wagner, where Wotan the god, when his wife Frika rightly asserts that his chosen agent, Seigmund, cannot be allowed to consort with his sister Sieglinde, laments, 'How can I create a man who will be free?', a cry which reflects the dilemma of gods who inhabit a world of their own apart from that of their creatures. Authority and freedom are only possible if the parties involved share the same system (world). By contrast with Wotan, this is supremely exemplified for Christians who can experience freedom because God-in-Christ became one with the human race through the incarnation of Jesus. He shared the same human system and accepted the consequences of being a man who in the end was rejected by his own people.

In conclusion, in terms of this chapter it enables us to conceive of the church as an example of open systems thinking, with all the concern about resources and communication in relation to the current postmodern context; and the Kingdom of God which exemplifies the sustaining systems thinking model, whose values become significant in giving meaning to society and its culture. The confusion of church people, including clergy, may be due to their inability to recognize these differences between the church and the Kingdom of God which these concepts illuminate. It is perhaps significant that revisions of the Anglican liturgy have tended to focus baptism as being more concerned for entry into the church than as promising membership of the Kingdom of God.

Understanding the church requires the language of perceiving reality in open systems thinking; perceiving the Kingdom of God in sustaining systems thinking needs the language of metaphor. As Jesus said in his parables, 'the Kingdom of Heaven is like . . .' The church as a whole can then be seen as the servant of God in enabling society to take on the characteristics of God's Kingdom, of love, joy, freedom, justice, truth, righteousness, in pursuit of sustainability.

References

1. Barry Palmer, 'Learning and the Group Experience', in Gordon Lawrence (ed.), *Exploring Individual and Organizational Boundaries* (Wiley, 1979), pp. 169–92.
2. Gregory Bateson, 'The Logical Categories of Learning and Communication', in *Steps to an Ecology of Mind* (London: Paladin Granada, 1973), pp. 250–79.
3. John Heron, *Feeling and Personhood* (London: Sage, 1992).
4. John Donne, *Devotions* (1624), 17.
5. Erving Goffman, 'Role Distance', in E. Goffman, *Where the Action Is* (Allen Lane, 1969).
6. Mara S. Palazzoli, Gianfranco Cecchin, Giuiana Prate and Luigi Boscolo, *Paradox and Counterparadox* (Jason Aronson, 1978).
7. Peter Checkland, *Systems Thinking, Systems Practice* (Wiley, 1981).
8. Humberto R. Maturana and Francisco J. Varela, *Autopoiesis and Cognision: The Realization of the Living* (BSPS, 42; Reidel, 1980).
9. Bateson, 'The Logical Categories'.
10. Gregory Bateson, *Mind and Nature: A Necessary Unity* (London: Wildwood House, 1979), p. 228.
11. Ludwig von Bertalanffy, *General System Theory* (Harmondsworth: Penguin, 1973).
12. George Goyder advocates this approach as early as 1951 in *The Future of Private Enterprise* (Oxford: Blackwell, 1951) and developed it in *The Responsible Company*, (Oxford: Basil Blackwell, 1961) and *The Responsible Worker* (London: Hutchinson, 1975).
13. Charles Hampden-Turner and Fons Tropenaards, *Mastering the Infinite Game* (Oxford: Capstone, 1997).

14

The hidden depths of organizations: people in working relationships

Correspondence between Norman Todd and Gillian Stamp

Introduction

We have been searching for correspondence between our disciplines for more than ten years now. This search has not been an 'academic exercise' but specifically for the purpose of offering people with whom we work – together and separately – 'tools for their heads' which can illuminate, clarify and help them to put into words their experience of being a person in a working relationship.

Dear Gillian,

I remember you giving a talk to a group of bishops about the structure of organization. 'The hidden depths of organization', you called it, and produced a diagram which scared most of the audience, though some of them were intrigued. Either reaction was because most of them had not got beyond thinking of an organization as either a machine or a body. They were used to thinking of the church they belonged to as a body rather than a machine. This idea, which St Paul had borrowed from the Greeks and used to describe the church in his letters – a single body with many members working in harmony and co-ordinated by the head – is not the only way of imagining the church but it is the one most favoured today. The Turnbull report on the organization of the Church of England is called 'Working as One Body'. An MBA thesis on the central organization of a diocese reported an interview with one of the senior clergy, 'Nice man, much happier with church as an organism than as an organization.' I wonder why the church does not more often think of itself as a company, a sister- brother-hood of breadsharers. Perhaps because it would mean facing up much more honestly to the realities of human relationship, which is what St Paul was doing in much of what he wrote. We use the word 'synod' with its emphasis on finding a common way and then pretend that it should work with the automatic integration of a healthy human body. In practice it becomes more like a parliament with protagonists at sword's length.

The human body metaphor is a very common, almost universal, way of getting our minds round the experience of belonging to an organization. It is as part of our language. An army unit was a fine body of men – now of women and men. An operational unit is the arm of the law. The centre of planning and execution is the headquarters. It is there in the very word 'organization' itself – the organs of the body. We organize our experience of belonging, and oddly double the metaphor by referring to a 'corporate body'.

Before I return to the 'hidden depths of organization' I must just refer to the way we now think about the 'hidden depths' of the human body. We would not have much confidence in a doctor who relied only on the knowledge of the human body possessed by a doctor in the time of St Paul – even if he was St Luke, the 'beloved physician'. As laymen we may still think of the exterior of the body as they did, but internally we use a very different picture. We know that the members are co-ordinated by a complex nervous system; operated by an interactive muscular system, fuelled by a vascular system linked with a digestive system and a respiratory system; and protected by an immune system though we do not know much about how it works. There are other systems, too. And each system contains sub-systems and all work together for the common good as long as the body is healthy within a sustaining environment.

In some ways this modern way of thinking about our body as an organization of systems is still helpful. Any organization consists of interactive systems and sub-systems. Deming defines a system as 'a network of interdependent components that work together to accomplish the aim of the system'. He might have added that the aim is something that could not be achieved by any of the sub-systems alone. 'Appreciation for a system' is the first of Deming's four essentials for 'profound knowledge' for 'transformation from the present style of Western management to one of optimisation' (*The New Economics*, MIT, 1986, p. 96.)

However, it is never wise to depend on only one metaphor, for metaphor depends, as does analogy, on likeness and difference, not on identity. John Adair warns against overdependence on a single metaphor. 'Learning about leadership comes mainly from widening one's span of analogy. People with a narrow span of analogy tend to rely – consciously or unconsciously – upon one or two metaphors' (*Great Leaders*, Talbot Adair, 1989, p. 60).

A range of metaphors is described by Gareth Morgan in *Images of Organizations*' (Sage, 1986) and summarized in the chapter headings: organizations as machines, as organisms, as brains, as cultures, as political systems, as psychic prisons, as flux and transformation, as instruments of dominion. No doubt others could be added. It is only fair to add that the last two chapters of his book are: 'Developing the Art of Organizational Analysis', and 'Imagination: A Direction for the Future'.

It is much better today, however, to study organization in its own right. This is why I find your matrix diagram of hidden depths so helpful. It encourages me to ask whether we could find a generic name for all organizations, a name which does not depend on a metaphor from something else. For this I am forced back to the idea of relationship or interaction. In any organization units are interacting whether individuals or groups. If the units are impersonal we tend to say they interact. If they are people then we say they relate. Perhaps no person can be a person except as in relationship, that is, in organization.

That is it! *People-in-relationship* (PiR). What interests me is this: 'Is there a necessary form of PiR which results from the nature of people and the way in which they relate?' Your 'hidden depths' matrix suggests to me that there is. If there is, then we have a way of referring to all human groupings that is not dependent on metaphors other than those which are anyway inherent in all language.

I always find it helpful to think of, or imagine, the way in which any human phenomenon may have come about. It is a way of describing phenomena in terms of their imagined genesis. In this case I remember my own experience of the growth of the voluntary PiRs I have been involved in, mostly voluntary bodies or pressure

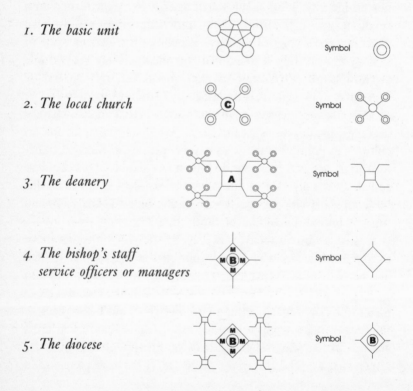

1. The basic unit   Symbol

2. The local church   Symbol

3. The deanery   Symbol

4. The bishop's staff service officers or managers   Symbol

5. The diocese   Symbol

groups. It is also the way I imagine the early church growing, or for that matter any newly planted idea or project.

One person has an enthusiasm which she wants to share, so she relates to someone else willing to listen and involves her in the enthusiasm. They draw in a third person and the PiR continues to grow, held together by the relationships powered by the common enthusiasm.

Line 1 of diagram: the basic unit — the group of disciples sharing a common enthusiasm.

This is the basic unit of any and every PiR. The limit, it is usually agreed, is about twelve people. Beyond twelve they start talking about splitting and forming two groups. When they do this they soon find that to keep in touch they need a co-ordinator of some sort. Otherwise they grow apart because the common enthusiasm – their very *raison d'être* – cannot be maintained and developed appropriately within changing circumstances. They get out of touch. The more the enthusiasm catches on, the more successful the movement as more basic units are formed and the need for a co-ordinator with some administration and finance increases.

Line 2 of diagram: the local church

With continuing growth of the PiR the co-ordinator will find that she has reached the limit of what she can do and has to face the PiR with the need to split and form two of these secondary units. In the Church of England this is when a parish church (the PiR) becomes too big for one priest and parish administration. Of course the reverse process can also take place, when parishes have to be amalgamated or united but – staying with the build-up of PiR – there comes the growth in the number of these second line units and the inevitable need to keep them co-ordinated. A new third level co-ordinator has to be chosen and given appropriate administration and finance.

Line 3 of diagram: the deanery.

Again, with continuing growth, another line of enablement is required to hold all the line 3 units together in common purpose of shared enthusiasm, and a new co-ordinator is required. However, this new line is represented in the diagram by line 5, not line 4. The reason for this is that the PiR now requires a much wider provision of administration, finance, education and training and planning. This constitutes a line between lines 3 and 5. Line 4 is a necessary constituent of a PiR of this size. It enables level 5 to form and continue effective co-ordination and preparation for the anticipated future.

Line 4 of diagram

The service officers and planning officers planning and training for the immediate future.

Line 5 of diagram

The diocesan bishop with strategic co-ordination (oversight, foresight, delegation, but also with some undelegatable power or authority).

Of course different PiRs will have differing proportions and styles of this basic and essential form, but all the roles and functions will be there. Even if two of the co-ordinator functions are carried by the same person it is important that everyone see the functions as clearly discrete. The person who is both area dean and vicar has two different sets of relationships to manage, and could be required to send a letter from himself as area dean to himself as vicar. It would be interesting to see if he puts it in the waste paper basket.

Yours sincerely,
Norman

Dear Norman,

At long last I am replying to your letter about the 'hidden depths' of organization. There are two, interwoven reasons why my reply has been so delayed. The first is that I have been 'doing it' – working alongside people in various enterprises and parts of the world as they try to think about the 'hidden depths' of their organizations. This is part of their efforts to increase effectiveness in response to very tough competition and unexpected influences, opportunities and pressures coming not only from 'left-field' but also from directions no one even knew existed! The second is a hesitation on my part sparked by your comment about how the idea of the 'hidden depths' 'scared most of the audience, though most of them were intrigued'.

These reasons led me to reflect on what it is about some of the models we have developed that makes them 'work' for people. 'Work' in the sense that the person can immediately use the model to make sense of his or her situation, think about it in a different way and then, sooner or later, do something about it. These models become 'tools for my head' - parables? – that people can use.

The phrase 'tools for my head' was given to me by a young Aboriginal man in Northern Australia many years ago. I was at a meeting of a community group whose chairman had invited me to work with them on patterns of work and life as the community faced more and more pressure from commercial and tourist groups. At the beginning of the meeting, this young man came up to me and said, 'What have you brought?' I replied rather feebly that I had brought nothing, just some ideas, some experience with other people in traditional communities, and he wandered off looking both bemused and irritated. At the end of the day he came back and said, 'I will tell you what you've brought; you have brought me tools for my head.' For me that was a perfect distillation of what I was trying to do then and have been ever since.

It is important to understand why some of the models I offer people become tools that are readily used, while others are seen as 'scary' and shut away at the bottom of the toolbox (or thrown away) and yet others are 'intriguing', shiny, but the person cannot see what can be done with them. There is a clue in my use of 'immediate': the connotation of doing something quickly is obvious, less so is the connotation of an insight that does not need any mediation or interpretation – is 'im-mediate'.

For many reasons the 'hidden depths' diagram scares, intrigues and needs explanation – an echo of the complexities it tries to represent perhaps? It is an attempt to model both levels of work process and the patterns of connection between them. The levels provide a framework for distributing decisions so that they are made by the people closest to the action – a clear echo of the theological principle of subsidiarity. The connections between them create the conditions for people at each level to support purpose by making decisions with grace and competence and learning from them.

Perhaps if I had made the links with the image of organization as body, the model would have been less alarming, more immediate for the group of bishops. When I use the models with people in business who carry extensive responsibilities I usually use commercial, economic or business language and it would have been more thoughtful to 'situate' the diagram for the bishops.

This puts me in mind of two ways I describe the work we do; both have the quality of 'immediacy'. One is to say that the work is about turning 'what everyone knows' into 'common knowledge'; the other is to say that it is about three 'ands': the enterprise *and* the environment, the person *and* the enterprise, the person *and* the inner resource on which she or he draws to make decisions.

A couple of days ago two people came to see me to brief me about a conference on management of primary health care teams at which I am to speak. They are both 'practice managers' with GP practices in two different areas of London: in one a proportion of the population is transient and often deprived; the other area has a more settled population for whom it is easier to plan and provide services. Both managers are very committed and work very hard to fulfil a role which is poorly defined and unbounded so they never really know when a task or project is complete. One consequence is that they are not able to 'complete and contemplate', learn and give meaning to what they do beyond knowing that it is very important and likely to become more so with the growing emphasis on primary health care.

As we talked about the role of practice managers and of the conference, I introduced some ideas about the levels at which decisions 'belong' and the conditions needed for those decisions to be properly informed and robust. It was as if light bulbs had been switched on for them. They began to sit differently, to look less pale and strained and to say in response to some of my quick sketches 'Of course, it's obvious . . . and, and . . .' Rapidly and enthusiastically they extended the frameworks to give meaning to other issues that had been foggy, not amenable to being thought about before. They knew all about what I was saying, they lived it every day and moment of their working lives but they had no language, no way of turning both the riches and the pain of their work into 'common knowledge' with which they and their colleagues could go forward.

The delicacy is to create tools which speak both to a general idea that can widen understanding and to the specific experience of each particular individual. The general idea can so readily seem – and be – 'abstracted' in the negative sense and too distant from the particular to give meaning to it; the response to such a model is 'that's too academic'. Equally, the particular can be trapped in a moment, a situation; the response is usually 'we don't do it like that here'. To feel as if you have been told 'you are one of these' is both demeaning and comforting; demeaning if it is heard as 'you are "just" one of these', comforting if heard as 'others have also felt this way'. That is the tricky part of the balance.

Reflecting on this experience, I think you are wise to say that it is better to study organization 'in its own right' and am sure you are right to home in on relationships as the key. The models we use in Brunel Institute of Organisational and Social Studies,

(BIOSS) that 'work' immediately all depict relationships: the model of being 'in flow' – energized through a dynamic balance between what one is asked to do and one's sense of what one can do – makes instant sense. The model of tasking, trusting and tending (that you call 'the three Ts') is immediately recognized as the way people would want to work together – both inside an organization and with suppliers, contractors, distributors.

So to return to one of your questions, is there a necessary form of people-in-relationships (PiR) that results from the nature of people? What never ceases to amaze me is that 'flow' and the three T's make sense for people in a wide variety of cultures and wisdom traditions and very diverse organizations. There are many indications that the essence is in 'relationship' but not only as it refers to people. For example, in a fascinating book called *Leadership and the New Science*, Margaret Wheatley writes about creating complexity from simplicity – 'strange as it may seem . . . to make a fern of curving, intricate complexity, all that is required is . . . the simple rule that the seed shape is free to repeat itself at many different levels of scale, that it is placed in an upright direction and that it connects with what is already [there]. From this combination of a few simple rules and high levels of autonomy – of order and chaos working in tandem – emerges the beautiful complexity of a fern.'

This is a particular kind of relationship and I hear the longing for it again and again when people are talking about their working lives – 'If he will just tell me what he wants, what the limits are and then leave me free to decide how to achieve it.' The wish for 'a few simple rules' and 'high levels of autonomy' – a boundary so that one knows the space within which one has freedom to take responsibility, use initiative, make decisions. This wish to give of oneself in work is quite extraordinarily powerful in people even when, as we have found in our work in Poland and South Africa for instance, it has been repressed, suppressed and depressed. The wish – almost a longing – lies latent, blooming forth as soon as the limits are clarified and the field defined. The 'simple rules' link with the notion of tasking people – sharing intention, why something needs to be done and setting the boundaries; the autonomy links with the notion of trusting them to use their discretion in making decisions to forward the purpose. Tending is about taking the effects of time seriously, keeping paths clear so that each person, each process and the purpose can move along it with ease together and 'beautiful complexity' can emerge. This is the essence of what complexity theorists call 'self-organizing systems' – those that arise when the wider system is 'far from equilibrium', dynamic and probably not very comfortable for the people in it. Do you remember my constant turning to Hannah Arendt's descriptions of human systems as characterized by 'nativity', irreversibility and unpredictability?

I find I have slipped from your idea of PiR to a pattern of relationships that is the core of my working life – PiWR (people in working relationships). Perhaps the reason is the autonomy/rules idea because my approach is much influenced by Elliott Jaques' definition of work as 'the exercise of discretion within prescribed limits'. All the questions of who prescribes, who has the power to do so lead one to thoughts about ownership and the power of institutional investors in the world of business. This is becoming more and more of a factor in the lives of people in employment – or those pushed out of or seeking it – and as we write to each other, we need to be wary of idealizing organizations – either secular or religious. In my experience many, many PiWR are very vulnerable precisely because of the power of institutional investors for whom figures are the primary reality. Come to think of it, P-in-R or is it, as you point out, P-in-I (interaction). There are, as you know, some indications that other considerations are also coming to play a part in the evaluations of businesses – the whole idea of 'stakeholders' – but the reality for the moment is numbers, and you and I have to be as realistic about that as about human nature. People are opportunistic, have and pursue their own agendas, are 'political'. Writing a piece for an encyclopaedia of management thinkers about Elliott Jaques made me aware all over again that the main theme of his work has been that it *is* possible to design social institutions in such a way as to support the most constructive and not feed the destructive aspects of human nature. Someone once asked me whether I thought it was possible for an institution to be designed to foster original grace rather than original sin. Elliott would claim so, in my better moments I would too, but . . .

To come back to your PiR 'held together by the relationships powered by common enthusiasm'. I really like that phrase, it is what so many organizations seek to achieve through a 'vision statement'. But, like so many things once put into words, it becomes 'just words' and not a source of power, of *dunamis*, but often of cynicism. 'Enthusiasm' is an interesting word – 'filled with a god' is how my dictionary defines it. It has so many echoes of the three Ts and the coherence that emerges and is sustained when people are trusted to use their judgement and the path for emerging complexity is kept clear for them through tending. And of a comment by an economist called George Shackle who created a theory of decision-making in uncertainty: 'if I were asked what is the central object of study in economic theory, I should say that it is the meaning and the means of coherence in human action . . . how actions ought to be mutually constrained so . . . that . . . resources may be pushing together in the same direction.'

And now I appreciate for the first time your point that the need for a co-ordinator in the basic unit arises 'because the common enthusiasm cannot be maintained and developed appropriately within changing circumstances'. What a lovely definition of leadership that is for an organization that treats its people as people and not as objects or part people as in 'hands', 'grey matter' or 'items of maritime equipment'. The key is 'within changing circumstances'. If nothing ever changed, there would be need for administration and finance, for management to keep things going, but none for leadership to tap the 'hidden depths' and make provision for coherence to thread through uncertainty.

I am not sure that organizations 'happen' because of the nature of people and the way they relate. Both Elliott and I would feel that they will be effective to the extent that their leaders take account of that and, as I've said above, design can either contribute to people's paranoia or to their capacity for mutual respect and collaboration. But the secular organizations with which I work come into being as the result of the desire on the part of some group(s) to make money. Shareholders carry the risk by investing their money – usually through institutional investors so that small shareholders have a very limited voice in what happens. Executives manage resources, optimally, in such a way as to minimize that risk but, more and more, executives pursue their own agendas which may or may not align with shareholder interests. Hence 'reward packages' that are tied to stock options and thus to the overall outcome of the enterprise in creating wealth. A recent article in the *Financial Times* raises the question about how these will feel to senior executives when the value of their company declines.

The step from the basic unit to the local church in your model is now much clearer for me. Can you tease out a bit further the step to the deanery or group? The administration and finance come anyway and weigh so heavily on people, it would be really helpful to see more clearly – and thus help others too – the work that needs to be done to maintain the common enthusiasm.

Thinking about line 3 of your diagram reminds me of someone telling me recently about the need they had uncovered in their parish for 'body-building' work. He then went on to describe what you and I would see in our shorthand as a vulnerability in the third level of work. He explained that the parish priest was very good at the pastoral work with individuals (especially with those leading home-based lives) and good at doing things one by one. But he could not 'make the connections necessary in a large parish'. I link this directly to 'your line of enablement' required to hold all the units together. You and I would make that link readily; the tricky bit is then to use your model to help people see the wisest way to address such a vulnerability. The solution that parish had chosen was to raise the money for a curate in his second curacy to come and 'take on the body-building and report directly to the PCC'. I tried to help them see that this would, in effect, create two parish priests and that this could be difficult. But the response was that the two would have to learn to work together. I am sure they will try, but know from experience just how difficult it is to do that when responsibilities and reporting lines are not clear.

Thinking in this way about the steps between your lines blurs the distinction I have previously felt between PiR and PiWR. Perhaps people always are working when they do anything together – my thoughts turn to my daughter-in-law and her baby daughter as they work together so well at breast-feeding.

So then the question arises of the differences in work when one is a mother, employed, given a stipend, self-employed, a 'portfolio worker' or a term I came across the other day, 'a non-regular worker'. For so long – and still in many organizations – employees have been treated as objects or at best, as dependent. But, as we have discussed before, there is now an economic imperative to treat people as people: each individual as an adult, a source of creativity, imagination, ideas and enthusiasm; and individuals co-operating, 'powered by common enthusiasm'.

So the genesis of religious organizations around common enthusiasm makes sense. What seems to be the case in secular organizations – as we have discussed before – is that, as people, and their gifts, knowledge and skills *as people*, become the vehicle for creating wealth, so the nature of people (as individuals and working together), of what it means – and takes – to be 'powered by common enthusiasm,' becomes a matter of concern or interest.

It is ironic that it is increase in uncertainty – which so many of us find so difficult to cope with – that is driving this need to treat people as people. One of my sons calls this 'fighting fire with fire' – opportunity with enthusiasm. A recent book by two American academics called *Built to Last* (James Collins and Jerry

Porras, Century Business, 1992) is directly relevant to 'powered by common enthusiasm'. It is an account of studies of (mainly US) companies that have been outstandingly successful in creating value for shareholders. Their key finding is that each of these companies has – and clearly states – fundamental reasons for existence beyond just making money. The authors describe this purpose as 'a perpetual guiding star on the horizon, not to be confused with specific goals or strategies'. They go on to say that these companies do not have charismatic leaders, nor fancy strategies, but are committed to something that is very long term, hold close to their basic values and change only at the edges. Sounds familiar!

Back to the group or deanery, your line 3: 'line of enablement' is another lovely phrase and you link it directly with the common purpose of shared enthusiasm. I don't understand your explanation of the lines; could you elaborate? Would it be good to write little stories about each of the scales of complexity? And you might think of doing something we have tried, which is to make a sort of checklist of the signs that a step from one to the other is imminent as a way of helping people think about how to prepare.

Moving to line 4 of your diagram: I recall you telling me that above level 3 there is change and the move is to what becomes level 5. Level 4 then has to be inserted as the communication between them using messengers. I think you suggested these could be angels ascending and descending. You also referred to the mistrust of those who work at this level – as directors, archdeacons – partly because they have apparently been 'elevated' from the struggles of level 3 and below. You pointed out that the mistrust is also caused by money and this reminded me of a comment made to me about the move between the third and fourth levels in my 'hidden depths' model – 'it is the shift from the language of people and things to the language of strategy and money'. For me this is the intrinsic vulnerability of line/level 4. As you say, it is all about change, and in many organizations that is seen as strategy and money with 'people's attitudes' as an unfortunate matter to be 'dealt with'. This feels a long way away from angels or even messengers!

You describe the purpose of level 4 as stewardship and I think it is the stewardship of the hidden depths that is the essence; and yet it is so often lost or submerged in the stewardship of money with that, these days, becoming cost control. For instance, the different ways in which common enthusiasm has to be maintained when each individual is not known, when everything is in the language of money, when putting 'lived culture' into words loses the spirit. Through symbols, yes, but how? As you know I have often thought that this level is both very 'full' in the church – with archdeacons, suffragans, some rural deans, diocesan officers – and yet also strangely 'empty' in terms of powering through common enthusiasm.

So, emerging between us is a fresh way of thinking about people working together; about co-ordination for common enthusiasm; about how common enthusiasm can be sustained in increasing complexity. From your perspective the energy comes from 'an enthusiasm to be shared'. Is that an enthusiasm about belief? About salvation? From my perspective, the energy also comes from an enthusiasm but, in secular 'for profit' organizations this is for creating wealth. The common factor is that both enthusiasms can be realized only through people. But, at this stage of capitalism, they are subservient to money. Witness the frequency with which production is moved from one country to another. A comment which I may have mentioned to you before sums this up: 'production will have to be moved to dollar denominated currencies'; no mention of people or place, that a site means a community, a region, a nation.

Let me know what you think about all this. In the meantime, I will be mulling over ways in which the 'hidden depths' can be described while maximizing the intriguing and minimizing the scary aspects.

With best wishes,
Gillian

Dear Gillian,

In my first letter I expressed my awareness of the hidden depths of organization (as a living process rather than as a thing) in the form of the way in which it might be built up from its inception, as, for example, the early church, a missionary church, or a voluntary organization. However, for the most part, we are confronted by, or enclosed within, organizations that are already formed. I realize that over-emphasis on the possible genesis can distract from study of the present phenomenon. The 'as if' language has, at least, to merge with the 'what is going on now' language. Your paper on Elliott Jaques describes how his theory of 'Levels of Work' – which I think, correspond to my diagram – was developed from his study of the target completion times in the various sub-systems of actual organizations. Therefore it makes sense that you should ask me for some examples of my experience in the organization 'church'.

In the UK (and remember my experience is of the Church of England) we normally meet, or belong to, a local church gathered mainly from within the parish boundaries, or, in other denominations, from a different catchment area. In very small rural parishes this church may be a level 1 unit of face-to-face relationships, that is, a primary group, but usually the vicar inherits a level 2 structure in which the level 1 units have largely disintegrated. She or he therefore spends considerable effort in re-establishing them. The parochial church council is divided up into committees, the congregation into study groups, street groups, house groups, youth groups, men's groups and so on. Even the Methodist Church has lost the class meetings which were an essential part of its 'method'. In the house church movement, on the contrary, the level 1 units multiply and then have the problem of staying within the common enthusiasm. Longer established congregational, or gathered, churches such as the URC and the Society of Friends have developed their own variety of the common structure.

Level 3 in the Church of England is the deanery with the area dean (it used to be rural dean) as leader. The area dean is nearly always also a vicar and wears the two hats. Part of the weakness of this level 3 in the Church may well be due to the difficulty of dealing with the condition of the area dean as 'first among equals'. Both he or she and the other clergy experience difficulties. It may be as simple (or complicated) a matter as how to deal with the jealousy we all suffer from. Jealousy is sure to occur also in secular organizations, but I suspect that there the much clearer distinction between the lines of management means that it is institutionalized and even utilized as a form of ambition and competition. In the church it is often denied whereas it should be confessed.

The main finding of your research on deaneries was to show that they are of two types, one like a large parish and the other like a small diocese. This is caused, I assume, by a confusion of levels, with the dean either a glorified vicar or a diminished bishop. It is certainly true that most area deans are keen to share what they refer to as 'episcope' (episcopal oversight) with the bishop. I think that the confusion is mostly among the clergy; lay people are much more used to level 3 structures at work and cannot understand why they do not work effectively in the church.

The confusion of levels in which I have had most experience (I was never an area dean) is around level 4. This level, I have suggested, exists to effect a sharing of the enthusiasm for work between level 5 and the rest of the organization. This is necessary because the straight-line sharing (or management) through area deans has to be augmented with strategic enablement through thinking, information gathering and analysis, education and training and communication. The level 5 leader (bishop, superintendent) needs several 'advisers' with specialist remits, education (children, youth, adult), social responsibility, evangelism, liturgy, spirituality. They vary from diocese to diocese, but perform the same level 4 function. Some of these advisers may be part time, dividing their time with normal parish duties. Thus they also wear two hats, of levels 4 and 2.

A similar confusion of levels can occur when someone moves from 4 to 5, she or he tries to continue practising a function from their previous work. A man who was very good at evangelism, or social responsibility or education and then becomes a bishop may seek personal satisfaction by 'keeping his hand in'. But he will only de-skill the person who should now be doing it and avoid developing his own satisfaction to one that is appropriate in his new level – being a good overseer of the whole, including his former responsibility as part of the whole.

It seems to me that, seen in this way, level 4 is identical with what, in the army, would be called 'staff', a description also used for the bishop's senior helpers, or at least some of them. John Adair, in 'A Staff College for the Church of England', *Theology*, May 1962, who wrote from experience, described the staff college at Camberley thus.

> The syllabus fell into two broad inter-related parts: the study of the way large units achieve their aims in warfare and an analysis of the staff officers' work in connection with these operations.
>
> Staff officers were on the staff of a commanding officer and were responsible for seeing that his decisions were well informed and his orders understood and carried out.
>
> The young officer [at Staff College] comes to see the army in a new way, as a developed complex organism, designed to respond as a body to such situations as the enemy might impose upon it!
>
> During their study of warfare they become aware of the need of any large army for some form of general staff to act as a nerve centre of the body, to co-ordinate its various members in the common task.

Adair also makes the point that an important result of proper staff training is that by the time they are promoted to senior positions, officers have an understanding of how the army works, how their staff should serve them, how to lead effectively and achieve the required results. How the army works, how the business works, how the church works, how this organization works – this seems to be the important contribution of level 4. Yet it is all too easy for people in this level to rouse resentment from those in levels 1 – 3. I suspect that it is because they appear not to be doing the real work – fighting the enemy, earning the money, worshipping God.

Sometimes they themselves feel this – that they have a cushy job, they are not at the coal face. I wonder if you think that one reason why consultants are so often used now to do level 4 work is that they can draw off some of the odium and take it with them when they leave. I am sure that there are other reasons. But consultants are concerned with the way the organization works.

So one of the problems in the inner depths of organizations is the lack of understanding between levels. In your account of Elliott Jaques you write, 'The essential, frequently misunderstood, point is that these levels are of work and not of status and grading.' The problem has to do with one of the 'ands' of your last letter, in particular the 'and' between the people in any two levels of work. The conjunction's function is a fascinating one, both joining and separating. I hope to write about it later in greater detail, but for the time being merely say that it should be part of level 4's responsibility to see that this understanding of how the organiz- ation works is extended appropriately to everyone in it and that this should include an awareness of the facilitating interaction between levels. This is just as true for voluntary organizations as waged, for religious as for secular.

You ask what the lines in my diagram represent. They are the actual communication between the units of each level and the next level above or below, that is, they are two-way communications. Thus, each parish is in two-way communication with the area dean and hence stays in the common enthusiasm with other parishes. The deaneries are in two-way communication with the bishop – but the staff of level 4 are part of that communication.

Do you think that this communication at all levels is largely a matter of appreciating the three Ts appropriate to one's neighbouring level? Thus, if the vicars understand and sympathize with the Tasking, the Tending and the Trusting of the area dean and vice versa, then the essential work communication is taking place. Of course, it is the vicar's job to see that this understanding is shared with the various level 1 groups in her or his parish. It is easy for this communication within the whole organization to break down and need healing, but in as much as it is operating I think that in a completely human way we could say that it is in communion. There is a kind of hum or purr of contentment.

This seems similar to your 'tools for the head' applied to organizations. It involves having a working model of what is going on and links with what I wrote about a reflective style of spirituality in the first MODEM book. It can lead, I suggest, to a shared awareness within the organization which is rather like self-consciousness. It includes what is meant by culture, a complex of tradition, norms, controls, but lets them point beyond themselves (or within themselves) to a felt awareness of 'all-rightness', or it might be 'not-all-rightness'. I wonder if the Acts of the Apostles is, among other things, an account of the church becoming conscious of itself as a body; developing a self-consciousness which is also evident in the Epistles quite a lot of which are about relationships within the new community. And St Paul in one place (Colossians 2:5) says that when he visits the church he will find how 'well ordered' it is. The Greek word may have a military connotation. St Paul was certainly concerned with the hidden depths of the church, including, I think, what we are calling the work levels of organization.

Before I finish I must respond to your mention of 'making money' as the motivation within the organizations you come up against professionally. This is not the place to examine the morality of making money – it has been done admirably by Peter Selby in his book, *Grace and Mortgage* (DLT, 1997). The point here is whether the enthusiasm (treasure on earth or treasure in heaven) changes the basic structure of PiWR and the need for some kind of management. I am suggesting that it does not, but want to hear your opinion. What is different is the nature of the relationship, acquisitive or gracious. In all the organizations we meet or belong to there is a mixture, just as there are mixed motives in all of us. It is certainly mistaken to identify the good with Christianity as practised anywhere or any time (except by Jesus Christ) and to demonize 'management' as, rather surprisingly, the religious affairs editor did in *The Guardian*: [the] 'tools of managerialism are a sinister totalitarianism and are primarily about extending control, and a centralisation of power' (25 October 1997). Surely, the managerial disciplines can be used for either earthly or heavenly treasure. The important thing is the nature of the relationships within the common structure, whether they are predominantly for health and commonwealth, or not. But more of that when I have digested your response.

Yours sincerely,
Norman

Dear Norman,

I have been pondering about so many of the ideas and thoughts in your last letter and have allowed them to wander around in the back of my head waiting for the moment when some clarity might emerge. But I am departing for a week's work in India on Saturday and so need to reply even though some – perhaps most – of my responses are still only 'half-baked'.

The most consistent way is probably to reply point by point starting with your comments – in both your letters – about 'possible genesis', going on via 'common enthusiasm' to 'confusion between levels' and then 'lack of understanding between levels'.

Reflecting on understanding organizations through your

'thought experiment' of possible genesis – starting from the simple and building the more complex – took me back to that paper you have always been so warm about, describing the differences between executive and corporate hierarchies. In that I made the point that the defining characteristic of hierarchy – in mathematics, information and living systems – is to subsume levels one within another, to include each in something larger, that is, build from the simple to the complex. The common understanding of social hierarchy is a particular kind of subsuming – subordinating in a top-down control relationship, 'making of a lower order, dependent'. So most people both understand and 'practise' hierarchy in the way described by the comment you quoted – 'the tools of managerialism are a sinister totalitarianism and are primarily about extending control and a centralisation of power'.

As you know, this view of social hierarchy as 'top-down control' is being more and more frequently challenged as businesses – and other organizations – realize they must become more sprightly in a turbulent world and that their primary vehicle for that is people – people being imaginative, intuitive, willing to learn, in short motivated or, in your phrase 'powered by common enthusiasm'. As secular organizations grapple with treating people as people – not out of altruism but commercial necessity – they are coming to the view that control has to be distributed, not abdicated but carefully and appropriately distributed so that knowledge can be gathered and decisions made at the places where they 'belong', are best informed, can be made with grace and competence and will have most impact.

A fascinating book about the complementarity of machines and living systems puts it very clearly: 'The law is concise: distributed control has to be grown from simple local control. Complexity must be grown from simple systems that already work.' This is directly relevant to the pattern of understanding you have built by starting from how the common enthusiasm can be sustained. And also to the emergence of 'the beautiful complexity of a fern from a few simple rules'.

You will remember that, in my paper, I also referred to the approach to hierarchy of the anthropologist Louis Dumont – 'hierarchy integrates a society by reference to its values'. There is a link here with your comment about St Paul's concern for the 'well ordering' and the 'hidden depths' of the church.

That leads me to the point about what the subsuming level(s) should/can/do provide for if subsumed. If you think of the level 1 unit of face-to-face relationships being 'subsumed' with level 2, one of the functions of that is, as you say, to reintegrate, to cohere the common enthusiasm and restore boundaries so that the enthusiasm and energy can connect with the world outside rather than diffuse into it and thus be lost. You put this so clearly in explaining that the need for a co-ordinator in the basic unit arises 'because the common enthusiasm cannot be maintained and developed appropriately within changing circumstances'.

You mention that lay people are familiar with the functions of level 3 in the business world and cannot understand why they are not effective in the church. In my experience, many secular organizations have rendered level 3 very vulnerable through what is euphemistically known as 'downsizing'. The consequences of level 3's diminished capacity to subsume can be clearly seen in the way the capacity of level 2 deteriorates. It can no longer produce imaginative, multi-faceted professional and/or technical responses to particular situations. All it is able to do is to 'fire-fight', produce *ad hoc* responses to the presenting problem, sort it and rush on.

Subsuming is, of course, another way of putting the principle of subsidiarity – that the more general does not control the less but acts as a subsidiary context for it – serving to help, assist or supplement. A passage from Hans Küng about the local church puts this beautifully,

Since local communities are not only parts of the Church, but are themselves churches . . . they have a right to autonomy in respect of the universal church. In the Church, whatever each individual can do with his or her own power should not be done by the community; whatever the [subsumed] community do not do, the supreme authority has no need to do. The behaviour of the community in regard to the individual and that of the superior community in regard to the [subsumed] community, is subsidiary. This is the meaning of the principle of subsidiarity, which allows as much liberty as possible and as much association as necessary. But this implies too, that no community has the right to shut itself off like a sect. [This is your point about the primary groups and the parish.] Its autonomy is not absolute, but it is in many ways relative, inasmuch as subsidiarity carries with it an obligation to a solidarity with other communities, with the regional church and with the universal church.

It is interesting that one of the definitions of subsidiarity is 'to sit behind in reserve': not an easy stance for many people managing and leading organizations, but one that has clear echoes of 'the servant leader' – not subservient but there in reserve.

I could write so much more about subsuming or what I often call 'making provision' for the well-being of each level, but I don't want this to be too long so I shall turn now to the idea of 'common enthusiasm'. Three points put me in mind of some interesting recent research into successful companies – 'success' defined in quantitative terms of increase in shareholder value. First, your pertinent question as to whether the content of the enthusiasm changes the basic structure of PiWR; second, your idea that what is different is the nature of the relationship – gracious or acquisitive, for health and well-being or not; and third, your characteristically wise comment that in all organizations there will be a mixture just as there are mixed motives in all of us.

The Industrial Society recently published the findings of a study of 1,000 employees in a range of different organizations. The employees rated desirable traits of leaders on a sliding scale. At the top came the ability to show enthusiasm; then came support for other people, then recognizing individual effort; agreeing targets and taking decisions were at the bottom of the list. The Institute of Work Psychology at the University of Sheffield has recently published a seven-year longitudinal study on the market environment and organizational characteristics in over 100 UK manufacturing companies. The aim was to determine what factors principally determine company effectiveness. Far and away the most significant predictor was concern for employee welfare; strategy explains 2% of change in profitability and 3% in productivity. Unsurprisingly, the conclusion is that 'if managers wish to influence the performance of their companies, the most important area they should emphasise is the management of people'. As you know, much of the thinking about leadership is coming to focus on treating people as people: PiWR.

There are many such studies that echo your notion of common enthusiasm and some that make it clear that you are right when you suggest that whatever the enthusiasm, there is a basic structure of PiWR. I referred to one about 'visionary companies' in my last letter and how they were found to have a 'core ideology – core values and purpose beyond making money'. The authors demonstrate that while profitability is a necessary condition for existence and a means to more important ends, it is not the end in itself for the visionary companies. 'Profit is like oxygen, food, water and blood for the body; they are not the point of life, but without them, there is no life.' The genius of the 'and' lies in ideology and profits. The authors conclude that 'the authenticity of the ideology and the extent to which a company attains consistent alignment with the ideology counts more than the content of the ideology'. Their notion of the 'genius' of the 'and' echoes your reminder that 'and' joins and separates.

Another very interesting survey was reported by the accountancy firm Price Waterhouse at the recent global economic forum in Davos. They surveyed chief executives in 377 of the world's leading corporations. One of the biggest changes identified by the survey is in the way chief executives prioritize their time. Nearly half said they devoted more of their energies into reshaping cor-

porate culture and motivating employees than in monitoring the
financial position of the company or liaising with customers. Only
6% of those surveyed claimed to have a fully integrated corporate
culture that crossed national boundaries and values. 'The creation
of such a unifying force among employees is regarded as a key
objective by most chief executives' – 'powered by common
enthusiasm'!

Just one thought: does it help to think of ordained and consecrated people in the church having a dual responsibility – to
sustain the fellowship of believers and to maintain the order that
defines their fellowship? The first aspect is about doctrine, the
processes that teach, preach and define the boundaries of acceptable belief. The second is the whole web of care that holds, supports and, where necessary, disciplines each member. I think this
implies that the more a level subsumes, the wider and deeper is
this dual responsibility. Is this a way of thinking about episcope?
I'm not sure whether it helps but feel that, in your hands and
mind, the idea might develop.

Following the sequence in your letter brings me to 'confusion
between levels'. Again, I learn so much about the levels framework
from the ways you are using it. My research on deaneries and the
view that there are – or were – broadly two types came about
by looking carefully at what they were doing in relation to the
communities they served rather than their 'place' inside the structure. It was the 'and' between the church and the social and
economic environment that seemed to make the difference. So,
from my perspective, it was not so much a confusion between
levels as different kinds of need in the environment and/or outreach to them that distinguished the two types. The smaller deanery is doing the level 3 work – externally with an 'extended
community' and internally – and, as you will recall, often finds
itself overlapping a group or team if such exists.

The larger deanery is doing or reaching towards the level 4
work, doing completely new things in a much more amorphous
community, where we found that individuals would often take

advantage of the anonymity to go to a church 'just to see what it was like'. The larger deanery sometimes added to the confusion in level 4 of which you write so tellingly in that the area dean – in relation to the outreach of the deanery – may be coming close to the boundaries of an archdeaconry, can even seem to be in the same space/level of work as the suffragan bishop. Although I am not closely in touch with deaneries these days, it seems to me that more are of the level 3 than the level 4 type now and this may be because the 'crowding' became too uncomfortable at the same time as the weakness in the level 3 work became apparent. A very sensible response to this would have been to shape deaneries to do the level 3 work in the world and in the church. You may be making a similar point when you say in your last letter that sharing or management through area deans has to be augmented with strategic enablement through thinking, information gathering and analysis, education and training and communication.

You will recall that the theme of level 4 work is 'strategic development', bringing into being everything that will be needed for effectiveness – of mission, worship and ministry – in the changes likely to occur within the next three to five years. Your description of the advisers at level 4 fits this well. Could it be that they are not always encouraged to reach outward and forward and find it easier (and perhaps more acceptable to level 5?) to keep their attention on the inner working of the deaneries which could, probably, do what they need to do without too much 'control' from 'above'. Put another way, deaneries might be effective in direct proportion to how far they are subsumed (included in something larger) and how far they are subordinated (made of a lower order, dependent).

Now I think about it, there seems to be a particular difficulty for level 4 in subsuming rather than subordinating. I realize that I am seeing this in four or five organizations at the moment. I am not sure why this should be; perhaps because of your point that level 4 is about sharing of enthusiasm and it is not easy to ensure a two-way communication of that. You describe it as 'between level 5 and the rest of the organization' and I know you do not mean that is only one way, but maybe level 4 is especially vulnerable to something happening – or not happening – that turns sharing into control. I am really rambling here, but could it be to do with the 'abstraction' of the level? Not doing 'the real work' as we have said before, having to hold together the activities that need to remain as they are to maintain continuity and the activities that have to be added or taken away to engage with change. And having to manage or control scarce resources. In my pondering on all this, I realize that my thoughts are turning more to confusion within a level and to your point about lack of understanding between levels than staying strictly with confusion between levels. I am reminded of an adviser who combined level 4 and level 2 work and like a mother who works outside the home, always felt he was either in the 'wrong place' or driving in 'the wrong direction', leaving the specialist role to rush back to the parish when there was more to be done; 'abandoning' the parish for a meeting he knew would be very stimulating.

You are right that the 'staff' contribution is 'how the organization works'. In a business this is the economics of provision of services or production of goods, so everything – and everyone – is, as I said in my last letter, put into figures, into quantity. So the work is very vulnerable to losing the qualitative, the sense of a person 'behind' each figure. Could it be the abstraction, the 'standing back' that makes sharing enthusiasm so vulnerable to becoming control, two-way communication becoming unilateral, subsuming slipping into subordinating?

If level 4 is able to subsume rather than subordinate, then 'how the organization works' becomes, as you say, the stewardship of the hidden depths, the mutuality of understanding between levels. Then what level 4 can do for level 3 is to put the 'culture' into words without losing the spirit, it can make sure systems are consistent, that initiatives are shared across deaneries and parishes, that the specialness of each unit is appreciated and knows where it fits in the whole; and it can hold change and continuity together so that neither comes to predominate, so that death and resurrection can be an institutional reality.

I have said before that level 4 is often too full of people trying to do the work and yet, often strangely empty in that the more people employed in level 4 work, the more the cry from people in the subsumed levels that 'we do not know where we are going'. Is that one of the clues that the intention to subsume and make provision has become – or is experienced as – subordination and control? This is not through any individual desire for power but through the intrinsic vulnerability of level 4 work perhaps especially when there seems to be even more change than usual to live with.

Turning now to the shift from level 4 to level 5 (or, indeed, any pair of levels). You will recall that some years ago we designed a work journal designed to support people through this kind of transition. Probably the most helpful part of it is where we ask the person to think about and write down: two things he/she has left behind with regret, two left behind with relief, and two he or she knows should have left behind but has not yet been able to. It is sometimes useful to add two things that will be completely new and to refine that by asking about two new things that are likely to be exciting and two that arouse anxiety. I use these 'triggers' frequently with people as they make transitions and they really seem to help the process of leaving behind the familiar and taking on new responsibilities. Sometimes people have been longing and longing for the new role and are surprised to find themselves almost disappointed when it actually comes because, at first, it seems somehow less than they thought. For others, the new role may seem so huge and overwhelming that they shrink smaller and smaller just in contemplating it. Somehow thinking about relief, regret and challenge and putting the thoughts into words make it easier to move forward.

Now to respond to the last point in your letter about lack of understanding between levels. 'So one of the problems in the hidden/inner depths is the lack of understanding between levels'

– the 'and' between the people in any two levels of work. This 'and' nests inside people and the organization emerging only when people are aware of levels and the connections between them that make a whole. Another echo of your timely reminder that 'and' both joins and separates. If one thinks of each of the levels as a separate entity, then 'or' rules and there is no whole, no 'wholeness', no well-being.

What an excellent idea of yours that part of level 4's responsibility is to see that the understanding of how the organization works is extended appropriately to everyone in it, and that this should include an awareness of the interaction between levels. My first thought is that, as you know, we think not only of the levels of work but also of the levels of the capability needed to do the work with grace and ease. The theme of the work of level 4 is strategic development and of the capability modelling. Should one criterion for the effectiveness of level 4 be the extent to which the 'models' created and communicated become tools for people's heads? So often, as we both know, level 4 feels cut off both to those working in it and to people in the first three levels. Is this because communications about 'how the organization works' or has to change to continue to work, are not always immediate in the way I described in my first letter? Communications may be in language which does not touch or even make sense to people and/or they may be couched in financial terms which appear completely impersonal. Often, especially when people are pushed and anxious, they appear to want to be told what to do; it is not enough to provide them with a tool. Perhaps they are steps: a model which may or may not become a tool; then a tool; then the question, 'what can I do with it?' or 'what should I do with it?' I feel as if I'm edging back towards parables again . . . this deserves further thought. Do you have any ideas?

I really warm to your idea of seeing communication as part of appreciating the three Ts appropriate to one's neighbouring level, probably levels. As you say, if vicars understand and sympathize with the tasking, trusting and tending of the area dean and vice versa then the essential work of communication is taking place '. . . the hum or purr of contentment pervades'.

The first 'T' of 'tasking' has at its core the sharing of intention – why something needs to be done, where it fits in the whole; and then it is about setting boundaries of time when completion is needed, of what resources will be available and the quality standards of what is to be done. The second 'T' of 'trusting' honours the person as a person with the wish and the capacity to use their own judgement in forwarding the work for which they are responsible. The third 'T' of 'tending' keeps an eye on, and keeps the paths clear so that people, processes, and purpose can hum along contentedly and competently.

So, as you say, the three Ts are three strands of communicating (rather than communication) that sustain the flow of the work, the discretionary energy of people and the inevitable fragility of permanence as time passes.

In BIOSS we have written quite a bit recently about 'tending upwards', making sure that the person who depends on you to get their work done has the information she or he needs, in an appropriate form to do what he or she needs to do. In organizations rife with 'politics' it is much harder to encourage people to tend upwards. They have become so accustomed to having demands for information made of them that they are inclined to comply to the minimum and to present information in such a way as not to 'upset the boss' or in such a way as to make it difficult for the boss to find out what is 'really going on'.

You and I are edging our way towards a pattern – or perhaps patterns – of leadership which are emerging in the space between us. I will always remember your trying to help me to suspend my certainties and to enter the no-person's-land between us so that we could really work together rather than side by side. I have not been able to overcome my tendency to try to lure you into my space but have learned so much from you about venturing into and working in ours.

I end with a quote which seems apposite. Apparently Henry

Ford once said, 'Why is it I always get the whole person when what I really want is just a pair of hands?'

As always, looking forward so much to your reply, but knowing I have delayed you.

With all best wishes,
Gillian

Dear Gillian,

As I read your last letter I kept writing 'yes', 'yes' in the margin. There really is a correspondence between the church and secular organizations which throws light on both.

The one direct question you ask is about how people in level 4 can actually do their work. This, as I understand it having attempted to do it, is putting into practice the strategic planning of level 5. How can the organization be prepared for the changes which will become necessary? How can everybody in every sub-system be moved from the mind-set where they are now to that of where they will have to be for the next phase of the organization's life? This must include changes in level 5 as well as in 3, 2 and 1 – which can be a bit tricky if the bishop thinks he was given all the answers at his consecration. You must know the equivalent in your world. The work (of 4) must be based on a sympathetic understanding of present attitudes and knowledge; awareness (perhaps in the Jungian sense of 'where something is going, of what the possibilities are, without conscious proof or knowledge') of the future implications of the continuing enthusiasm; and imagination informed by the methods of effective adult learning.

You wonder if parables might be the method, a very interesting suggestion. The parable is an art form which creates a hiatus in our normal flow of assumptions or mind-set. I naturally think of Jesus as the master of this form, but all religious leaders use it. It is a kind of paradigm shift, but the hiatus is in the context of, or is an invitation to, a more fundamental (or superordinate) form of experience. The disciples of Jesus often had to ask him what a parable meant. There had to be continuity and discontinuity out of which there emerged a penny-dropping awareness of what the shared enthusiasm meant in a new situation. It is similar to the preacher's continual search for telling sermon illustrations. (I remember a student once telling me he had a wonderful sermon illustration, but was not quite sure what it illustrated.) In some situations it is possible to involve the hearers in inventing their own parable. Another variation is to work with conceptual models, of which my diagram and also yours of 'hidden depths' are examples, though they do not work with everybody. Again it is important that the learner should be able to make the conceptual model her own and in doing so can often help the teacher to grow her own awareness. Some would advocate the writing of 'documented management systems' which can work well if the actual workers are fully involved in writing them and monitoring to keep them up to date. They can be particularly useful when the people are working voluntarily and in their spare time.

So we see an organization as an intricate and potentially beautiful, network of relationships ordered to achieve the purpose of the whole. Now I want to open up another aspect of what is going on, looking more closely at how people relate and how units of organization relate. It may be like examining what happens in the subatomic particles when atoms combine to form molecules. What joins up with what, or does not join up with what?

'No-man's-land' is the evocative name given to that terrible space between the opposing front trenches of armies at war, the divide into which either side enters on pain of death. It is the space in which the other person is totally destroyed, unless he surrenders, submits to the dominion of the other. It is an ominous region of threat. I always remember that story of how, on the first Christmas Day of the 1914–18 war, men were somehow able to meet and play a game of football in No-man's-land and then return to killing each other the next day. How did the first venturing forth take place? Who took the first step – chanced his life? Created, at least for a day, some common ground out of No-man's-land?

Of course, warfare is the most extreme case, but there is a sense in which the space between people starts as a no-person's-land into which they have to enter. In the recent past there were a lot of common assumptions on which people at work could depend, mainly that they could for the most part trust each other. Now there is much more caution. From various businesses and professions people tell me they have to look over their shoulders to protect their backs. So there has to be a much more conscious negotiation as there would be after a tentative truce across no-man's-land. To do this we have to suspend our own certainties while we try to explain them and then listen while the other tries to do the same with his. We are searching for coherences between us, assumptions which are close enough to rouse some hope of agreement. This is finding common ground, changing a barrier between two closed offensive/defensive minds into a corridor in which realistic risk taking and trust can develop.

This process has to happen in all relationships between one person 'and' another. It is the 'and' again which keeps separate and joins at the same time. At work we relate to get the work done – achieve the purpose for which the PiWR exists. It is possible to have a working relationship with someone whom I do not relate to as a friend where the purpose would be mutual gratification of a different order. This has often happened to me in the church and must happen frequently in business. Once I had to act as a go-between for two colleagues whose antipathy would otherwise have made their working relationship ineffective. For them I was the 'and'.

Those two men were able to stay in their working relationship because they were, through me, honest with each other. All relationship depends on sufficient honesty to keep the dialogue going. It is destroyed by deceit. I used to ponder why Jesus commended Nathanael as 'an Israelite in whom there is no guile' (John 1:47). It must be because it enabled a relationship to begin and grow. 'Guile' in the Greek is derived from bait or a lure used to catch something. Then I realised that speaking with a forked tongue (like the serpent to Eve) is destructive of relationship. And the opposite of guile would be to speak together with a common voice. And this is what Jesus said gets things done in a most mysterious way. 'Truly, I tell you, if two of you agree on earth about anything you ask, it will be done for you by my Father in heaven.' (Matthew 18:19). This common voice has the same root as 'symphony'.

The city whose citizens have this common voice relationship must come close to what St Augustine describes as the 'City of God'. Opposed to this is the city of the world where relationship is maintained by guile and domination, the denial of God (good) and of others. The City of God is empowered by God as an act of grace, 'willing a new fellowship with himself and amongst the beings he has created'. And its fulfilment is within the heavenly city, 'beyond the possibility of alteration, the angels and saints abide in such a fellowship; their virtue is not the virtue of resistance and domination, but simply of remaining in a state of self-forgetting conviviality.' (Milbank, 1990)

These two cities are St Augustine's beautiful and profound analysis of the two ways of life which are present in all human experience and appear in religions and philosophies (Milbank, 1997, 106f.). Developing a postmodern analysis even suggests that the struggle lies within the original metaphor of language itself. If he is right, and I think he is, then within the deepest hidden depths of an organization, within the language of relationship itself, there is the struggle between bondage and freedom, good and evil, love and indifference. This seems to be the experience of many business people who talk to me about the agonies and joys of their work.

In his next book (1997), Milbank links this fundamental divide with language as the development of metaphor. 'Original metaphor implies either a primal personification of nature ("paganism") or else a primal response to nature as a personal address ("monotheism").' And he quotes Vico on the double origin of language, godly and demonic.

Although it is hard work wrestling with Milbank's precise philosophical presentation of his arguments, I find it rewarding for it introduces a little more precision into my faith. Within the hidden depths of organization, within the very language by which people relate, there are two opposing principles of bondage and freedom, of good and evil. Though they are often thought to be equal and opposite powers this is not really so.

My experience of the world – including actual warfare – and of the church, does not allow me to claim that all the bondage is in the former and all the freedom in the latter. The tares and the wheat grow in both as in the persons in both. But there is a difference. The work of the church is explicitly the creation of the free organization within the purpose of God as it is revealed in the life of Jesus. The work of the world may have some of this too, but it is not the exclusive aim. 'Then they said to him, "What must we do to perform the works of God?" Jesus answered them, "This is the work of God, that you believe in him whom he has sent."' This means to me, that we aim to live our relationships including those at work according to the teaching and example of Jesus.

This is in fulfilment of the 'Law' of the Old Testament which includes what we might call the godly organization of society. It is also fulfilling the prophetic hope expressed, for example, in Psalm 85:

> Steadfast love and faithfulness will meet:
> righteousness and peace will kiss each other.
> Faithfulness will spring up from the ground,
> and righteousness will look down from the sky.
> The Lord will give what is good,
> and our land will yield its increase.
> Righteousness will go before him,
> and will make a path for his steps.
>
> *The New Jerusalem Bible*

We are not thinking of an ideal church, but the actual church in the world – militant here on earth. I quote Milbank again: 'Salvation is available for us after Christ, because we can be incorporated into the community which he founded'; 'the new community belongs from the beginning within the new narrative manifestation of God.' Hence the metanarrative is not just the story of Jesus, it is the continuing story of the church, already realized in a finally exemplary way by Christ, yet still to be realized universally, in harmony with Christ – and yet differently – by all the generations of Christians.

Thus, the actual PiWR of the church is crucially important. It provides itself the only evidence of its claim to be the People of God. And this is true not only in the local church of levels 1 and 2, but also of 3, 4 and 5, and beyond these to the levels not mentioned so far in this correspondence: 6 (national) and 7 (global). We worship God in Christ (our work) by embodying his will in the total organization and in our relationship with the rest of the world.

This leads us to the all-too-obvious failure of the church to be and do what it should. The treasure is in earthen vessels, not in the sense of a spiritual treasure contained within an earthenware vase, but contained within the actual earthenware of human PiWR. In a strange way the failure of the church can still point to the glory of God by its negative example, but negative is not very convincing. When the church recognizes its failure, is sorry, confesses its sins and seeks to amend its life, then the negative is converted to positive. This is, I imagine, what your secular clients would call 'review'. The process seems to be identical, though I am not sure whether the secular organization actually repents.

The church differs in having a plethora of formularies for self-examination, repentance and amendment of life, but it does not apply them in detail to its own organization. It is its practical earthen actuality that the church should review, repent and amend: in each and every relationship within and between its units and layers, all the systems and subsystems of its PiWR. I believe it could be done and the start of the church's third millennium of existence seems to me to be a good time to do it. We should not ignore the lessons we could learn of how to do this from the world. And his master commended the dishonest manager because he had acted shrewdly: for the children of this age are more shrewd in dealing with their own generations than are the children of light (Luke 16:8).

So what does all this imply for those who lead – find the way – in organizations? They have to find the way to achieve the primary task; find the way in which the organization works; find the way in which it is bound together in working relationships. And they have to find the ways to share this knowledge appropriately throughout the organization. There's a wealth of practical wisdom in that 'appropriately'. In this they have to elicit the enthusiastic insights of everybody into the best way of finding the way.

There is no doubt that Jesus strongly contrasted the way the bosses of his day exercised their authority and the way his disciples were to lead by graceful service. (Matthew 28:25–28; Luke 22:24–27) This difference corresponds with the contrasting forms of relationship already described. Is it the leader's role in any organization to move as far as possible from relating by control to relating by the constraint of mutuality and grace? And how far is 'possible'? The answer must depend on whether it helps to get the work of the organization done. In the church the grace relationship is part of the whole work. Even here it is possible to argue about the need for punishment as did St Augustine. In the world the work does not have the ultimacy and all-embracingness of the church's work.

As already admitted, the world can find an urge towards what the church aims at and describes in its own traditional language. But it can follow the urge only so far as it will pay off. The church is not yet purified of worldliness including its unreconciled divisions. Leaders in the world and in the church can increasingly learn from each other.

Yours sincerely,
Norman

Dear Norman,

Your last letter had an interesting effect on me. First, I felt as if I was being drawn into your world – most unusually because it is I who tries to draw you into mine much more often. And then I found myself feeling protective of the church in your descriptions of its 'failures' and wanting to ask you to forgive it. Overall I felt very unsure about how to reply. Was there anything to add, to take further your clear ending about how leaders in world and church can increasingly learn from each other'?

First I reread all our letters to see what themes would emerge, but eventually decided to respond to phrases or points in your last letter that were especially telling for me. The first is that marvellous sentence about how we have to 'suspend our own certainties while we try to explain them and then listen while the other tries to do the same'; the second is a consistent theme through all your letters about 'tares and wheat' and the mixed motives in each of us; the third about finding 'the way'. Each warrants a letter in its own right so all I can do is just take your points a tiny bit further – in our shared landscape, I hope, rather than back into my field.

Suspending our own certainties while we try to explain them and then listen while the other does the same is something you and I have worked hard at. The mystery of suspending certainties while, at the same time, trying to explain them is worthy of much deeper thought. Our commitment to our respective disciplines sometimes makes it difficult to suspend, to explain and not to try to enthuse each other with our own way of looking at things, of making sense of them. Reflecting on this, it seems to be when we hear echoes in each other's imagery that we are best able to move forward together – support for your point about parables and their 'penny-dropping awareness'; why does that suddenly make me think of waiting to hear the other shoe drop? It seems to me as if we have come towards wearing the same lenses to look at the nature of work and of people-in-working relationships. Now we must guard against the idea that our lenses 'see more clearly' than others.

The suspending of certainties and all your comments about 'no-person's land' makes me think of a way I use the tripod of tasking, trusting and tending to help people think about working relationships, especially when they are entering into a joint venture or are in one that is going wrong. The key idea here is that the financial and other costs of such relationships can become prohibitive if the transactions between the parties do not run smoothly. More often than not the parties come from different cultures and economies, speak different languages and have different agendas and expectations of what they want to get out of the joint venture. One such is a joint venture where one party is made up of Japanese and British partners, the other is a regional government in China. So the stage is set for high transaction costs which can limit the trade-off of sharing investment in high risk ventures.

The starting-point for reflection on these joint ventures is the need for and how to achieve 'vigilant trust' – not 'a warm and fuzzy feeling' but careful, openly watchful awareness of the other. In my experience, the more common state of mind is 'wariness' – accepting that everything possible must be done to forge a working relationship, but not being sure sometimes even where 'no-man's land' is and where it might be entered. The idea of vigilant trust and its implications for reducing the costs of transactions (making them into and keeping them as relationships in our language) links directly with the notion of 'social capital'. A recent article from the World Bank is very clear about the need for social capital to support people and make it possible for them to make the most of loans of working capital and sustain an enterprise.

Vigilant trust must be supported by tasking which anticipates and can budget for transaction costs by sharing intention, clarifying resources and completion time. In the early stages of a working relationship (or when things are going off track) tasking can become 'specifying' – laying down every last detail, telling people exactly how things are to be done, constraining the space in which the parties can be trusted to use their own judgement.

Vigilant trust must also be supported by tending – the work that minimizes the costs of transacting through time. This is particularly difficult to do when the parties are from different cultures, vast distances and each has their own agenda to pursue – an agenda they may or may not have made completely clear to the other party. Again, in the early stages and/or when things begin to go wrong, tending deteriorates into 'contracting' – trying to deny what lawyers call 'incomplete contracting', the inevitable ambiguities that will crop up as the relationship progresses – by crossing every 't' and dotting every 'i', in effect, by more and more contracting! Many writers on 'social capital' refer directly to the high costs of lawyers in some cultures and to the control of that in societies where there is a greater likelihood of vigilant trust and the low-key, often unnoticed tending that sustains it.

Again I find your image of the journey to the promised land so powerful when trying to help people change their understanding and behaviour from wariness to vigilant trust, specifying to tasking and contracting to tending. As people make this journey, the inevitable outcomes of the 'wariness tripod' – opportunism, redress and fixity or passivity – begin imperceptibly to shift towards coherence, review and discernment.

Working with this version of the three Ts in our landscape has helped me to a much deeper understanding of what you call the 'tares and the wheat', the mixed motives in each of us. This is a further reminder of the need to face up honestly to the realities of human relationship – I find myself thinking here of Macmurray and the influence his ideas are now having on UK government.

In your second letter you spoke of differences in the nature of the relationship – acquisitive or gracious – and made the point that in all organizations there will be a mixture, as in each of us. I have been pondering on that alongside Elliott's idea of the 'paranoiagenic' organization where suspicion, mistrust and guile (to follow your idea) are rife and original sin flourishes; and the 'pistogenic' organization that builds on original grace, induces confidence. 'Pistogenic' is a very unwieldy word which seems to refer to the Greek for faith or religious belief. I have no idea why he chose it and it has not been taken up as far as I know, but the root meaning is very interesting. I have also being mulling all this over in the light of reading Buddhist philosophy, where acquisitiveness is seen as only one of the ways we try to persuade ourselves we can create fixity in an ever-changing world. The Sanskrit word used for craving is *trishna* – thirst.

This led me to wonder whether perhaps we are thinking about elements of grace and thirst in working relationships (thirst for certainty when faced with change, for power, possessions, control). This idea came to me while travelling to Paris on Eurostar where there was no etymological dictionary for me to look more deeply into this pair of words, but the 'pairing' still felt right. Imagine the shock of recognition when I looked up 'grace' to find that the Sanskrit root means to be warm, to glow, to rejoice and also to yearn. So, we glow, we yearn and we thirst – it sounds very human to me.

The next step was to think about conditions for PiWR that would take account of grace and thirst, fostering the former and containing the latter. Or – and this is just a random thought – satisfying thirst with 'enough'; with the responsibility, the reward the person feels to be 'just right' for them (strong shades of Elliott again with his ideas of 'felt-fair' pay – the amount felt by the person to be fair for the responsibility she or he was asked to carry and the capability they had to do that). My mind went – yet again! – to coherence, discernment and review. Coherence as a shared understanding of the common enthusiasm such that it can power the organization, and each person can use it as the touchstone for their discernment, their judgement of where to place energy and attention or, as one of my business colleagues put it, 'to decide which hare to chase and for how long'. This is your point about sharing knowledge about the primary task and how things work 'appropriately throughout the organization' and your rider that there is a wealth of practical wisdom in that 'appropriately'. We have touched on this before in writing about the need to appreciate the three Ts in neighbouring levels.

The second outcome of discernment – navigating 'that shaded area between . . . our view of things . . . and the infinitely more complex and changing world', as Caron puts it – has a particular significance for grace and thirst. As you know, much of my work is with individuals as they reflect on and plan for the journeys of their working lives. As I mentioned in my first letter, the experience of being 'in flow' is one where the person is profoundly self-aware and utterly unself-conscious; the person feels well – in all senses. Although there is no religious connotation, one could describe them as being in a state of grace. Being out of flow leads immediately to thirst – thirst for more or less challenge so that they can be back 'in flow', for power, for the apparent comfort of giving up completely, for status.

All the more important then for a leader to provide and sustain conditions in which each person can be discerning and with the touchstone of coherence can use his or her judgement. You remember that the third outcome of the three Ts is review; not so much as repentance but as an in-built capacity to learn from what has and has not happened and thus to strengthen the organization's understanding of 'how it works'. My thoughts on this are far from clear but it may be my feeling for what constitutes review – focusing on the event, the deed and not the doer, and the need to forgive and not to blame – that aroused in me the completely unexpected feeling of wanting to protect the church against your comment about 'the all too obvious failure of the church to be and do what it should'. I felt I wanted to say 'it's trying and is faced with so many pressures, expectations and opportunities in such complex circumstances'. And I realized that is true for all the social institutions we in BIOSS work with. Here is a very apposite comment from a thoughtful writer. (Karl Weick) about organizations: 'when trying to map an unknowable, unpredictable

world, there is a temptation to overconfident knowing or over
cautious doubt'. This swinging from knowing to doubt must he
even more difficult when an important element of the work is to
spread a 'truth'.

This takes me to the third of your themes that affected me
particularly strongly – your comments about a leader needing to
find the way to achieve the primary task, the way the organization
works, the way it is bound together. I am not sure if you meant
'the' underlined as I have written it but that was how it seemed
to me and it gave me pause. Partly because it seems so important
for all of us to know that 'our' way is 'a' and not 'the' way to see
things, make sense of them, act on them (in this I am not necessarily subscribing to the relativism of everything, just reminding
about how each of us constructs the reality in which we operate).

Then there is another pause re 'the's because one of the reasons
we find the idea of levels helpful is because it makes it possible
to consider differences. For a long time we in BIOSS have
used the idea of 'level-specific'; for example, having information
systems that are designed for the specifics of a particular level.
Recently a colleague from India started to speak of 'level-wise',
for me that has just the right connotations – especially, perhaps,
for thinking about leadership and how it could be exercised at
and for different levels.

As you know, much of my work is about supporting individuals
as they move into new levels and take on new leadership responsibilities, being with them as they garner wisdom about the new
level – these days this work is known as 'executive mentoring',
one could also think of it as being a 'companion in doubt'. Many
years ago I put together some descriptions of the vulnerabilities
that are intrinsic to each level simply because of the nature of the
work to be done. My experience is that the first thing the person
becomes aware of as she or he takes on the responsibilities of a
new level are those vulnerabilities. A frequent response is to feel
overwhelmed, incompetent and to respond either by trying to
control whatever we can and deny the validity and significance of

what we cannot or – and maybe simultaneously – to retreat into the familiar, into parts of work we do understand, can get our arms around. This is a restatement of Weick's comments about being overconfident and/or over-cautious; you made a similar point in your second letter when you wrote about moving from one level to another. There are also echoes of stumbling, even falling from grace.

For example, we see level 4 as the link between levels 3 (where the 'real work' is done) and 5 (where the 'strategic intent' is shaped). One of the intrinsic vulnerabilities of level 4 is that relationship between the 'real work' and the 'strategic intent'. If the strategic intent (the long-term direction of the common enthusiasm) is unclear and/or poorly or ambiguously communicated, people in level 4 simply cannot be act as 'messengers', 'angels ascending and descending'. But someone coming new into that level of work may begin to think that their difficulty in being an angel is an indication of their personal incompetence rather than an intrinsic vulnerability of the work for which they are responsible. If they can look at the situation in that light they are better able to see it for what it is, look for the coherence that could or should be provided from level 5 and even ask for it to be provided. This would be coherence about the primary task, about updating people in level 4 about changes, possibilities and seeking their advice about what change at what pace is realistic in deaneries and parishes. When this coherence is provided by level 5, the vulnerabilities are contained and disintegration – fierce resistance to change, crowding of deaneries and parishes in the name of coordinating their activities – can be prevented.

Looking at it from another perspective, what provision does level 4 make to contain the intrinsic vulnerabilities of level 3? One vulnerability is the balance between cohesion and introducing new ways of doing things – forms of worship, evaluation of quality of work, for instance. Another is the vulnerability of the balance between proper pride in established and familiar practices and clinging to them. There are three strands to the coherence that people at level 4 supply – as they sit behind in reserve, they can sensitively put the culture that is lived in house groups, parishes and deaneries into words without losing their spirit; they can do everything possible to keep hold and signal the importance of the personal in all the impersonality of figures, returns, statistics; and they can convey an equal honouring of the given, the new and those ways of doing things that have to come to an end.

This letter will grow far too long if I go through each level in this way but I will just sketch the coherencies that level 3 can provide for level 2 where the intrinsic vulnerabilities include the expectation that the person will stand for and be an exemplar of the purpose when they may not be fully in the picture about it. Or they may disagree and decide not to go along with it. The 'down-side' is the risk of 'shutting off like a sect'; the up-side the centuries-old freehold and freedom of the parish priest. So level 3 can provide coherencies that demonstrate the necessity of two-way communication and honour each person, each situation as part of the whole.

In super-simple terms subsuming, including in something larger (as you have hinted many times) is all about 'and' – joining and separating. What a pity there is not a verb 'to and'. Do you remember Whitehead's comment, 'We used to think if we knew one, we knew two because one and one are two. We are finding that we must learn a great deal more about "and".'

This returns me to tares and wheat, grace and thirst – much, much more to be thought about all that. Perhaps it is in and through these (and other) 'ands' that 'leaders in world and church can increasingly learn from each other'. They can also learn from history and other traditions as the comments below suggest.

There are three essentials to leadership: humanity, clarity and courage. 'Humanity without clarity is like having a field but not ploughing it. Clarity without courage is like having sprouts but not weeding. Courage without humanity is like knowing how to reap but not how to sow' (Fushan Yuan writing about leadership in tenth-century China).

A leader is a person who has an unusual degree of power to project on other people his or her shadow, his or her light. A leader is a person who must take special responsibility for what is going on inside him or herself, inside his or her consciousness, lest the act of leadership create more harm than good' (the Quaker scholar Parker Palmer).

With very best wishes,
Gillian.

Appendix

During this correspondence we have each felt the pull of the other out of our home territory and beyond the no-person's land between us – our landscape – into the actual professional territory of the other. When this has been pointed out by the other, we have each realized what we have been doing.

We have both worked hard at suspending our own certainties while trying to explain them and then listening while the other does the same. Our commitment to our respective disciplines sometimes makes it difficult to suspend, to explain and not to try to enthuse each other with our own way of looking at things, of making sense of them. Reflecting on this, it seems to be when we see echoes in each other's imagery that we are best able to move forward together.

We hope we have modelled the correspondence that is necessary between companies, churches, nations and national factions. But in writing like this we must beware of falling again into the use of only one metaphor, now not of the body but of the person.

So how do PiWRs relate? This new 'relate' (from the Latin *ferro, ferre, tuli, latum* – to carry and be carried) has to be looked at in its own terms. What actually happens, and what word could be found and coined?

Bibliography

Adair, J. May 1962 'A Staff College for the Church of England', *Theology*, 1989 *Great Leaders*, Talbot Adair.

Caron, P. 1996 *Discernment Beyond the Church in Discerning Together* (*The Way*, Supplement).

Cleary, T. 1989 *Zen Lessons: The Art of Leadership* (Shambala).

Collins, J.C. and Porras J.I. 1996 *Built to Last* (Century Business).

Csikszentmihalyi M. 1990 *Flow*. (New York: Harper and Row).

Kung Hans, 1971 *Why Priests?* (London: Collins).

Jaques, E. 1976 *A General Theory of Bureaucracy* (London: Heinemann).

Kelly, K. 1994 *Out of Control: The New Biology of Machines* (London: Fourth Estate).

Macmurray, J. 1961 *Persons in Relation* (London: Faber and Faber).

Milbank, J. 1990 *Theology and Social Theory* (Oxford: Blackwell).

Milbank, J. 1997 *The World Made Strange* (Oxford: Blackwell).

Palmer P.J. 1990 *Leading from Within* (Indiana Office for Campus Ministries).

Selby, P. 1997 *Grace and Mortgage*, DLT.

Shackle, G.L.S. 1988 *Business, Time and Thought* (London: Macmillan).

Srivastva, S., and Cooperrider, D.L. 1998 *Organisational Wisdom and Executive Courage* (San Francisco: The New Lexington Press).

Stamp, G. 1998 *Elliott Jaques* (IEBM Handbook of Management Thinking).

Stamp, G. 1983 *Executive and Corporate Hierarchies* (BIOSS Publication).

Wheatley, M. 1994 *Leadership and the New Science* (San Francisco: Berrett-Kohler)

Bibliography: a personal A-Z selection

BERNARD KILROY

The following offers a very personal 'desert island' package, arranged by subject matter, just to whet the appetite. It does not pretend to be comprehensive or definitive. However, it is intended to complement the bibliography in MODEM's previous book: Nelson, John (ed.), *Management and Ministry*, Canterbury Press Norwich (1996), p. 227 (abbreviated below to *M & M*). Other cross references below are to bibliographies of the chapters in the present book, for example (ref. Ch. 5 n. 7).

A for **ANXIETY**, defence against which is held to be the unconscious purpose of so much in the personality (ref. Ch. 7 n. 15, **Webb, K.**, *The Enneagram*, p. 3), in groups (ref. Ch. 7 n. 17 & 18 referring to Bion, W. and Stacey, R.D.) or in organisations (ref. Ch. 7 n. 19 Menzies-Lyth, I., *Containing Anxiety in Institutions*).

B for **BROTHER LAWRENCE**, the seventeenth-century French monk, author of *The Practice and Presence of God*, Hodder, 1981, who in his monastery kitchen discovered an overwhelming delight in God's presence, and so for many has become the model for fulfilment in work. (Another version of his book is arranged as daily readings). B might have been for the Beatitudes, the ultimate source for the Unconditional Positive Regard which has now become a touchstone of modern management.

C for **COMPLEXITY**, as in Battram, Arthur, *Navigating Complexity* (ref. Ch. 7 n. 1) at the biological and micro-biological level as the source for new ideas about relationships and organizations. Also for **CONFLICT**, all too common in community, considered by Avis, P., *Authority, Leadership and Conflict in the Church* (ref. Ch. 9 n. 2). Paul Avis is, coincidentally, General Secretary of the Church of England's Council for Christian Unity.

D for **DIALOGUE** of a comparative *statistical* kind which churches and congregations need to have with their mission contexts through the Australian type surveys in Kaldor, P., *Shaping the Future* (ref. Ch. 7 n. 8). Otherwise, see also the *UK Christian Handbook* (ref. Ch. 8 n. 30). Dialogue as a constructive method of leadership and as an alternative to adversarial debate is referred to in *Self-Organising for Success* (ref. Ch. 7 n. 3), and also in *Senge* (**Y** below).

E for **ENVIRONMENTAL SCANS** which all forward-looking organizations carry out of future lifestyles. The inspirational classiccs by Alvin Toffler, *Future Shock*, and John Naisbitt, *Megatrends*, may seem dated now. Mercer, David, *Marketing Strategy: the challenge of the external environment*, Sage/Open University, 1998, and Northcott, Jim, *The Future of Britain and Europe*, Policy Studies Institute, 1995, are imaginative and matter-of-fact. One needs to include the hidden world of microscopically continuous creation, as in Capra, F., *The Web of Life* (ref. Ch. 7 n. 12) or the new paradigms of thinking in Kelly, K., *Out of Control* (ref. Ch. 14 n. 7).

F for **FEMINISM** and its benefits for us all, beyond the narrow focus of equality in, say, Helgesen, S., *The Female Advantage* (ref. Ch. 7 n. 14), which incidentally contains an excellent summary of Henry Mintzberg's classic research in the 1960s which analyzed how top managers (all male!) then really spent their day (striving!) For Masculinity, see under **H**. For relationship, a feminine and Trinitrarian emphasis, see under **P**.

G for **GURUS** in management thinking and passing fashion, a useful summary arranged by subject in Kennedy, Carol, *Managing with the Gurus*, Century, 1994, taking on from an earlier book of hers, *Guide to the Management of Gurus*, Century, 1998, revised. For groups and their behaviour, see **A** and **Z**. For the still young in ideas G.O.M. guru, see almost anything by Drucker, Peter, especially *Managing the Non-Profit Organization*, Butterworth Heinemann, 1990.

H for **HERO**, usually alone and Herculean, embodied in Machievelli, Niccoló, *The Prince*, Penman, Bruce (ed.), Everyman, 1992, a still living archetype of the Reniassance leader, and where some of our hidden agenda in the West's version of civilization may come from. A very readable and seminal foil is Nelson, James, *The Intimate Connection* (ref. Ch. 7 n. 14), for a much needed post-macho re-invention of masculinity for the next Millennium.

I for **ISHIGURO, Kazuo**, author of *The Remains of the Day*, Faber, 1989, the Booker Prize winning novel (and subsequent film) which movingly portrays the employee (the butler of a grand household) whose identity and emotions are almost totally subsumed into his work. Otherwise, for *Innovation* through Henry, Jane & Walker, David (eds.), *Managing Innovation*, Sage/Open University, 1991, a useful reader; or for *Intrapreneurship*, through Arbuckle, Gerald A., *Refounding the Church: dissent for leadership*, Geoffrey Chapman, 1993, for sheer stimulus.

J for **JESUS CHRIST**, in juxtaposition, in whose image all leadership should proceed and be modelled, but about which there is so little specific information gathered together. I have in mind a contemporary study of leadership, equivalent to Lake, Frank, *Clinical Theology* (abridged), DLT, 1986, (Chapter 2), which proposes Christ as the [psychological] 'norm' for the study of the 'normal' person (as in Nash, Wanda, *Christ, Stress and Glory*, DLT, 1997, on personal stress management); or a similar attempt at another [societal] 'norm' by MacFadyen, Alistair, *The Call to Personhood: A Christian theory of the individual in social relationships* (ref. Ch. 8 n. 38). I have been recommended Gonzalez, (Fr) Luis Jorge, *Jesus the Leader*, Monterrey (Mexico), 1995, which combines theology with the learning community (from Anglo-American Bk Co., 01267 211880).

K for **KAIZEN**, the Japanese for 'continuous improvement', a less restlessly anxious version of which might be the concept of 'continuous learning' for both individuals starting with Pedler, Mike, *A Manager's Guide to Self-Development* (3rd edn.), McGraw-Hill, 1994, or 'organisational learning', starting with Pedler, Mike, *The Learning Company* (2nd edn.), McGraw-Hill, 1997.

L for **LEADERSHIP** and its elusive qualities, the classical and perhaps Classical (Graeco-Roman) handbook for which is Adair, John, *Effective Leadership: a self-development guide* (revd. edn.) Pan, 1988, a radical and inspirational contrast being Owen, Harrison, *Leadership Is . . .* Abbot Publishing, 1990.

M for **MANAGERIALISM**, the opposite of the values and processes for which **MODEM** exists, and the justifiable fear of many in the Church. The tendency is very capably explored, mostly in the secular public sector, in Pattison, Stephen, *The Faith of the Managers: when management becomes religion*, Cassell, 1997.

N for **NEW TESTAMENT CHURCH**, most refreshingly yet scholastically explored, including in its social and political context, in the magnum opus of Brown, Raymond, *An Introduction to the New Testament*, 1997, and which I would complement with Frend, W.H.C., *The Early Church* (3rd edn.), SCM Press, 1991, because written as if by an 'outsider' historian.

O for **ORGANIZATIONS** as organisms, brilliantly portrayed in Morgan, Gareth, *Images of Organizations* (2nd edn.), Sage, 1997, which is a good foil to the ever popular Handy, Charles, *Understanding Organizations* (4th edn.), Penguin, 1993, which can leave one replete but unfocused. (His much shorter *Understanding Voluntary Organizations*, ref. Ch. 6 n. 13, is very digestible.) The diversely blessed personality temperaments which comprise these mysterious bodies are appreciated in the original Briggs Myers, Isobel, *Gifts Differing*, Davies-Black/Oxford Psychologists Press, reprinted in 1995, but see also Ch. 7 n. 15.

P for **PASTORAL**, of so many definitions; hence, Carr, Wesley, *Handbook of Pastoral Studies*, SPCK, 1997, offers an ideal springboard, supplemented by the richness of Schillebeeckx, Edward, *The Church with a Human Face: a new and expanded theology of ministry*, SCM Press, 1985, and so many other topical publications in each chapter's bibliography in our present book, e.g. ref. Ch. 7, n. 7 & 8, as well as the once seminal Kerkhofs, Jan, *Europe Without Priests?*, SCM Press, 1995. Greenwood, Robin, *Transforming Priesthood: a new theology of mission and ministry* SPCK, 1994, is especially valuable for using the Trinity as a model of relationship as the basis for the faith organization.

Q for **QUESTIONING** the conventional and 'rational' approach to problem-solving via Proctor, Tony, *Essence of Management Creativity* (ref. Ch. 7 n. 22) or Morgan, Gareth, *Imagin-i-zation* (ref. Ch. 10 n. 4), since the Open University's excellent text, Martin, John (ed.), B882 *Creative Management: Block 2 – Techniques*, ISBN 07492 7917 6, 1998, is not generally available. A foundation handbook is Buzan, Tony, *Use Your Head* (ref. Ch. 7 n. 22 also, and see n. 20 for de Bono, Edward).

R for **REFLECTIVE PRACTICE** as used so effectively for 'Avec' type of work consultancy by Lovell, George, in *Analysis and Design* (ref. Ch. 7 n. 21). Schön, Donald (ref. Ch. 6 n. 27) also remains excellent value.

S for **SPIRIT** as the most acceptable word-bridge with the 'New Age' and between faiths. In this field Handy, Charles, *The Hungry Spirit*, Hutchinson, 1997, can be a stepping stone to the vast and varied field of spirituality (*see also* **W** *below*). S could have been for **STRATEGY**, for which see Ch. 7 n. 2 and Johnson & Scholes in *M & M* bibliography; also **E** above.

T for **TENTMAKING**, specifically Francis, James & Francis, Leslie, *Tentmaking: perspectives on self-supporting ministry*, Gracewing, 1998, an anthology of new articles from different churches worldwide. Links might be made also with the growing evidence of popular faith throughout history in scholastic works like Duffy's (ref. Ch. 7 n. 10).

U for **UNCHANGING CHURCH**, the argument of Clark, David (ed.), *Changing World, Unchanging Church? – an agenda for Christians in Public Life*, Mowbray, 1997, an anthology of papers across the range of social responsibility from the CIPL network. Also for **UNCERTAINTY**, blessed companion of faith (while uncertainty remains the only certainty in business), explored by a previous Archbishop of York who has been the saving Grace of many a General Synod debate: Habgood, John, *Faith and Uncertainty*, DLT, 1997. Relates closely to the blessing of mystery by the feminist theologian Grey, Mary, *The Wisdom of Fools? seeking Revelation for today*, SPCK, 1993.

V for **VIRTUAL CHURCH**, the coming to terms with which is taking time, in spite of landmarks explorations by Davie, Grace, *Religion in Britain since 1945: believing without belonging* (ref. Ch. 6 n. 1) and the Diana phenomenon.

W for **WORKPLACE SPIRITUALITY**, for which West, Norveen, *Friend of the Soul; a Benedictine spirituality of work*, Cowley, 1997, is an attractive approach in individual terms. Rather more comprehensive and solid is Schumacher, Christian, *To Live* *and Work: a theological interpretation*, Marc Europe, 1987. Other valuable sources are the *Faith in Business Quarterly* from the Ridley Hall Foundation and Industrial Christian Fellowship, Ridley Hall, Cambridge CB3 9HG; the Industrial Mission Association's *Agenda*, 81 Collingwood Cres, Bosgrove Park, Guildford GU1 2NU; the CCBI's *Unemployment and the Future of Work* report, Inter-Church House, 35–41 Lower Marsh, London SE1 7RL.

X for **EXASPERATION** and the book of prayers featured in the *Church Times* under the heading 'Let me not see "add toner"', Lord', containing this and other prayers against being overwhelmed by modern life's little frustrations (though none against the humour of this book): Steele, Jay and Bayne, Brett, *Bless This Mess*, Workman/Melia Publishing, Maidenhead.

Y for **YIN and YANG**, the two complementary opposites in the Tao perspective of reality, most closely mirrored in the holistic approach to practical management by the Buddhist boardroom guru, Senge, Peter, *The Fifth Generation Fieldbook*, Nicholas Brealey, 1994. This book is not to be confused with the ubiquitously quoted but much heavier going similar title by the same author. Collins, J.C. and Porras, J. I. in *Built to Last* (ref. Ch. 14 n. 3) use the Yin and Yang symbol to denote the integrated vision of successful companies. Heider, J.. *The Tao of Leadership*, Gower, 1994 and Messing, B., *The Tao of Management*, Wildwood House, 1989, are each compilations of inspiring values, though not actually in application; the fashion can entice without satisfying.

Z for **ZEN** (of course), especially Hunter, D., *The Zen of Groups*, a useful handbook which recognizes that groups can have a wayward spirit of their own, born of the kind of anxiety mentioned in **A** above.

About the contributors

Adair, John

Leadership development consultant and writer of thirty books on leadership, management and history including *The Becoming Church* (SPCK, 1976). Visiting Professor in Leadership Studies at the University of Exeter. Read history and theology at Cambridge and obtained higher degrees in both subjects at London and Oxford. He developed his Action-Centred Leadership model—widely used in industry and the armed forces—while involved in leadership training at Sandhurst and the Industrial Society. He was the first Director of Studies at St George's House, Windsor Castle where he established the 'staff college' case for future leaders in the Church of England. He acted as management consultant in the Dioceses of York and Chichester and was deeply involved in senior development activities both in the Church of England and subsequently the World Council of Churches.

Bemrose, Christopher

General Secretary of the International Federation of L'Arche Communities – a group of over a hundred communities in twenty-eight countries based around the needs of people with learning difficulties. He lives in Trosly, Northern France. Previously a Partner in Compass Partnership, a leading management consultancy working with the not-for-profit sector. Member of MODEM.

Brierley, Peter

Executive Director of Christian Research, an independent charity serving Christian leaders by research, publications and seminars on leadership and management. Editor of *Religious Trends* and joint editor of the *UK Christian Handbook*. A former Civil Service statistician and Programme Director of the Bible Society. Started MARC Europe. A member of MODEM.

Burkett, Christopher

Ministry Review Officer in the Diocese of Chester, Vicar of Whitegate with Little Budworth and occasional lecturer and writer in the sociology of religion. Since 1992 he has edited the quarterly international prayer journal *Encounter* for the United Society for the Propagation of the Gospel (USPG). Member of MODEM.

Collinson, Leonard

Director of Collinson Grant Consultants, Forum of Private Business (23,000 members), Newsco Publications and Universities' Suprannuation Scheme (assets at £17.5 billion). Chairs Manchester Diocesan Committee for Church in the Economy and the Network for Professionals. Former Director of Manpower for Plessey Telecommunications and Office Systems. Member of MODEM.

Cummins, Julian

A non-stipendiary priest in the Diocese of Ripon and Managing Director of Avista, a public relations and promotions firm in Leeds. An Honorary Visiting Fellow at the Bradford Management Centre. Author of *Sales Promotion* (2nd edn., Kogan Page, 1998). Member of MODEM.

Grundy, Malcolm

Archdeacon of Craven, Diocese of Bradford, Founder of the journal *Ministry*. Author of books on the relationship between Christianity, work and community. Formerly Senior Industrial Chaplain in the Sheffield Industrial Mission; Director of Education and Community for the Diocese of London; Team Rector of Huntingdon; Director of Avec; a Deputy Chairman of MODEM.

Harpham, Alan

Independent management consultant in programme and project management and executive coach. Part-time Chairman of APM Group Ltd, the trading arm of the Association for Project Management and a Deputy Chairman of MODEM. Formerly managing director of Nichols Associates (part of the Nichols Group). Previously directed Cranfield's MSc in project management and before that was Overseas Contracts Manager (M & E) for John Laing. Former churchwarden, lay co-chairman of Elstow Deanery and member of the St Albans Diocesan Synod, past Chairman of the St Albans and Oxford Ministry course. Founder member and first chairman of MODEM.

Henshaw, David

Chief Executive, Merseyside Borough of Knowsley. Also Clerk to the Merseyside Police Authority, Vice Chairman of the Merseyside Training and Enterprise Council, Deputy Chairman of the Mersey Partnership, Non-Executive Director of SOLACE International, Chair of SOLACE Enterprises, Honorary Secretary and Junior Vice President of the Society of Local Authority Chief Executives.

Hawley, Anthony

Team Rector of Kirkby and Area Dean of Walton in the Diocese of Liverpool. Formerly Director of Charterhouse-in-Southwark, a social and youth work agency for change, in London. Twenty-eight years of ordained ministry in the Church of England. Member of MODEM.

Kilroy, Bernard

A Roman Catholic consultant and facilitator for ministry using Avec methods. Tutor for Wesley College's (Bristol) MA in Theology and Ministry and for the Open University's MBA; previously Chief Executive Officer of Haringey Council's Housing Services; Shelter Executive Trustee; writer and broadcaster on public expenditure. Member of MODEM's Management Committee.

Nelson, John

Anglican layman working as management consultant with the Diocese of Liverpool. Formerly Head of Department of Management Studies at the former Liverpool Polytechnic (now John Moores University). Edited MODEM's first book, *Management and Ministry: Appreciating Contemporary Issues.* Honorary Secretary of MODEM.

Reed, Bruce

Director of the Grubb Institute of Behavioural Studies which he founded in 1969. An Australian who first studied architecture and was then ordained in the Church of England. His continuing interest is to work with people on how the meaning of faith can be expressed pragmatically in life situations through working extensively with the churches. He published his theory of oscillation in *The Dynamics of Religion* (Darton, Longman & Todd,

London, 1978). In 1990 he was awarded a Lambeth Degree in recognition of his work.

Rolls, Jayme

Dr Jayme Rolls died shortly after submitting her chapter. Lately President of Rolls & Co. Inc., Connecticut, USA. Organizational psychologist, author and educator, with a PhD in organizational transformation. Lately Director of the Leadership Institute at Manhattonville College, USA.

Stamp, Gillian

Director of the Brunel Institute of Organization and Social Studies (BIOSS). Works as a consultant on strategic and individual development in the private and public sectors in the UK, US, Africa, India, Australia, Europe, SE Asia. Worked with the Church of England on issues arising from synodical government (with Norman Todd) in workshops for recently consecrated bishops, with the Reformed Rabbinate and with the Methodist Church. A Member of the Council of St George's House, Windsor. Member of MODEM, former MODEM Trustee.

Todd, Norman

Anglican priest, now part-time freelance consultant on spirituality, psychotherapy and ministry. Experience in parish ministry and diocesan level adult education. Until 1995, Archbishops' Advisor for Bishops' Ministry. Graduate in science and theology, a doctorate in psychology. Canon Emeritus of Southwell. Associate member of BIOSS. Former member of MODEM's Management Committee and former Trustee.

Welch, Elizabeth

Provincial Moderator for the West Midlands Province of the URC. Member of the Central Committee of the World Council of Churches. Grew up in South Africa. Ordained to URC ministry and a served at the ecumenical Church of Christ the Cornerstone, Milton Keynes, 1983–96. Member of MODEM.

Wraight, Heather

Assistant Director of Christian Research, an independent charity that supports Christian leaders by helping them understand and interpret the context in which they minister. Joint editor of the *UK Christian Handbook* and *Atlas of World Christianity*. Previously Director of Radio Worldwide, the radio programme production and communications training arm of WEC International.